MEN-IN-THE-MIDDLE

MEN-IN-THE-MIDDLE

Conversations to Gain Momentum with Gender Equity's Silent Majority

Kori Reed

PURE INK PRESS

Paperback ISBN: 979-8-9875866-0-0
Ebook ISBN: 979-8-9875866-5-5

Library of Congress Control Number: 2023911364

Cover design by Nikola Tikoski

Published by Pure Ink Press
www.pureinkpress.com
July 2023

To my husband, who encouraged me to spend intimate, one-on-one time with more than thirty men ... virtually.

(For a few years, I gushed about, vacationed with, and even fell asleep at the keyboard analyzing detailed interview notes.)

CONTENTS

Leading with curiosity and listening with empathy liberates conversations, connections, and collaboration.

"There are relationships waiting to be healed. There are conversations you haven't had, stories that need unraveling. And if we all do that in our backyard, in our office, in our families—have the difficult conversations—miracles happen."

ELIZABETH LESSER, OMEGA INSTITUTE

SUPER SOUL SUNDAY WITH OPRAH WINFREY

APRIL 27, 2014

PLEASE READ THIS FIRST

Before you read these chapters, here are some key notes to help set the context for themes and ideas throughout the book.

Anonymous Interviews

Per my agreement with the men I interviewed for this book, I have changed their names to protect their identities. Expert interviewee identities are included with permission, and all secondary sources quoted are cited in the bibliography.

The Complexity of Gender-Related Research

I interviewed men—people who identify as male—about gender equity in the context of male-female interactions. I acknowledge that gender has become a beautiful, complex mosaic that requires a deeper dive into the niche and subcategory areas for greater understanding. It is my hope that we continue to see more research and conversations to explore other niche categories within the context of gender.

Word Choice Matters

- **Sex vs. Gender:** "Sex" is determined at birth based on anatomical and physiological markers. "Gender," on the other hand, involves how a person identifies. Someone who identifies with the gender that they were assigned at birth is called "cisgender" (Newman, 2021). For the purposes of this book, the primary context is interactions between cisgender males and females. The framework of leading with curiosity, asking questions, and having conversations can apply to other dynamics too.
- **Equity vs. Equality:** Equality is a foundational, core American value. Core values, according to a 2014 write-up for the online learning platform Study, are a set of beliefs on which our country founded the American government. The authors also point out that we don't always live up to these ideals. The six American values are liberty, self-government, individualism, diversity, unity, and equality—the latter being the idea that all people must receive fair treatment with dignity and be able to embrace opportunities for education, economic success, political involvement, and a fulfilling life.

While you will see both words—equality and equity—my personal focus and preference is on the equitable outcome and not the activity of ensuring all have the same or equal of everything. As you will see in some quotes, journalists and researchers frequently use the words "gender equality," and I stayed true to the language they used. When I interviewed men for this book, I initially asked questions in the context of equality. My thinking evolved over time, and I now prefer the term "gender equity." The back-of-the-napkin illustration below helps visualize the change in thinking. Men and women are different, and so are their strengths, needs, opportunities, and experiences. **Equality** is about providing or treating all people the same, even if the sameness would not make them equal due to different circumstances. **Equity** acknowledges imbalances exist—not everyone starts from the same place—and people might need something a little different to be successful. Men and women are different by design, and when working together, are a dynamic duo for change.

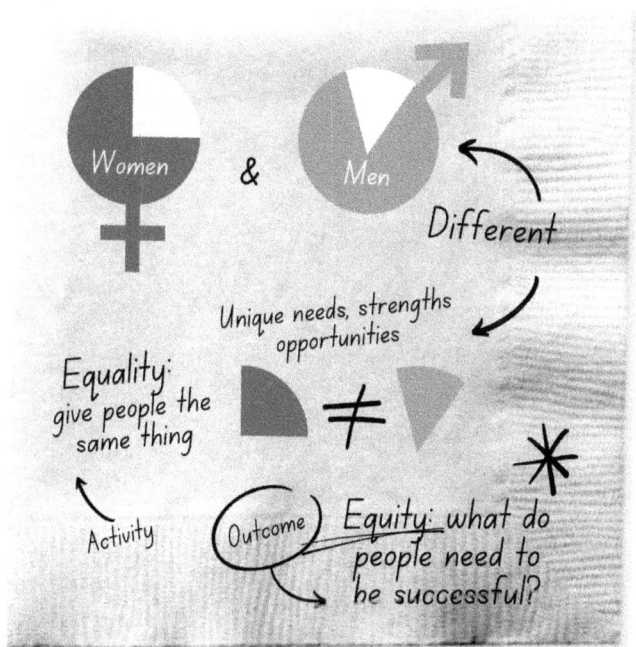

Women & Men

Different

Unique needs, strengths opportunities

Equality: give people the same thing

Activity

Outcome

Equity: what do people need to be successful?

- **Empathy over Antagonism:** Since the original interviews for this book, I have had a number of conversations with both men and women about the insights gained, the pursuit of gender equity, and other topics that often go undiscussed. Both men and women have shared visceral reactions that polarize the issue related to trust and intent; these range from "here we go again, I am on the defense" to "are you excusing that behavior at my expense?" I understand both perspectives. My goal is to open a conversation about gender equity among Men-in-the-Middle AND with others for a better collaboration for progress. Seeing and hearing perspectives creates more empathy-driven conversations. The words in this book are not intended to be condemnations for a group or individuals, but commendations for those willing to step up to change the narrative for a better tomorrow.

AN INVITATION TO A NEW WAY

Frank's enlightenment came as a bombshell.
This transformation sparked curiosity, conversations,
a quest for change, and a path toward collaboration.

On a Friday night early in 2020, Frank, a senior director of procurement at a Fortune 500 company in the Midwest, watched an eye-opening movie scene unfold on his large-screen, in-home television that made him as uncomfortable as the thought of talking with his adult daughter about her sex life. The movie storyline depicted a man in a position of power at a company inviting a young, up-and-coming female employee into his office. The woman in the movie was about the same age as Frank's daughter.

The man in power issued unprofessional, disturbing-to-watch commands to the employee, from "stand up and twirl" to "hike your skirt up" higher and higher to expose her underwear. Frank confided that seeing this intimate scene unfold at a slow pace—in the contrasting context of power and pain—made him want to turn away and turn it off.

As the movie kept playing, Frank's mood shifted from uncomfortable and enraged to awakened when he looked at his wife and daughter across the room. The three of them were watching the movie *Bombshell,* a 2019 biographical docudrama directed by Jay Roach and inspired by the real-life sexual harassment allegations brought against Roger Ailes, the former chief executive and chairman of Fox News.

After celebrating his daughter's first corporate job as legal counsel, Frank decided to have a movie night with his family. *Bombshell* did not make his top-ten list of movies to watch, but at his daughter's request, he agreed to an evening of theater-style popcorn and a beer with the two women he loved. He admitted he kept his phone close by, just in case he needed an out if the movie got to be too much of a woman-centered flick.

Instead, he got hooked.

Almost a week after the movie's release, New York-based journalist, Jill Filipovic, wrote an opinion piece for CNN explaining the impact of scenes like the one Frank described. "Reading about sexual harassment dulls it," she explained. "Seeing it is a crucial reminder of how repulsive and destructive sexual harassers can be."

Frank recalled his thoughts after that disturbing scene invaded his home theater television: "If there are still men who do this type of behavior in the office, it has to stop. Heck, I remember my first years at a company when the norm included scantily clothed women serving drinks at a sales meeting. It's not okay. Just because I wanted to look away during that scene did not mean the behavior went away. I looked at my daughter, thought about her career, and felt compelled to do something."

Frank said the film ignited a passion in him regarding the issues of harassment and gender equity in the workplace. "By the end of the movie," he shared, "I mentally gathered a list of people, including my female boss, whom I wanted to talk with at the office on Monday, humbly inquiring about rumors and stories of men and women working together in our own office that I had ignored."

That weekend, he and his daughter went back and forth in conversation on various related topics, ranging from sitting through uncomfortable dinners with male colleagues to being talked over in meetings by men she had worked or gone to school with, as well as gender equity in general. He also called his son to ask about his experiences related to office behavior. The movie and consequent discussions shifted Frank's perspective. He felt much greater awareness and wanted to talk about his realization with others. He even considered joining the #MeToo conversations.

While this book is not solely focused on #MeToo, and the author does not intend to perpetuate a name, shame, or blame mindset, the elevated gender-related conversations during that time frame did provide a context to study perspectives. The volume of comments heightened awareness and reactions from a wide variety of people.

Bombshell came out more than two years after #MeToo went viral, signifying a social movement against sexual abuse and sexual harassment. #MeToo appeared more than nineteen million times on Twitter from October 2017 to October 2018, editors at the *Columbia Journalism Review* reported in the 2019 article, "The Reach of #MeToo."

A 2018 SurveyMonkey poll referenced in a FiveThirtyEight website article by Koeze and Barry-Jester disclosed that:

- 77 percent of men surveyed had heard about the #MeToo movement.
- 30 percent reported changing behaviors in response to the movement.
- 60 percent of men agreed that society puts pressure on men in an unhealthy or bad way.

Over time, #MeToo got more inclusive of other gender-related discrepancies in the office. A 2018 *Wall Street Journal* article by Vanessa Fuhrmans, "What #MeToo Has to Do with the Workplace

Gender Gap," linked harassment and the gender divide. Fuhrmans wrote, "In fact, management experts and executives say harassment can be a direct side effect of a workplace that slights women on everything from pay to promotions, especially when the perception is that men run the show and women can't speak up."

With #MeToo, the office became a hotbed of conversation, controversy, and criticism. The topics expanded from inappropriate interactions to all gender-related inequities and discrimination in the year that followed. #MeToo made its way into the media too, grabbing the attention of those who weren't directly affected by the movement. For men like Frank, who never really thought about the reason for the movement, the movie docudrama inspired greater interest.

Note: Frank's story highlights the prospect of collaboration, not condemnation.

From Elevated Conversation to Deflation

When Frank returned to the office on Monday, he saw an opportunity to discuss the topic in the break room as his co-workers refilled cups of coffee before the weekly staff meeting.

"Have you seen the movie *Bombshell*?" Frank asked one of them.

His colleague looked at him, paused, and cleared his throat as a sign of discomfort before attempting to answer in a timid, hesitant manner.

"Are you talking about #MePhew?" a third man broke in, uttering the made-up word "#MePhew" to replace "#MeToo." He snickered and emphasized the "Phew" with a back-of-the-hand gesture to the forehead.

The colleague Frank first approached smiled, looking relieved, as the third man continued. "I'm glad there weren't cameras or social media around when I started in sales. Wow! Some of the things we did, I am embarrassed to say. I'm *glad* we didn't get caught!"

Frank later shared: "Those two laughed with a smirk as they walked out of the break room to attend the staff meeting. I knew that laugh. It is that awkward moment, among the guys, when you know you would not intentionally do anything scandalous, but then doubt creeps in that you might have said or done something even worse."

Frank followed behind the men and paused in the doorway to the conference room. He looked at his colleagues gathered for the staff meeting, perplexed by the stark contrast between the weekend conversations with his children and the break-room exchange.

He started to question himself. Was this the right venue to continue the conversation? Watching *Bombshell* enlightened him to consider the implications of #MeToo in his own office. However, listening to his male colleagues reminisce about once-acceptable behaviors opened his eyes to what Frank now knew as complicit behavior.

When Frank noticed his sole female supervisor among a team of ten male direct-report employees, he looked around the room again. He thought about his motivation to bring up the topic in the workplace. "I didn't think my female supervisor, the *only* female supervisor on this team and in the western division, would appreciate me asking her about her views on gender equity, harassment, and discrimination and whether more women should be in the workplace," he said. He viewed it as not his conversation to have.

From Apathy to Action

Frank is not alone in his detachment from conversations on harassment and gender equity in the workplace. Catalyst, a nonprofit organization that helps accelerate progress for women through workplace inclusion, found in their 2022 report titled "Engaging Men: Barriers and Gender Norms" by Geoffrey Kerr and Alix Pollack, that 74 percent of the men they interviewed said apathy toward issues of gender equity is a factor in men's lack of action. When I spoke with Frank, and other men who thought like him, to dig in and uncover the "why" behind that view on gender equity, three primary interrelated reasons emerged that also aligned with existing research:

1. **Uncertainty**: What should men say? How may they come across in mixed-company meetings, especially at the office?
2. **Ambiguity**: What is their role in the gender equity conversation overall? What could be presented as a solution?
3. **Complexity**: How will others respond? How does each party benefit from gender-equity conversations at the office?

Many men I spoke with thought their "maleness" excluded them from the conversations on gender equity. They felt that "women's issues" were not their personal battle, and it was not their place to speak out.

After this insight, I was driven by my own curiosity and felt compelled to interview more men and do additional research to gain a better understanding. I shared these collective insights at a 2021 hybrid TEDxLakeShoreDriveWomen event with a speech titled "#MeToo Silenced the Men Who Can Make a Difference. What Now?" When I realized I had way more content than a ten-minute-idea-worth-spreading talk, I decided to expand the concept and write this book.

Despite the elevated awareness following the global spread of #MeToo, harassment in the office, pay and promotion gaps, and discriminatory practices—stated or implied—continue today. However, we can change the narrative and invite men and women to see gender equity as a leadership issue owned by all and speak out. This type of communication is about empathy, greater understanding of perspectives, and promoting positive connections among male and female colleagues to align for better outcomes for all.

The numbers tell an interesting story, highlighting the importance of encouraging men to engage in the gender-equity conversation. According to the 2022 United States Census Bureau "QuickFacts," males represent 49.5 percent, just under half, of the population; however, they represent the majority of leadership roles in corporate America. *Women in the Workplace 2022*, an annual study of the state of women in business published by McKinsey & Company and LeanIn, reports that men hold 74 percent of C-suite or executive-level offices in corporate America today (Thomas et al., 2022). Since men hold a disproportionate amount of power positions, they have more impact on work-related decisions, from policy and pay to promotions and performance evaluations.

Many men may want to see more women in executive ranks, but there is a barrier. A 2020 Pew Research Center study on gender by Juliana Horowitz and Ruth Igielnik showed almost 60 percent of adults believe we need to do more for gender equality, nearly a 10 percent increase from the time prior to the viral #MeToo. However, that same report also showed three in ten American men think women's gains in the workplace have come at the expense of men, looking at it as a loss as opposed to an opportunity for all. This is described as a zero-sum game mentality—the idea that when one group wins or makes progress, another must lose (Merriam-Webster, 2022).

This insight prompted my interest to learn more. I realized that men do have thoughts about gender equity, even if they do not often outwardly express them. For example, men like Frank don't discuss gender equity at work, yet we learned Frank does have his own views on the issue. I made observations and derived a hypothesis. If we listen to understand and engage men in gender-related conversations in the office from a place of empathy, we may be able to break through that barrier; then we can make even more progress on the gender-equity movement.

Because men hold the most leadership positions, they are powerful stakeholders and potential influencers in the conversations about gender equity in the workplace today. In the spirit of collaboration, the ideal state is for men and women to work in alignment and raise these issues together. To do this, we need men to speak out and use their voices to reframe gender equity as a leadership issue, shifting the paradigm of a zero-sum game mentality to a gain for all.

This issue affects men too.

Earlier, I mentioned a survey on the website FiveThirtyEight that showed 60 percent of men agreed that society puts pressure on men in an unhealthy or bad way. There is more to that story. In that same survey, nearly 25 percent of respondents said men are taken more seriously than women at work, but most said there were no advantages. The majority of men who answered the survey said men are at greater risk of being accused of sexual harassment, sexism, or racism (Koeze and Barry-Jester, 2018).

While most sexual harassment victims are women, men are harassed too. In his 2019 *USA Today* opinion piece titled "For Male Survivors of Sexual Assault — Like Me — #MeToo Can Help Change Culture of Silence," Jacob Bruggeman wrote these powerful words: "#MeToo has upset many American men, but avoiding conversations about masculinity and sexual assault makes it difficult for male survivors to get help too." Bruggeman's words reinforce the idea that avoiding conversations by staying silent rarely leads to sustainable progress on equity for men and women.

Some men have their own stories as victims of harassment, but the national and even global narrative is that men abuse power or design systems to benefit themselves. #MeToo elevated stories predominantly about men who took advantage of situations or offended women but not conversations with men about gender-related issues in the workplace and their viewpoints on change for good. My purpose in writing this book is to unearth conversations people aren't or don't want to have about gender equity but need to have to make a meaningful, positive impact.

For me, it is about inspiring conversations that fuel connection and ignite change for good; this requires creating a safe space for open, honest dialogue that leads to shared understanding and common ground.

From Personal Experience to Purposeful Curiosity

To this day, I vividly recall a specific moment early in my professional career when I felt extremely uncomfortable in the office with a senior leader. While I wrote an announcement on a deadline, he stood behind me, bending over at the waist to get a better look at my computer screen. He was breathing near my ear and massaging my shoulders at the same time. I felt torn. I wanted to do a good job, even if it meant dealing with some discomfort. At the same time, I wanted to stop sitting there ignoring my discomfort, creeped out by this man being in my personal space and massaging my shoulders. I wanted to run away from the situation. I lacked the confidence, language, or perceived support to say, "Please take your hands off my shoulders and back up so that I can focus."

I stayed silent.

At my age now, nearly three decades later, the words seem like a simple request, but the situation still challenges me today. What if I had spoken up? Would I have progressed in my career as I did or been labeled difficult to work with, or worse? I did not expect a situation like that in my early twenties and did not know what to do. I dismissed it and forged ahead, but I still remember, years later, how uneasy I felt at that moment.

Over time, I progressed in management at large Fortune 500 companies, starting in manufacturing plants and moving to headquarters, working predominantly with men. I also worked a stint at a salt mining company, where the demographics included an 85 percent male workforce. With academic degrees and a professional background in journalism and corporate communication, I have managed large-scale change communication in times of uncertainty, including mergers and acquisitions, and prepared leaders to deliver good and not-so-good news to employees under ambiguous conditions. I have also counseled employees and company leaders during the complexity of crises, from labor-force work stoppages to a reentry plan after a gun-shooting incident at a manufacturing plant.

My interest in gender equity was piqued at the intersection of my professional and personal life. At age five, I wanted to be the first female president of the United States or a police officer like the one played by actress Angie Dickinson in Gerber's 1974 series *Police Woman*. I also knew I wanted to be a mom who worked outside the home. As a teenager in the late eighties, I wanted to be a working mom married to an at-home husband.

Gender equity, sex-role stereotypes, and inclusive conversations have always interested me. That passion lives on in me now, as the mom of four children, two girls and two boys, now all in or near entering the workforce. There are six years between the oldest and the youngest child, and each child was born in a different state due to required relocation for my career moves. My husband of nearly thirty years and I aligned on a plan when he traded his marketing manager job to be an at-home dad about six months before the birth of our second daughter. Over the course of two decades, he adeptly managed a household for a family of six and was supportive even during our four moves to four states.

I know what it is like to feel the pressure of being a breadwinner and being attached to your cell phone, even at family events or holidays. I also know what it is like to be the odd one out in an office meeting, at a business dinner, or even at a mixed-company party when female colleagues spoke about school drop-offs, packing lunches, and even finding childcare for overnight business trips.

I had little to add to those conversations and did not take that for granted.

A conversation I did have something to add to, however, was the #MeToo movement. At its height, I noticed how women like me would join together to share stories about their experiences. We read about powerful men like Roger Ailes and Hollywood mogul, Harvey Weinstein, who both made headlines for unwelcome, lewd behavior toward women. We didn't hear similar stories, commentary about the events, or ideas for positive change from the men like the ones I had worked with nearly every day of my career. They stayed silent.

Inquiry to Insights from the Middle

I went to the source to inquire why. I intentionally invited men into a conversation about the impacts of gender in corporate America, post the height of #MeToo. I hired a professional researcher and enlisted a trusted friend. We interviewed a variety of men, from CEOs to rising managers at U.S.-based companies, acquiring hours of transcripts to analyze.

Studying their words and comments, I looked for patterns and insights. An intriguing bell-shaped curve emerged from the qualitative research. Most of the men's perspectives fell somewhere in the middle, far from the extremes of either outwardly, vocally championing women or treating women like sex objects in the office.

After applying secondary research to the interview insights, I discovered that these "Men-in-the-Middle" had much to unpack about gender-related issues in the office. As it turns out, they had a lot to say! We listened, acknowledged men's experiences, and got below the surface-level dialogue. Imagine that. These men had opinions and ideas for improvement but did not speak out about them until we asked. I have changed the names and identifying details to protect the privacy of these individuals, but I share many of their stories in this book.

The goal is to highlight these ideas and behaviors as specific examples of what some men shared and had learned. Picture a virtual idea-sharing session: men sitting around the lunch table or high-top rounds at a bar, brainstorming ideas about improving gender equity—that would be awesome! It would be even better if men and women had collaborative conversations about the impacts of gender and ways to make it better for all.

Validation in the Voice of a Courageous, Vulnerable Man

Even though I recorded hours of interview conversations with men and spent more hours poring over the transcripts and analysis, I faced uncertainty about how to proceed. I value authenticity and integrity. How would I come across as a woman talking about men's thoughts and perspectives about the emotive topic of gender equity? The doubt even delayed my progress in talking about it and publishing this book.

Then, in October 2020, I came across the opening line of a book review by William Carmichael, a corporate training leader with a master's degree in business and a doctorate in instructional design. Carmichael started his write-up for *HR Professional Magazine* with a commission for men to engage in gender equity conversations:

In all probability, I will anger some of our male readers with my opening remarks. That we men in the workforce ... yes, 'us guys,' created the gender disparities that exist today. And not just created it. We have the audacity to perpetuate it! Somehow, we feel that gender inequality is a women's issue; therefore, we never feel any responsibility to fix it. We talk a good game about promoting an inclusive environment, but our actions are not so convincing.

Carmichael took it a step further, displaying vulnerability when digging below the surface to understand the *why*. So, why do men's actions not match that belief? Why aren't more men speaking up and out? Here is Carmichael's take:

To be completely honest, I think most men, myself included, feel a bit excluded from the #MeToo movement. It's not that we don't feel it is important ... we do! It's just that we don't feel it was a positive catalyst to move men to action or to make badly needed behavioral changes in the workplace. If anything, it moved some of us in the opposite direction, thereby aggravating already chronic gender disparities.

I spoke with Carmichael directly to learn more. As a consultant and corporate trainer, he has seen leaders, with good intentions, remove the phrase #MeToo from diversity and inclusion discussion meeting agendas. When he asked why, the leaders explained they didn't want to make people too uncomfortable. In essence, Carmichael said they shut down a much-needed conversation before it even started.

"It's not about covering it up," he clarified in reference to his comments. "The men just don't want to talk about it. Either they don't want to get into a discussion that makes it seem like they don't know what they are talking about or don't know what to do about it."

Carmichael also shared this conversation with a male colleague after he read his book review:

Colleague: "Have you gone out of your mind?"

Carmichael: "Well, do you want to talk about it? Do you want to talk about the book review or the broader topics of #MeToo or gender equity?"

Colleague: "No," and he quickly changed the subject.

"I think he did his due process as a man by giving me a hard time as if I was a traitor—to men," Carmichael said as he recalled the interaction. "I was surprised he did not want to challenge me, and certainly, I was not ready for him to just stop the conversation when I invited him to talk about it."

Uncertainty, ambiguity, and the complexity of gender dynamics in the workplace related to role identity and masculinity can make gender a scary subject for men to wade into and even weigh in on, not just in the United States but across the globe.

Osman Faruqi, a Pakistani-born male journalist who writes in Australia, explained why in the 2020 *ABC Everyday* article, "Why Is It So Hard for Men to Link Their Personal Behavior to Gender Inequality?" He wrote, "Men see the pay gap, sexual harassment, and gender equity, but a lot struggle to reconcile the link between their own individual actions and the bigger gender issues."

He also quoted Jess Hill, a female investigative journalist who wrote about domestic abuse and violence:

I think for a lot of men, it is an extremely confusing time. There's a big conversation about gender roles, and men are fifty years too late for it. Until now, men have believed the system was working for them. Now we can see that's not true, and it's making them feel angry and confused.

Communication is an antidote for confusion and anger and, in the context of gender equity, involves both women and men.

Engaging Men-in-the-Middle

Effective conversations, especially difficult ones, clear up confusion. It's time to open more dialogue, share perspectives, and engage more men in the discussions on gender equity. Engaging men and women together in the dialogue is an opportunity to strive toward positive change.

This book has three main parts:

1. **Collaborators for Change:** This is the business case for Men-in-the-Middle to speak out for gender equity. From curious conversations to actionable insights, these chapters explore what some men say about gender equity in one-on-one anonymous conversations outside the office. We study successful collaborators for change from history, the impacts of silence, and the opportunity for men as stakeholders to be gender equity disruptors.

2. **An Undiscussed Perspective:** Through interview comments and secondary research, this part of the book explores and acknowledges the uncertainty and other deeply ingrained issues men face that create discomfort and often go undiscussed. Toxic masculinity and bias are challenges for men too and can impact their mental health. Gender-related issues at work affect men too.

3. **A Lens to Move Forward:** Finally, to shift the gender equity narrative to include men, the last few chapters apply the

tenets of the Prosci® ADKAR® change model. Awakening an *awareness, desire, and knowledge* of the challenge, we look at what it means for men to expand their *abilities* to promote and engage in gender equity conversations as well as supporting behaviors. We end by sharing the good, pragmatic things men are doing but are not talking about to *reinforce* opening a dialogue for change.

This book is primarily geared toward people who work in a corporate environment and want to give voice to the male perspective to freshen the dialogue on creating an inclusive culture. While I did not speak with all men, I gleaned some valuable male-mindset insights that align with broader themes found in research from academic journals and mainstream business sources like *Time* and *Forbes*.

Equity is a conversation for both men and women. The challenges women face, from harassment and bias to inequity in pay and promotions, are well documented and discussed in the media and at the office. Yet, despite the awareness, the gaps remain, and it will take men and women working together to make progress toward equity.

Men represent the *majority* of C-suite and leadership roles and positions of influence in the organization, yet they are the *minority* regarding gender equity story sharing. Research also shows that men face challenges too, but these are often not discussed. Men mask mental health issues related to work-life balance. Men report feeling *less* safe than ever to speak out about gender-related matters at the office for fear of being accused of harassment or misconduct. Men have experiences with and perspectives about gender-related topics, but those seem to stay in the cone of silence, which is addressed in chapter three.

Being seen, heard, and included are important to all humans. I share a lens here based on conversations and research. If you, the reader, don't feel seen or heard here, you are encouraged to raise your voice and share your views. I am more interested in the conversation than I am in being right.

In the pursuit of greater understanding, reading men's comments, stories, and research on the male mindset might open the door for new perspective sharing and inquiry to encourage dialogue versus shutting it down, creating a path for progress.

Learning happens in conversations.

Historically, cisgender white males have set the norm, which is why we do not typically look to them as case studies on a path to change regarding equity. After all, why should we examine the status quo on the journey to a new approach? As society evolves and demographics change, however, this group continues to hold the majority of power positions that influence organizations, impacting policy, promotions, productivity, and more. Therefore, their silence on an issue can be a barrier to progress, which is the primary reason I suggest we probe and study this group.

This book is also a good source for women who want to engage the men in their lives—colleagues, mentors, boyfriends, husbands, sons, and more—in conversations about gender-related issues. When men don't speak about gender, we miss:

- a chance to hear from a stakeholder group
- the opportunity to address the root cause of the silence
- an invitation to engage the very people who are in positions to influence change

Seeing situations from a new lens opens a fresh dialogue. These are the conversations that can lead to change.

Each chapter ends with key takeaways and questions to get the dialogue going, whether it is an all-men's book club, a women's employee resource group, or a mixed-company diversity and inclusion meeting. If you are reading this book alone—which is okay too—the questions are there to ponder in self-reflection.

The goal is to ignite momentum-gaining conversations about gender equity. The Men-in-the-Middle represent the silent majority. When we see and hear perspectives with a mindset of empathy and understanding for all people, it leads to better collaboration. True equality is not solely about women. It impacts all of us. Men-in-the-Middle are an important part of driving a vision for equity in its truest form, as a leadership issue where success multiplies for a better tomorrow for all.

So, let's start with the curiosity that sparked the conversation.

CHAPTER ONE

FROM CURIOSITY TO INQUIRY

*Robert advocated for a time when women will lead the
way—regarding influence, pay, promotions, opportunities,
and more—before reaching a state of harmony,
equity, and balance between men and women.*

"I know it sounds odd today, but I would rather be in the imbalance
with the majority of women in charge of organizations for a while,"
said Robert, a former leader at a midsize, midwestern company
who now runs his own business. "Once women have been in power,
and we each have that shared perspective of power, we can say, let's
stop downgrading each other and get to it. Then we will learn what
balance really is," he explained.

For Robert, gender equity is a matter of physics and energy in
motion in the form of a pendulum, swinging from one extreme
to the other before returning to its natural state of symmetry. He
supports a swing toward *women in charge* as an essential first step
on the journey to harmony, balance, and equity among genders.

Based on the current data, Robert's vision would require a big,
bold shift. While there have been small gains in the talent pipeline,
women remain underrepresented across the corporate ladder (Burns
et al., 2021). In 2022, Statista showed that 85 percent of Fortune
500 CEOs are male, and this is even after four years of growth

in female CEOs (Buchholz and Richter, 2022). Men dominate leadership roles in corporate America and influence most major decisions that impact business performance and career advancement.

Robert sees this shift in leadership responsibility and accountability as a necessary step on a path to a better way, one based on a shared experience and, therefore, greater empathy.

"So, if I could wave my magic wand, I'd like to see an imbalance of power in women's favor before we get to balance," Robert continued. "I would love to say, 'It's okay, women. You are in charge. You run the world for a while.' I think we would see some great changes happen."

Robert is one of the men from managers to CEOs at medium-to-large companies across the United States who I interviewed about gender equity in the workplace shortly after the peak of the social media #MeToo movement.

At that time, after decades of silence, women spoke out to share and amplify stories of unjust, inappropriate, and inequitable treatment in the office. Among a flurry of story sharing and chatter by women, from the break rooms to the media, I observed that men, for the most part, did not participate. Their silence among the buzz in the office caught my attention.

The male voices—whether in response to the news, revealing their own experiences, renouncing behaviors, or recommending a fresh approach—seemed to be missing. Why does that matter? Men hold the majority of power and influential positions to make a difference.

The contrast in reactions between men and women intrigued me. Was there apathy behind men's silence or something else that kept them from speaking out? I had to find out.

As it turns out, there was more to the story. In one-on-one, anonymous interviews, men, including Robert, had a lot to say about gender equity in the office. We just had to initiate the conversation.

We Ask Men: The Interviews

Leaning into my curiosity about men's perspectives, I enlisted a team of like-minded professionals. Having worked in consumer-packaged goods companies for many years, I turned to my friends in marketing analytics for advice on how to understand men's mindsets in the context of gender equity. Market research professionals study and gather insights about a target audience. I have observed their work and seen them present information multiple times, creating profiles based on research. They are experts at eliciting information to develop a much deeper understanding of how the target thinks and feels about a particular product, brand, or situation. I felt asking questions and analyzing the data in this same way would lead me to the answers I was looking for.

At my own expense, I hired a professional market researcher from Fusion Marketing Power, Donna Malone. My husband described that as taking my natural curiosity to new heights! Donna created a process for consistency, including a skillfully designed interview guide, starting with general questions first and then easing into the potentially awkward stuff as the interviewees got more relaxed and comfortable.

The interview guide started with these types of general questions:

- What picture would you pick (from the photomontage of twenty-five images like the six below in Figure 1) to best depict your workplace culture today? Tell me why. Discuss the differences.
- What is most important to you in your work life? What gets in the way of achieving that?
- What parts of your day do you look forward to the most? The least? Why is that? Can you tell me a recent story of a day that went particularly well?

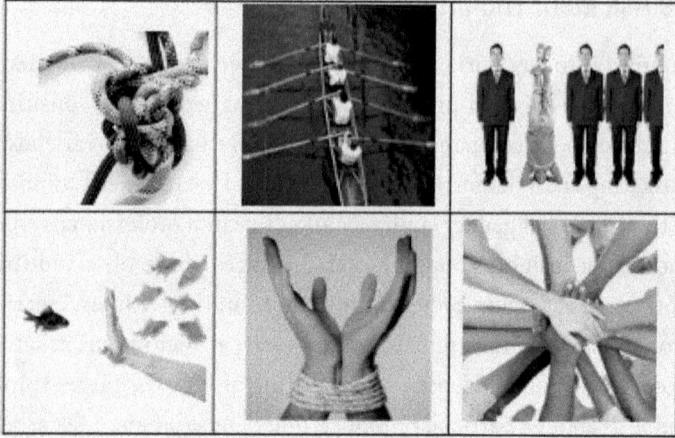

Images curated by Fusion Marketing Power

Figure 1: Sampling of images from the photomontage shared with interviewees.

Next, the guide shifted to general, gender interaction-related questions:

- What two pictures from the photomontage best depict the gender interactions at your company? Pick one that represents gender interactions today and one that represents gender interactions two years ago. Why those? Why not two different pictures?

- What percent of time are you typically interacting with others? What percent of your day are you interacting with men versus women? Has it always been that way, or has it changed recently? Why is that? How do you feel about that?

- Have you ever seen or been privy to a situation when you felt uncomfortable with male behavior around women? Describe it. How was it resolved? How did you feel about its resolution?

Near the end of the guide for the hour-long interviews, we got more personal with the questions:

- In what ways do you personally engage in the gender-equality topic? What, if anything, is holding you back from being an active spokesperson and championing women on issues like equality, representation, etc., in the workplace?
- How has the #MeToo movement impacted your feelings or interactions with women in the workplace, if at all?
- Have you discussed gender issues with someone in your immediate family, like your spouse? Daughter? Sister? Niece? Why or why not? What do you discuss?

In addition to the market research professional, I enlisted a trusted friend who has a master's degree in business administration and shares my passion for unearthing new conversations below the surface level, where the most awkward and uneasy-to-discuss topics remain. We came up with the code name "Project Sandbox" to signify our intent to experiment and explore ideas in a safe environment with the goals of sharing knowledge, perspectives, and perhaps even changing the narrative based on new input and insights.

The three of us reached out to our extended, collective networks of male colleagues, specifically focusing on men who worked in professional roles in corporate America, from managers to CEOs of medium-to-large companies across the country. We invited men to have one-on-one, one-hour-long phone conversations, under the condition of anonymity, about gender and gender equality in the workplace post the height of #MeToo.

We sent out the first email invites to more than one hundred men. We were not sure if any of them would want to have a conversation about gender. So, in alignment with market research practices, I added funding to my "curiosity project budget" to provide one-hundred-dollar gift cards as a participant incentive.

Thirty men within our parameters, representing several industries across the country, agreed to talk with us. The three of us divided and conquered the interviews, using the interview guide for consistency. We also added a couple of mixed-gender focus groups in the Midwest to get another angle and compare comments in context. The men let us use their words and tell their stories in exchange for a gift card and the promise that we would camouflage their identities. I changed the names and masked identifying characteristics to keep my end of the bargain.

I analyzed the transcripts and backed the findings of our primary interviews with secondary research to contrast, compare, and put their comments into context. My curiosity turned into a project needing to be managed. In the following pages, you will see a blend of interviewee perspectives and stories, other secondary research, and my own firsthand experiences.

I learned that, for the most part, men are aware of current events and the shift in dynamics pre- and post-#MeToo. They are feeling the change and responding to it—whether through quiet conversations about what's going on or sitting with their discomfort in silence.

Before we get to the deeper analysis of the interviews, let's look at the context of events and brush up on some useful information that unfolded prior to us reaching out to the men.

A Quick Refresher: #MeToo and #TimesUp Movements

In the introduction, I shared a 2018 survey by Koeze and Berry-Jester that revealed nearly one in four men had never even heard of #MeToo. Let me share a quick refresher if you are one of those men or are unaware of *all* the milestone moments of the movement. In 2017–2018, the hashtags "#MeToo" and "#TimesUp" elevated the voices and stories of sexual assault victims and highlighted the ongoing pursuit of gender equity in the workplace. The hashtag #MeToo symbolized solidarity; no victim had to face harassment or discrimination alone.

At this point, to ensure there is no confusion for the readers, the symbol "#" before a word or phrase is known as a hashtag in social media, starting with Twitter and expanding to other sites. Anything after that symbol classifies or categorizes the text (Merriam-Webster, 2023). Hashtags indicate something is part of a larger discussion and serve to unite and connect people discussing the same topic or at events (Cormier, 2022).

A timeline of the viral spread of #MeToo and #TimesUp:

- **October 15, 2017:** Actress Alyssa Milano reignited the #MeToo movement, founded originally by activist and survivor of assault Tarana Burke in 2006, with a tweet encouraging sexual assault and harassment victims to share their stories. A friend prompted Milano after the spread of sexual assault allegations against Hollywood producer Harvey Weinstein. As of the writing of this book, Weinstein is in prison for sex crimes (Sayej, 2017).

- **October 17, 2017:** Milano, who woke up to #MeToo trending as number one on Twitter, sent a new tweet crediting Tarana Burke for the #MeToo movement. The movement continued to grow (Sayej, 2017).

- **December 18, 2017:** *Time* magazine announced "The Silence Breakers"—those who spoke out and propelled the #MeToo movement—as the Person of the Year (Zacharek et al., 2017). This included both Milano and Burke, among others.

- **January 1, 2018:** More than three hundred Hollywood celebrities began using #TimesUp in their posts and described it as the action-based arm of #MeToo. #TimesUp expanded the conversation from sexual harassment and assault to include a society free of gender-based discrimination in the workplace, including safety and equity (Langone, 2018).

- **January 8, 2018:** The day after the 2018 Golden Globe Awards, #TimesUp became the biggest trend of the award show, watched by more than three million people. Hollywood female celebrities wore black in solidarity and support (Richards, 2018).
- **October 4, 2018:** The United States Equal Employment Opportunity Commission credited #MeToo for the first increase—by 12 percent—in a decade of sexual harassment cases filed by workers (Wiessner, 2018).
- **October 18, 2018:** #MeToo also raised awareness for many people who had not experienced sexual harassment. Most of us could not escape the sheer volume of people sharing stories on social media feeds with #MeToo. A year after the first #MeToo prompt, Pew Research Center found that #MeToo showed up more than nineteen million times on Twitter. This is equivalent to more than 55,000 uses of #MeToo per day that year (Anderson and Toor, 2018).

You are officially caught up on #MeToo and #TimesUp 2017–2018, the year that elevated consciousness and conversations. The visible consequences of #MeToo spoke volumes, amplified voices, and either stopped lewd behaviors or gave a framework to call out what is acceptable and what is not.

Awareness to Action

Over three months, the scope of "acceptable" actions and behaviors expanded too. In October 2017, #MeToo sparked viral stories of sexual assault and harassment. In January 2018, #TimesUp framed sexual harassment as "a symptom of imbalance that has kept women from realizing true equality at work" (Time's Up Now, 2022). In the blend of #MeToo and #TimesUp, the conversations shifted from harassment and equal pay to the broader abuse of power that threatens financial, physical, and emotional safety for women—paid family leave, pregnancy discrimination, lack of representation of women and people of color in leadership, and more.

Referring to Robert's pendulum and energy in motion, picture the bob, the mass at the end of the wire, oscillating in tempo with a fast-moving metronome. The pendulum makes a ticking sound with each swing to the left or right, encompassing more space as the bob gains momentum:

- *Tick*: Sexual assault victims are encouraged to share their stories.
- *Tick*: Hollywood celebrity stories influence attention around sexual assault at work.
- *Tick*: Victim storytelling extends beyond Hollywood.
- *Tick*: Celebrities raise awareness on pay and gender discrimination in Hollywood.
- *Tick*: Pay and discrimination conversations span beyond Hollywood.
- *Tick*: The topics are wide-sweeping as the bob moves higher, encompassing all forms of gender inequities.

The actions and impacts related to the movements grew too:

- One year after #MeToo launched, 425 prominent people across industries had been accused of sexual misconduct, including a range of behaviors that covered serial rape, lewd comments, and abuse of power (Griffin et al., 2018). These men and what the accusations did to their careers made the headlines.
- Award-winning actor Benedict Cumberbatch, on the other hand, vocally took action to promote equal pay, sharing his

policy: "Ask what women are being paid and say, 'If she's not paid the same as men, I'm not doing it'" (Jones, 2018).

- Actor Bradley Cooper, the male cast members of the television show *The Big Bang Theory,* and other actors also pledged or adjusted salaries to support female peers (Rueckert, 2018).

While the #MeToo social media buzz has slowed in recent years, the action continues. In her 2022 blog, "You Think #MeToo Is Over? Think Again," for the website Employment Law Spotlight, lawyer Amanda Van Hoose Garofalo wrote about the United States Senate passing HR4445. This bill ends the Forced Arbitration of Sexual Assault and Sexual Harassment Act of 2021 and allows an individual alleging sexual harassment to bring claims to court. She said its design ensures companies can't hide behind the confidentiality the arbitration process provides, such as confidential settlement agreements that keep behaviors out of the public eye.

The movement went viral. It elevated voices. It raised awareness of inequities. It also led to action in the form of misconduct allegations, equal pay champions, and even some changes in legislation.

Equity remains elusive in the workplace, and there is a missing voice to help us move the dial sooner—men, especially Men-in-the-Middle, the majority.

From Extremes to the Middle

We heard—in both traditional and social media—about the extremes of gender equity, from the accusations and eventual conviction of Harvey Weinstein for sexual assault and abuse of a position of power to Benedict Cumberbatch's vocal support of equal pay, but not so much about what was happening right in the middle. Under the "Article & Advice" section on the website

Fairygodboss, writer Liv McConnell shared something that she felt "should be required reading for all men." She quoted a Facebook entry by a man named Indigo Nai in her 2017 post titled *This Man's Post Perfectly Sums Up What's Wrong With #MeToo*. In his 2017 Facebook post about #MeToo, Nai offered insights on what could be happening with Men-in-the-Middle:

> *Women are owning the internet today. Every woman I know is speaking up and reaching out, drawing others into the circle. They are all saying, '#Me too; I have been assaulted, too.'*
>
> *On the other side of the line, men are being uncharacteristically quiet. While women are raising their voices and implicitly asking if men will acknowledge their experience at our hands, we are saying nothing in return. Effectively, we are gaslighting women with our silence. We are pretending their experiences did not happen. We are implying that while there may be bad men, we must not be the men they're talking about. We are acting as if all the bad men stand on the other side of a line we have drawn in the sand. We refuse to see that that line in the sand is a circle we've drawn around ourselves …*

The phrase "with our silence" drew me in as it aligned with my experience. While my female colleagues and I swapped stories and support around the #MeToo movement, I noticed the men—those I worked with nearly every day, ranging from the heights of the executive offices at Fortune 500 companies to the depths of a salt mine a mile below the earth's surface—remained silent.

While some argued men were silent about gender issues before #MeToo, the silence seemed more pronounced amid the hype of the gender-equity movements that got near Super Bowl-sized media coverage. The contrast stirred my curiosity. Why weren't men speaking out about gender equity in the workplace?

My curiosity intensified as I interacted daily with male peers in the office. When I tried to engage Lew, a longtime male colleague I respected, in a discussion about #MeToo, gender equity, and his experiences, he shut down the conversation.

"Look, you will never hear me say to a woman at the office that her hair looks nice, or her outfit is great, or anything like that," he explained, with an expression I had not seen him previously display. It was like he was on the edge of uneasiness.

"Well, then you are being an ass," I replied viscerally, abruptly, and admittedly inappropriately.

I had worked with this man for more than seven years, and over that time, we had plenty of conversations and disagreements at work. We had also been to each other's houses for social events and met each other's spouses and kids. So it shocked me that he avoided this topic when we had previously debated so many other issues.

After I apologized for my knee-jerk reaction and name-calling, I attempted to explain my concern. "We rarely find solutions when conversations are shut down or silenced. If I think your hair looks nice or your shirt is a good color, I will say, 'Hey, you look great today.' That is just authentic to me, and it is just being nice."

I continued, "Besides, you and I have had far more in-depth conversations about politics and other subjects that had the potential to offend me way more than this. Are you in 'Camp Harry?'" [For those who haven't seen the movie *When Harry Met Sally*, the main character, Harry, declares that "men and women can't be friends because the sex part always gets in the way" (Reiner, 1989).]

He laughed at the movie reference but did not budge. "I am just not going to do it," he said, showing no sign of changing his mind or wanting to entertain further conversation. Instead, he ended the chat with, "It just takes one person to interpret a comment the wrong way, and I become falsely accused of sexual harassment in the workplace."

To my amazement, this concern for mistaken allegations of harassment surfaced during discussions and interviews with multiple men. With each conversation, I probed the storyline from a different angle. Frank's story in the introduction involved his personal encounter with harassment through the eyes of a dad who compartmentalized his role back at the office. Lew spoke to the lengths he would take to avoid anticipated reactions to a surface-level compliment about appearance. In chapter three, I introduce Jay, who shares Lew's concern and focuses on the uncertainty of feeling and being seen as "creepy" in the office.

While men were not speaking out at the office about the workplace harassment stories in the news, it appears they were thinking about it and had some feelings too.

I realized then that my colleague Lew, like many other men, most likely had not been included in the gender equity conversation before, so he didn't know how to participate in it. It was foreign ground for him, which made him nervous. It appeared to me that he didn't know how to join the discussion in a healthy way, where he wasn't full of fear over potentially offending someone. He worried he would be perceived inaccurately and be unable to correct any misunderstanding.

How can we be inclusive if we don't include men in the conversation about gender in the workplace? More importantly, how do we get to know what is really going on in the minds of men behind their silence, especially men like the ones I had worked with for over two decades?

The analysis of the one-on-one interview comments my team managed revealed some interesting insights that inspired even more research, from scholarly research to business publications and blogs. First, I started by dissecting the interview transcripts.

From Pendulum to Curve: The Interview Results

After examining, reviewing, and categorizing the volume of comments, self-described behaviors, and peer observations, an intriguing and somewhat normal bell-shaped curve distribution emerged, as depicted in Figure 2 that follows, with the majority at the median, another word for *middle*. I divided the curve into three major sections for simplicity purposes. I call the sections Side A, Side B, and Middle. On Side A and in the Middle section, the men identified with and owned the behaviors described. On Side B, however, where the behaviors could be interpreted as offensive, the men chose words to describe behaviors they had observed among their peers. They attributed those behaviors to others, not themselves. This is why I describe it as a somewhat normal bell-shaped curve. I did not ask them to identify which section of the graph they fell into; when I studied their comments, I grouped similar remarks in the analysis. The words and phrases I collected naturally aligned to a bell-shaped curve.

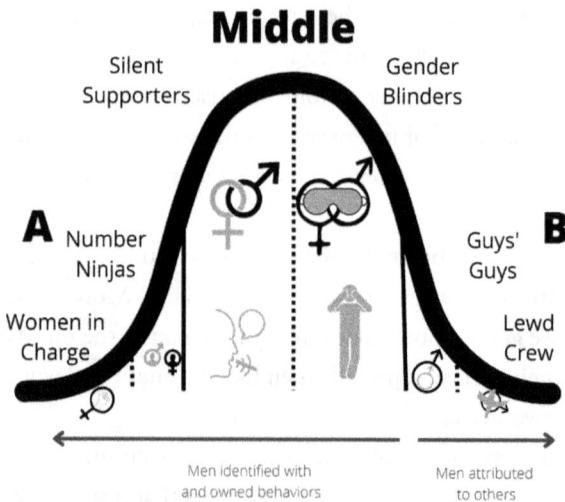

Figure 2: A visual representation of the modified bell-shaped curve derived from the analysis of the interviews.

Each section includes two subcategories for a total of six. I assigned a nickname or "handle" for each group along the curve, using their words to bring the concept to life.

Starting on Side A, we have the **Women in Charge** and the **Number Ninjas**:

- We started this chapter with a quote from Robert, who represents the Women in Charge group. **Women in Charge** believe we can only achieve true balance and equity when a group has experienced both the positive aspects and the challenges of having power. Men in this group say we could accomplish a lot if we put women in charge.

- The second group on Side A, closer to the center, are the **Number Ninjas**. These leaders looked at employee demographic numbers in their respective companies, identified gaps, and *did* something about it—either small steps or giant leaps. In college or grad school, specifically in IT or engineering classes, they did not see any women; but under their leadership, the respective companies increased diverse representation over time. Nevertheless, they acknowledge there is more work to do.

Now, let's go to Side B for the **Lewd Crew** and the **Guys' Guys**. On this side of the curve, we grouped the comments men used to describe peer behaviors that men attributed to others—not themselves—as unacceptable, including a range of activities. These comments align with how the Equal Employment Opportunity Commission defined sexual harassment in the 2013 United Nations WomenWatch document "What is Sexual Harassment?" Again, however, we stayed true to the language the men used.

- On the far side of Side B, we have the **Lewd Crew** or the Harvey Weinsteins of #MeToo. This is where the men interviewed called other men, their peers, "scum" for demonstrating unacceptable behaviors. (Weinstein was their example, and "scum" was their word, not a name or word I introduced.) "Five years from now," one man said, "I don't want to hear any more Harvey Weinstein instances. Still, if there are, we have a framework to stop it." He expressed an appreciation for #MeToo, calling out these behaviors and getting clear on the repercussions.

- Staying on Side B, but a little closer to the center, we have the **Guys' Guys**, a label the men assigned to male peers for behaviors ranging from calling a group of professional women "girls and gals" and telling sexual jokes to something called "Vegas Rules" or "Road-Code," which is a mix of "business travel, booze, bad choices, and bro code." One of the men said, "The macho thing gets old really quick. I don't want to feel like I am in a fraternity when I am at work."

Now it's time to look at what is happening right in the middle, where we see the majority. Nearly 85 percent of the views shared on gender equality fell into the middle two groups, the **Silent Supporters** and the **Gender Blinders**. As a whole, they spoke to the value of diverse, inclusive teams for better, creative problem-solving and work environments. However, the lens on equity is slightly different between the two.

- **Silent Supporters** have their eyes wide open to the gender imbalance in the workplace and are even willing to talk about it, just not at work. In a one-on-one conversation, these supporters spoke of strong women who have been a major influence. Some were raised by single moms. Others shared stories of wives or daughters who were told not to talk during a meeting or that being a tough negotiator makes a woman less likable. A significant portion of these men praised women for being good career role models and mentors. Supporters want a future where organizations have a balance at all layers, from entry-level to executive, and match the population of 50.5 percent women, according to the 2022 United States Census Bureau.

- Picture **Gender Blinders** with a blindfold. They don't talk about gender at work because they claim they don't even see it! This group takes great pride in a badge of *meritocracy*— the idea that the best candidates rise to the top regardless of age, race, or gender. Gender may not be something they notice or think about on an everyday basis; however, when we asked this group about gender equity, they shared some thoughts about improving it. One idea is to get more women to shift from staff leadership roles—like running Human Resources—to being responsible for lines of business with accountability for a profit and loss statement so that more women can be in the pipeline for C-suite jobs.

The Men-in-the-Middle

In the one-on-one interviews, Men-in-the-Middle, had a lot to say about gender equity, just not in the office; there, they remained silent. They have ideas but don't speak up, that is, without an invitation. Below are some of their comments and context based on additional research. As a reminder, the interviewees' names have been changed for anonymity.

- George shared an epiphany midway through our interview: "You know, I didn't even realize how passionate I was about this topic until I started talking with you."
  - Without an invitation to speak, some men have not even explored their own perspectives or opinions related to gender equity, including potential solutions.

39

- Thomas started the call with this statement: "I have been thinking about this for the last year and a half!" But he also said he does not talk about it at work because no one had asked him.
  - For Men-in-the-Middle, that means ambiguity about a male's role in advancing gender equity and uncertainty about whether there is a safe place to talk, ask questions, or share ideas.
- Frank expressed it this way: "I did not ask my sole female supervisor because I didn't think she would appreciate someone asking why she thinks it might be important that we have more women."
  - He felt there was complexity related to the anticipated interactions and reactions of both his male and female counterparts.
- Brady, a senior leader in market research, said, "I am cautious about how I joke anymore in the office. I am afraid I may say something someone may take out of context."
  - He felt unsafe bringing it up, and that led to silence.
- Conor, a mid-level leader, stated: "After all, I am not a woman, and gender is a woman's issue."
  - Avoiding the conversation altogether and staying silent is taking the safe road, an attitude consistent with the broader research on men and gender.

Is gender a woman's issue? Male is a gender too. Why should the entire male gender consider themselves irrelevant when sharing their perspectives on gender equity? Men-in-the-Middle, we need you to speak out and share your thoughts. When you stay silent, we also miss the good things you are doing in support of gender equity or even, more importantly, the innovative ideas men and women can create by working together to close the gaps. When we focus on the zero-sum game, we miss the abundance mentality of working together for better outcomes for all.

What's really holding men back from engaging in gender-equity conversations in the workplace, especially in a post-#MeToo era? In the analysis, it boiled down to "the F word"—*feelings*! Gauging insights from their words and secondary research, what's keeping men silent is the desire to avoid being vulnerable or misunderstood and a fear of judgment. Isn't it interesting, albeit from different angles of #MeToo, that men and women share these feelings? There is common ground, but different vantage points.

For women, the safety to speak out increased with #MeToo; the more women shared stories, the more others felt encouraged to speak out and overcome their fear. For men, however, the safety to speak out decreased with #MeToo. The more women shared their stories, the less men felt their voices mattered.

In the following chapters, we will explore that mindset and the perspective-taking concept, which the 2022 American Psychological Association dictionary describes as "looking at a situation from a viewpoint that is different from one's usual viewpoint" (Medin et al., 2008). It is a foundational skill that helps us relate to others and build relationships for good.

We will see the world, related to gender equity in the workplace, post the height of the #MeToo era, through the lens of the men I interviewed, specifically the Men-in-the-Middle. This book is a compilation of what I have learned while listening to men talk about gender equity in the context of #MeToo and #TimesUp. Taking it a step further, each chapter includes additional research to back up the one-on-one interview insights to gain a more expansive perspective of what the men are thinking and how they may approach the problem if or when asked. Unfortunately, the essence of balance and equity remains out of reach, especially if the majority-male population in the office remains silent in the middle, seeing gender as a women's issue.

Gender equity is in all of our interests. It is our issue.

When we dig below the surface and acknowledge the taboo topics and trials men face too, we discover whispers of wisdom, practical pointers, and interesting ideas that men can also deploy to move women and gender equity forward. This is beneficial for both parties. Through open communication, we can unearth the uncertainty and ambiguity at the root of the divisiveness. Let these words open a dialogue to move the gender-equity conversation forward among men and women.

Key Takeaways

- Men hold a disproportionate amount of power and leadership positions in organizations across the United States and, therefore, influence the majority of gender-related policies and decision-making in the office.
- #MeToo and #TimesUp movements have done a lot of good to amplify voices and stories of sexual assault and harassment victims, define repercussions for lewd and unlawful behaviors in the office, and increase the focus on overall gender equity in terms of fairness, safety, and economic parity.
- At the same time, the uncertainty and ambiguity about the perception of male-female interactions in the office have encouraged the silence among men—the silent majority—stopping them from engaging in gender-equity conversations and relationship-building that can drive positive change.
- When we intentionally invited men to talk about gender equity one-on-one, they had a lot to say and share. We need more men to speak up and out.

- While Men-in-the-Middle tend to agree that diversity of input leads to better decision-making, some see gender as a women's issue and not their conversation to have.

Questions to Discuss or Ponder

1. At the start of the chapter, Robert described gender equity as a pendulum swinging. How would you describe the current state of gender equity and gender-equity conversations in the workplace?
2. Do you engage in gender-equity conversations in the workplace? Why or why not?
3. Regarding the six groups within the bell-shaped curve, what stood out to you the most about the groupings and the language used by the men interviewed? Do you identify with one or more groups? If not, what "handle" would you ascribe to your group?
4. Do you see gender equity as a women's issue, or how would you describe it?
5. Ask yourself: What is one thing I can do to positively impact gender equity at the company I am working for today or an organization with which I am associated, as a volunteer, board member, advisor, etc.?

CHAPTER TWO

A TRIP BACK TO MOVE FORWARD

John said that one step toward solving the modern gender-equity mystery is to learn from history. He shared with me how getting the minority to work with the majority—those in power—will help make significant progress.

John, a seasoned company leader with a blend of private sector and academic experience, started our interview emphatically, sharing his perspective on how #MeToo rightfully exposed inappropriate behaviors in the office, bringing to light hidden gender inequities and power-related issues.

Then he paused, decelerated his pace, and lowered his voice as he built on his comments. "In the wake of #MeToo, there are also unspoken impacts on the mindsets of men working around women in the office," John said. "As in, if I say this and accidentally offend her, will she go to my boss? If I accidentally touch her in the wrong place, will I get a call from HR? If I say something at lunch in mixed company, and she thinks I am creating a hostile work environment, will I get fired?"

He added, "'Don't put yourself in a potentially bad situation.' Isn't that what we tell our kids? Once we see, hear, and acknowledge men's concerns, we can bring them into the gender-equity conversation, and not in an antagonistic way that makes them go silent or feel shame." Then he brought up, and encouraged me to study, the civil rights movement, the March on Washington specifically, when "the majority—those in power—and the minority worked together to make significant progress toward equal rights and pay."

History Lesson: Power, Influence, and Change

If you need to brush up on your history, as I did, here is a summary of the historic event (Study.com, 2015; History.com, 2022):

- In August 1963, more than a quarter of a million black and white citizens of all ages gathered at the Lincoln Memorial in Washington, D.C. to protest racial discrimination and support the Civil Rights Act legislation. In solidarity, they linked arms as they walked and chanted, "Equality now!"
- The March on Washington, known as the March on Washington for Jobs and Freedom, is regarded as a watershed moment in history. It influenced the passage of the Civil Rights Act of 1964, which gave federal law enforcement agencies the power to prevent racial discrimination in employment, voting, and the use of public facilities.
- It is the event at which Dr. Martin Luther King Jr., one of the "Big Six" civil rights leaders, delivered his famous "I Have a Dream" speech.

King advocated marching on the front line for racial equality through nonviolent protests and grassroots organizing. The activist believed that "men and women everywhere, regardless of color or creed, are equal members of the human family" (The King Center, 2022).

Behind the scenes, in between the visible protests, he strategically built relationships with those who could influence sustainable change at a higher level—those in power—which, in this case, were white men. Dr. King spoke with white ministers, targeted white moderates with his message, and worked with President Lyndon B. Johnson in 1964 and 1965 to push forward landmark civil rights laws designed to enact change. Paul Harvey, professor of American History at the University of Colorado in Colorado Springs, wrote in his 2018 article in *The Conversation* that Dr. King is underappreciated for his role as a radical advocate for economic equality for all. He pointed out that when Dr. King spoke at Vanderbilt University in 1957, he reassured all that the movement's aim was not to "defeat or humiliate the white man, but to win his friendship and understanding." Dr. King intentionally engaged white leaders with decision-making power to drive sustainable, lasting change via policy, working to find common ground (Harvey, 2018).

Okay, John, I see why you had me study the March on Washington to build strategic relationships with those in power for lasting change. I admired this principled, strategic move and continued to read and learn more.

The strategy of reaching out to those with influence did not stop with King alone.

In 2013, Krissah Thompson published a Washington Post article titled "In March on Washington, White Activists Were Largely Overlooked but Strategically Essential," where she delved into the partnership between black and white activists. Thompson wrote:

> *Gathered on July 2, 1963, at the Roosevelt Hotel in New York, the six men who led the nation's largest civil rights groups hashed out the details of the nonviolent show of force planned for late summer. In that meeting room sat the Rev. Martin Luther King*

Jr. and the NAACP's Roy Wilkins, the National Urban League's Whitney Young, the SNCC's John Lewis, and the Congress of Racial Equality's James Farmer. The seventy-four-year-old black union leader A. Philip Randolph was the elder statesman and march chairman who had brought them all together. They called themselves the Big Six, and their organizations all had interracial support but were predominantly black, as was their leadership ...

With less than eight weeks before the big day, Randolph and the others decided that they would add four more leaders to their roster: Four white men were invited to join ...

"It was a strategic move," says David Levering Lewis, a historian of the movement.. "Unless it could be shown quite graphically, dramatically, how important it was to white people that black people wanted change, we wouldn't have gotten there," he says.

Thompson explained how the March on Washington came at a moment when many white Americans felt personally disconnected from the civil rights movement, even if they supported the intended outcomes. They agreed civil rights were important for all, but few did anything actively to support the movement.

Does this sound similar to our Men-in-the-Middle from chapter one?

John challenged me to study this moment in history from another angle, one I had overlooked but found very relevant to the gender-equity conversation. Our Men-in-the-Middle, the gender blinders and gender supporters, said they agreed with pursuing gender equity in our one-on-one interviews and even had ideas for improvement, but they did not speak out at the office.

I went back to study the history of the March for additional insights. Thompson interviewed Rachelle Horowitz, who coordinated transportation for the March. Horowitz explained: "The idea really was to say to those people in the middle, white folks in the middle, 'You have to come and support this movement. You can't sit on the fence anymore.'" To reach those white folks in the middle, organizers had to ensure that something was in it for them.

The organizers found common ground: the need for jobs and decent wages. That way, the March represented a move to support wages, civil rights, voting rights, *and* racial equality. Participants also called for a massive federal program to train and place all unemployed workers—black and white—in meaningful and dignified jobs under the idea of "one for all and all for one" (Thompson, 2013).

After the March, King and other civil rights leaders met with President John F. Kennedy and Vice President Lyndon B. Johnson at the White House, where they discussed the need for bipartisan support of civil rights legislation. The Civil Rights Act of 1964 and the Voting Rights Act of 1965 both passed after Kennedy's death but are linked to the March on Washington as an influential moment in history.

While we can certainly point to examples that show that discrimination based on race continues to exist, the United States National Archives website describes the Civil Rights Act of 1964 as the most sweeping civil rights legislation since the Reconstruction period. Black activists identified apathy in white allies and built a sense of urgency based on common ground, paving a path toward action.

In contrast, the fate of the Equal Rights Amendment (ERA), designed to guarantee equal legal rights for all American citizens regardless of sex, remains unclear at the time of publication of this book, and a sense of urgency is missing (Cohen and Codrington, 2020).

These are two major movements in American history that took very different paths. There is an opportunity to learn from both the success of the Civil Rights Act and the stall related to the ERA.

Equal Rights: Women Advocates and Men in Apathy

Could men be the missing piece to equal rights based on sex? As established, men hold the majority of power positions in corporate America and can influence major decisions. Could women advocates build a sense of urgency with men based on common interests and pave the path forward? I tested male engagement at a dinner party I attended with mixed-sex couples I knew.

"What do you mean the Equal Rights Amendment hasn't passed?" asked one man I spoke with at the dinner table.

"No, it has been nearly one hundred years since its first proposal. There were numerous extensions to get to the thirty-eight states required to ratify it before it progressed on the path to making it an official amendment to the U.S. Constitution. It was not until January 2020, nearly fifty years after it passed, that Virginia became the thirty-eighth state to ratify it," I explained, referencing what I read in a 2020 *Time* magazine article by Tara Law.

"So, it's not a law that women have equal rights?" he inquired, almost incredulous.

"It's not a law that *sex* is a protected classification under the Constitution," I told him. "And for a moment of clarity, the term 'sex' refers to anatomical and physiological markers referenced at birth."

I continued: "There are other state laws, statutes, and case laws to protect rights based on sex, but without sex recognized as a classification in the Constitution, those laws are vulnerable to being ignored or reversed." I pulled up the EqualRightsAmendment website on my smartphone, showing him the proof, and read this statement: "The ERA would make sex a suspect classification protected by the highest level of judicial scrutiny."

"Then why are men, especially white aging men, the least protected group of all? And why are women taking men's jobs?" he asked facetiously, knowing this was a passionate topic for me.

"There is something in it for you too you know," I stated before launching into my case for change. "Having equal rights applies to men too. Consider family leave for men and paternal rights in custody cases typically biased toward moms. Think about men breaking into jobs *typically* reserved for women—nursing, dancing, at-home parents, or caretakers. Think about the freedom for men to express themselves as individuals, not defined by toxic masculinity or stereotyped as—"

"How about some dessert?" another friend at the party interrupted, worried we would break into an all-out debate.

My gender-equity sparring partner and I locked eyes, scanned the room, gave each other a nod and a smile, and agreed to move on. As we walked into a new room for the next course, he whispered loud enough for only me to hear, "Touché!" He acknowledged it to me and only me. I made a mental note.

We have some work to do.

Equality Now, the ERA-advocacy organization website, reports that 80 percent of people in the United States think men and women are guaranteed equal rights in the United States Constitution. On the website, in text that was edited in 2021, it says, "They're wrong. One short sentence would make all the difference to ensure people's protections under the Constitution, regardless of sex or gender."

That short phrase is a century in the making. I consulted several sources to condense a timeline of events regarding the Equal Rights Amendment, the proposed Twenty-eighth Amendment:

- **1923:** Alice Paul and Crystal Eastman of the women's suffrage movement proposed the ERA shortly after the passing of the Nineteenth Amendment, granting women the right to vote (ERA, 2022).

- **1923–1970:** Lawmakers introduced the ERA in every session of Congress for nearly fifty years, but it made little progress until the 1970s. Rep. Emanuel Celler (D-NY), chairman of the House Judiciary Committee, refused to hold a hearing on the ERA for more than thirty years (Cohen and Codrington, 2020).

- **1970:** A new class of female lawmakers prioritized the ERA (Cohen and Codrington, 2020).

- **1972:** The amendment passed both the House and Senate, exceeding the two-thirds majority votes needed to advance it to the next step in the process. Thirty-eight of the fifty states, or three-fourths, had to ratify it within a seven-year deadline before the amendment could become official (Law, 2020).

- **1972–2020:** Thirty states immediately approved the amendment. By 1977, an additional five states also said yes, and yet the ERA remained three states short of moving forward. After Congress voted to extend the deadline a few times, Nevada approved the amendment in 2017 and Illinois in 2018. The thirty-eighth state, Virginia, did not ratify the proposed amendment until January 2020, nearly fifty years after it passed in Congress.

- **2023:** As of the publication of this book, the fate of the ERA remains unclear. The process for adding an amendment to the United States Constitution outlined in Article V, and the time extension on this process, have raised some concerns.

Proponents say adopting the ERA will advance the cause of equality in the twenty-first century for men and women. For the first time, sex would be considered a suspect classification, like race, religion, and national origin currently are. However, some assume the deadline has passed, suggesting that activists may need to start over.

The text of the amendment adjusted slightly over the years to adapt to the times, but the main message remained constant. The final version Congress approved in 1972 and sent to the states for ratification reads as follows (EqualityNow, 2021):

- **Section 1.** Equality of rights under the law shall not be denied or abridged by the United States or by any State on account of sex.
- **Section 2.** Congress shall have the power to enforce, by appropriate legislation, the provisions of this article.
- **Section 3.** This amendment shall take effect two years after the date of ratification.

During the wait, other acts have passed in the name of gender equality, including the Equal Pay Act of 1963, the Pregnancy Discrimination Act of 1978, and Title IX of 1972—the latter protecting people from discrimination based on sex in education programs or activities that receive federal financial assistance (United States Department of Health and Human Services, 2021; United States Equal Employment Opportunity Commission, 1963, 1978).

For perspective, there are signs of progress:

- My own mother, who graduated from high school nearly a decade before Title IX, wanted to play volleyball, but the school said it did not have enough people or equipment for competitive leagues for women. Today, women's volleyball is a popular sport. In 2021, over one million viewers watched the National Collegiate Athletic Association Division I Women's Volleyball Championship, making it the most-viewed women's college volleyball match ever (Hruby, 2021).
- My female colleagues, who had children well before me, shared stories of a quick return to work—in two weeks

or less. But in 1972, the Equal Employment Opportunity Commission drafted guidelines that required employers to treat disabilities resulting from pregnancy and childbirth in the same manner as other temporary disabilities (Scholar, 2016). Even today, while companies may call it maternity leave, it is typically classified as a temporary disability and treated as such.

• Men and women do have some common ground. The Family and Medical Leave Act of 1993 granted certain categories of women and men up to twelve weeks of unpaid job-protected leave for the birth and care of a newborn, placing a child for adoption or foster care, and care for an immediate family member (Scholar, 2016).

The rights of a man caring for a family member were front and center for Ruth Bader Ginsburg well before she became Supreme Court Justice. Also known as the "Notorious RBG" or just "RBG," she is another historical figure who effectively advocated for common ground, primarily equality among men and women. With wisdom on her side, RBG did not get deterred by the ERA's slow progress. Expressed in a quote captured from a book and documentary film about her life, RBG said, "Real change, enduring change, happens one step at a time. Women will have achieved true equality when men share the responsibility of bringing up the next generation" (Carmon and Knizhnik, 2015; West and Cohen, 2018).

Equality for All: RBG for Men and Women

About eight months after Congress passed the ERA, then-lawyer Ruth Bader Ginsburg stood before the United States Court of Appeals in a case that challenged the phrase "equal protection of the laws" under the Fourteenth Amendment. In Charles E. Moritz v. Commissioner of the Internal Revenue, Ginsburg chose to represent a man who faced discrimination to show that addressing issues of gender equality are in the interests of men, too (Thulin, 2018).

The Internal Revenue Service (IRS) denied a tax deduction Charles Moritz claimed in 1968 for the cost of caring for his dependent, invalid mother, saying he was not eligible for the deduction as a single man who had never married. The IRS said the deduction is limited to a woman, a widower or divorcée, or a husband whose wife is incapacitated or institutionalized. In an appeal, the Tax Court upheld the government's position, rejecting the contention that the denial of the deduction to him was arbitrary or unlawful (Justia, 1972).

Moritz, via RBG, took it to the Court of Appeals, arguing discrimination on the basis of sex violated the Equal Protection Clause of the United States Constitution (the Fourteenth Amendment). The Tenth Circuit Court of Appeals overturned the decision and agreed that the tax code conflicted with the Equal Protection Clause of the Constitution.

In 2018, Participant Media released the movie directed by Mimi Leder, *On the Basis of Sex,* a story about RBG's life and battles for gender equality, which focused on the Moritz case. The pivotal scene in the movie captured a moment when the actor portraying Tenth Circuit Court Judge William Edward Doyle challenged RBG's arguments, saying the word "woman" does not appear once in the Constitution of the United States. In response, the actress playing RBG points out that neither does the word "freedom," referring to the original Constitution, before any amendments.

Later in the movie, RBG made it known that the intent of the law had not been to discriminate against men when she said, "It had been written at a different time when Congress could not have imagined a man, who had never been married, taking care of his mother" (Leder, 2018). She also explained that when she started at Harvard, there were no women's bathrooms, and women were just thrilled to be there and did not immediately recognize the injustice.

But times changed, calling for a fresh, revised way to look at these situations.

In the same courtroom scene, RBG argued a ruling in Moritz's favor could remove barriers that bar the next generation from pursuing dreams, not just for women but for *all* citizens, both men and women. She called for a time to rethink or reframe what equality looks like (Leder, 2018).

While movies can take poetic license, the screenwriter, Daniel Stiepleman, is RBG's nephew with firsthand knowledge of what RBG was like. Plus, according to a 2018 article by Tatiana Tenreyro in *The Hollywood Reporter,* Ginsburg edited the third draft of the script. She made sure everything was accurate but allowed some creative liberties in the story.

After being appointed to the Supreme Court in 1993, Justice Ginsburg continued her efforts to establish full gender equality under the Fourteenth Amendment on behalf of women and men. Before she died in 2020, the Notorious RBG had been interviewed several times and is cited in a number of sources, including these quotes from a variety of interviews:

- "… and if you are a boy and you like teaching, you like nursing, you would like to have a doll, that's okay too. We should each be free to develop our own talents, whatever they may be, and not be held back by artificial barriers" (MAKERS, 2012).
- "I don't say women's rights—I say the constitutional principle of the equal citizenship stature of men *and* women" (Academy of Achievement, 2020).

- "I didn't change the Constitution [in reference to the Fourteenth Amendment]. The equality principle was there from the start. I just was an advocate for seeing its full realization" (Weinberger, 2013).

We have two historical legends and two major historical events demonstrating how the fight for equity based on a common ground interest is effective. Furthermore, feminism, according to The Merriam-Webster Dictionary, is a belief in advocacy of the political, economic, and social equality of the sexes—[men *and* women]—expressed especially through organized activity on behalf of women's rights and interests.

For men who think gender equity is a women's issue, eliminating discrimination based on sex will benefit them too. Throughout the book, I provide "reasons to believe." For example, in a 1984 brief submitted to Congress regarding the ERA, Robert J. Gray, men's rights advocate, listed some legal benefits men will gain—rather mutual benefits for both men and women—when we have a society void of discriminatory practices. Here are some paraphrased excerpts from his writing:

- **Child custody:** The ERA will open the door to reexamine custody determined on "the best interest of the child," which differs from state to state. Currently, family courts grant sole custody to mothers in more than 90 percent of divorce cases.
- **Unwed fathers:** The ERA will provide rights to unwed fathers who want to support their children by being present and engaged during a child's time of development, financially and emotionally. Currently, most states only care about financial support. The ERA will guarantee a decision that is not clouded by obsolete sex-role stereotypes.
- **Career and family:** The ERA will mandate that women be paid the same as men for comparable work. When women

are paid fairly, the men married to these women will also benefit. As a result, it will be much easier than it is at present for men to take time off to raise their children or consider career changes.

The Equal Rights Amendment, which states that "equality of rights under the law shall not be denied or abridged by the United States or by any State on account of sex ..." includes rights for both males and females. True equality between women and men will not develop until we address the issues both sexes face.

My interview with John reminded me that we have a precedent of a minority group taking a strategic risk to open a conversation and engage those with majority influence by finding common ground and speaking out. The March on Washington that John pointed me to led to a major opportunity and change in civil rights legislation.

Now, one hundred years in the making, can we apply the same strategic foresight, identifying common ground with Men-in-the-Middle—who may be apathetic or silent—to advocate for gender equity?

The potential for common ground is there. It is time to look deeper at the "why" behind the silence for men. So far, Robert encouraged perspective-sharing from a place of power (in chapter one). John, at the start of this chapter, suggested we learn from history and engage men in the conversation without invoking shame. Both perspective-taking and finding common ground involve communication and working together to reframe the issue for a better path forward. Let's break through the silence in the next chapter.

Key Takeaways

- The black organizers of the March on Washington for Jobs and Freedom intentionally invited and engaged white majority leaders based on common interests including wages; this collaboration led in part to a successful March and the passing of the 1964 Civil Rights Amendment.

- Martin Luther King Jr., one of the March organizers, embraced a two-tier leadership approach in his lifelong fight for civil rights by marching on the front line in the form of nonviolent protests and employing the less-visible strategy of building relationships with those who could influence change at a higher level—those in power.

- The ERA intends to eliminate discrimination based on sex to benefit both men and women.

- In 1972, Congress approved the ERA with this language: "Equality of rights under the law shall not be denied or abridged by the United States or by any State on account of sex." In order to be added as an amendment to the Constitution, it required three-fourths of states to ratify it. It was not until 2020 that Virginia became the thirty-eighth state, crossing the threshold. At the time of publication of this book, the ERA's fate is uncertain.

- We can learn from exemplary leaders in history—from the leaders of the March on Washington and the work of the former Supreme Court Justice Ruth Bader Ginsberg advocating for both men and women—to engage Men-in-the-Middle to speak out from a place of common ground.

Questions to Discuss or Ponder

1. The chapter started with John saying that #MeToo affected the mindsets of men working around women in the office. Does that align with your experience? What have you observed?

2. Did the March on Washington example offer ideas on collaborating more effectively with your team or company?

3. What surprised you about the Equal Rights Amendment? What other questions do you have?

4. What are some areas of life where you and others can benefit from equal rights for both men and women?

5. What ideas do you have to move equity forward in a way that benefits men and women?

CHAPTER THREE

THE SPIRAL OF SILENCE

Jay finds it creepy to discuss body parts or brazen bar stories in mixed company. His answer is to eliminate compliments in the office, especially to "non-dudes," and avoid any awkward conversations.

Jay is a technology leader from the Pacific Northwest. A straight, married man, he recalls interacting mostly with guys in his college information technology classes, and today he continues to work and build his corporate career on teams primarily composed of what he calls "dudes."

The week before I interviewed him, one of Jay's male colleagues had been at a strip club over the weekend and shared his experience with others at the office. Jay looked at the people in proximity to the conversation. The group included mainly men, but a few women also sat within earshot of the discussion. He excused himself to go to the restroom, and the conversation ended.

"I get uncomfortable if I think others are listening, and I thought, holy crap, why did he do that?" Jay explained. "I struggle a bit because if it was just guys, would I have been as offended? ... I didn't want to offend the women I work with and near, so I walked away. Now that I am thinking about it, does that make me sound insensitive?"

As Jay contemplated his own reaction, he also shared an example of what concerned him regarding other interactions in the office. "It has always seemed weird to me about compliments in the office. I could never talk with a woman and say, 'That is really a nice dress.' That would sound super creepy. I mean, I would be weirded out if a woman looked at me and said, 'Hey, you look like you have been working out!' Maybe people can get away with it if they are not creepy, but I stay clear of it."

Then the uncertainty crept in a second time for Jay. After a short pause, he said, as if he had an epiphany in the moment, "There is a distinct possibility that I am being creepy, and I don't even know it!"

One of the other men I interviewed said he would feel sad if he wore a new suit to the office and no one noticed. However, nearly a dozen others agreed with Jay, specifically in the context of avoiding complimenting women on what they are wearing or anything related to appearance—hair, jewelry, shoes, and definitely not a dress or pants. The men usually did not use the word "creepy." Instead, they called it "awkward" as in they opted not to put themselves in an "awkward" situation. By not saying anything, they avoided it altogether.

The men addressed the awkwardness with silence.

Arielle Lapiano, a contributor to Ellevate Network—a community of professional women committed to helping each other—wrote about this behavior in her 2019 blog that got picked up by *Forbes*, titled "Dear Sir—Don't Let #MeToo Make You Afraid of Me." She shared that a male colleague apologized for accidentally touching her elbow. Then another male office peer called her after a tense but professional conversation to ask her if he had been rude. Still, another man checked in with her to see if he had crossed the line in any way when he complimented her on a new pair of funky boots. She called it an unintended consequence of the

#MeToo movement, a sign that men are unsure how to interact with women in the office.

Sheryl Sandberg, author of the book *Lean In: Women, Work, and the Will to Lead,* and Marc Pritchard presented more data that reflected this uncertainty in the 2019 *Fortune* article titled "The Number of Men Who Are Uncomfortable Mentoring Women Is Growing." They wrote about the analysis of survey results that showed senior men are exponentially more likely to hesitate to spend time with junior *women* than *men* in a variety of activities:

- twelve times more likely to hesitate to have a one-on-one meeting
- nine times more likely to hesitate about business travel
- six times more likely to hesitate to have work dinners

In a 2018 *Harvard Business Review* article, two corporate training experts, Candace Bertotti and David Maxfield, wrote about the adverse reactions to #MeToo. Sixty-five percent of men say it's now *less* safe to mentor and coach members of the opposite sex. One survey respondent wrote, "Men and women are not talking to each other. The environment is becoming sterile and completely unenjoyable at work."

While awareness is a good thing, the uncertainty leads to silence, and the silence extends beyond compliments to include the broader issue of gender-related topics. There is a perceived risk of speaking out, especially if the interpreted viewpoint is contrary to the popular one or out of the norm. It is new territory, especially since men have set societal norms in the office for such a long time.

Here is what that uneasiness looks like from the men I interviewed just after the height of the #MeToo campaign. These are direct interview quotes:

- "We are more afraid to say anything that might offend people. Way too many topics are completely off-limits now."

- "There is undoubtedly fear or concern over things we did or said in the past."
- "You must be cognizant of anything you say, so it is not misconstrued. One of my most respected male colleagues will no longer have a door shut during a meeting with a woman."
- "We are all on edge … How much latitude do we have to joke with people?"
- "There is heightened awareness about saying offhand remarks."
- "I am not saying anything because no one has asked me about my opinion on #MeToo or gender equity; guys won't step out of bounds without an invitation and don't want to take a chance."
- "There's uncertainty about addressing topics like the #MeToo movement or topics [men] don't perceive are directly relating to them or the bottom line, like gender."

I see you, Men-in-the-Middle, and I hear you. You, the reader, might even feel the same as these men. This desire to ensure you do not offend anyone or step out of bounds is respected and understood. Silence and avoidance, however, perpetuate the status quo of inequity.

A Brief Benefits Overview

In the process of silence, men might be leaving opportunities on the table for a better way. There are many benefits to having that gender-equity pendulum in the middle. In subsequent chapters, I continue to build on this idea. For now, let's briefly mention a few plusses. Academic researchers Andre P. Audette and Sean Lam have published their benefit-based research online in "The Gender Policy Report" and in the 2019 *Journal of Happiness*, which states that "improving gender equality and women's representation in the public and private sectors can significantly improve life satisfaction for all residents of a country, both men and women."

But let's make it about what is important to you, including the well-being of your children and your sex life. Yep, that's right. I said your sex life.

Let's start with the kids first. In 2021, the Child & Family Research Partnership at the University of Austin, Texas, issued a policy brief titled "The Importance of Father Involvement" (Osborne et al., 2021). The document cites several studies that support how active dads—measured by accessibility, engagement, and responsibility—positively impact children. For example, one finding showed that father involvement is linked to higher levels of academic preparedness and fewer school-related challenges (Rosenberg et al., 2006; Pruett, 2000).

In 2004, the United States Department of Health and Human Services' Head Start Bureau, focused on children from birth to age five, commissioned the National Head Start Training and Technical Assistance Resource Center to compile the extensive body of research on the perks of the dad-child interactions. The report, "Building Blocks for Father Involvement, Building Block 1: Appreciating How Fathers Give Children a Head Start," references several studies that show the dad-child relationship is different from the mom, and no less valuable. Active dads benefit young children in the following ways:

- Increased verbal skills, especially in daughters, and higher cognitive skills (Bing, 1963)
- More curiosity and problem-solving skills, including mathematical competencies for daughters (Biller, 1981; Radin et al., 1983)
- Increased intellectual, motor, and physical development (Parke, 1996)

- High levels of empathy and compassion as adults, as well as positive moral behavior (Sears et al., 1957; Koestner et al., 1990; Pruett, 2000)

Now, let's get to how you probably got those kids in the first place. In a 2016 study published on the American Psychological Association's PsychNet titled "Skip the Dishes? Not So Fast! Sex and Housework Revisited," researchers Matthew Johnson, Nancy Galambos, and Jared Anderson found couples enjoyed more frequent and satisfying sex for both partners when men made a fair contribution to housework.

I can tell you that in my home, housework can be an aphrodisiac! When I am on my laptop working on a project, nothing is sexier than seeing my husband in his three-quarter zippered pullover, sleeves pushed up to his elbows, exposing his forearms while doing the dishes. The forethought of waking up to clean dishes and an empty sink gets me excited.

Other research showed that when genders are more equal, men have more freedom about how they express themselves and leverage parental leave without fear of discrimination (Soken-Huberty, 2020). Another study showed dads who share household chores are more likely to raise daughters who aspire to less traditional and potentially higher-paying careers (Croft et al., 2014).

Since I mention careers, let's also acknowledge the benefits of pursuing gender equity in business. Multiple studies show a more diverse workforce is a competitive advantage and can bolster innovation, revenue, sustainability, and more (Reguera-Alvarado et al., 2015; Kim and Starks, 2016; Perryman et al., 2016; Liu, 2018; Chen et al., 2018; Post et al., 2021). The organization Catalyst keeps on its website a running list of evidence-based research called "Why Diversity & Inclusion Matter: Financial Performance," updated through June 2020. This includes a study by the Credit-Suisse

Research Institute that found companies in which women held 20% or more management roles generated 2.04% higher cash flow returns on investment than companies with 15% or less women in management roles (Kersley et al., 2019).

Many corporate leaders agree, including those at the board of directors' level. For example, the 2021 PricewaterhouseCoopers LLC's Annual Corporate Director survey shared that 75 percent of corporate directors say diversity enhances company performance.

Before we get to the good stuff, from business to personal gains, however, we need to break through and understand the *why* behind the choice men make *not* to address or speak out about the issues of gender equity. Then we can tackle how to work through that.

My research focused on the silence, or rather not speaking out about gender equity in general. Let's look at it from Jay's perspective. Jay, whose story opened this chapter, decided certain conversations are off-limits, especially in mixed company. He has gone to the extreme of not saying anything to cope with the discomfort of not knowing how it will be interpreted. For him, the potential benefits do not outweigh the risk. Let's examine that silence before we open a new narrative.

Dissecting the Spiral of Silence

In academic terms, this reluctance to speak out is associated with the *spiral of silence* theory, broadly described as withholding one's opinion for fear of being excluded or poorly perceived by those with a majority view (Hedge, 2022; Petersen, 2022). Political scientist Elisabeth Noelle-Neumann first proposed this political science and mass communication theory in 1974 to explain why a person may stay silent if they have a view that differs from a commonly held— and therefore more powerful—force of the popular perspective. (Noelle-Neumann, 1993; Davie, 2022).

If you apply this to Jay, he may fear that anything other than what is agreed upon by the majority of society will be met with aggression, dismissal, misunderstanding, etc. So, for him, the better choice is to avoid it altogether, to stay silent and out of trouble.

He is in the spiral.

A number of the men I interviewed described gender equity as a women's issue. However, they also have stated that they perceive gender-related issues as not their conversation to have. This means that, even though men are considered the majority in corporate America by numbers and influence, many are not using their positions of power to address the important issue of gender equity, even if it will benefit them too.

This was the case even before #MeToo. Post the height of the #MeToo and #TimesUp social media explosion in 2017–2018, however, the missing male voice became more obvious. The majority view included stories, mostly shared by women, about male behaviors described as unwelcome, ill-intentioned, or inappropriate. Yet, even as the #MeToo and #TimesUp conversations spanned beyond harassment to address gender equity, men's opinions remained mostly silent.

Noelle-Neumann developed the spiral of silence theory before the prevalence of social media. Still, researchers, including German Neubaum and Nicole Krämer, continued to study the spiral of silence more recently in the context of offline and online communication. Even on a social networking website, in the context of a personally relevant audience, people often hold back their opinions if they do not agree with the majority (Neubaum and Krämer, 2018). The researchers wrote:

> *If one's opinion is perceived to conform to the majority, individuals are more likely to express their stance than individuals who find themselves on the side of the minority—these latter people might*

lapse into silence. Thus, the minority group, in turn, becomes less visible in public opinion over time, while the presumed majority stance becomes more and more salient.

The authors argued how situational factors, including fear of isolation or being verbally attacked for expressing a divergent viewpoint, can hold people back from stating an opinion opposite or different than the popular view. As a result, the minority viewpoint stays silent to avoid conflict.

Regarding my research, it appears #MeToo encouraged victims, predominantly women, to overcome their fear and speak out in support of one another. This heightened activity created more fear for men in corporate jobs to speak out about harassment and gender equity, even though they have the most influence in the organization. In short, they hold the majority of influential high-level positions in companies, yet they are the minority when it comes to gender-equity storytelling.

The pendulum is swinging, influenced by timely events and circumstances.

Barbara Harmon's 2021 dissertation "Framing, Spiral of Silence, and Coverage of the #MeToo Movement" corroborated the findings of Neubaum and Krämer. Harmon wrote: "The spiral of silence explains that those who do not want to risk being secluded or outed for what they believe to be an unpopular opinion will remain silent rather than change the outcome."

Harmon's study focused on race differences and media bias toward covering the stories of celebrities and white female victims during #MeToo, making stories of black women and women of color the minority. Harmon wrote in her conclusion: "Those who already are in the limelight should not be the only stories told. There are victims who have far more to fear and a lot more to lose, but no one is writing their story and speaking for them."

All people have a story to tell, especially victims of marginalized populations who get less media attention. All victims, regardless of color or gender, deserve a voice. This is why Tarana Burke founded #MeToo, making it more than a moment in time and bigger than any hashtag.

I take a little liberty here, with respect to the spiral of silence and maybe even at the risk of my own isolation, to suggest a parallel thought for men, those who are not sexual offenders but are gender stakeholders. Male is a gender too. I suggest we expand our thinking, problem-solving, and perspective-sharing to include those whose stories have not been told, both victims and people in positions of influence, to make changes that help all involved. Let's talk with those who have *not* been speaking—the silent ones—specifically about gender-related issues post the height of #MeToo, and this includes men, especially if they can influence the outcomes.

Before I lose my women's champion card, which I am proud of, follow my logic. The majority speaking out on #MeToo are women sharing stories of their own experiences as victims. The majority of men in the media, the stories we hear about men, involve the ones facing allegations or men convicted of harassment or assault, also known as the offenders.

Let's also acknowledge, as I did in the introduction, that there are male victims in the #MeToo movement. The data shows one in four men experience unwanted sexual events across their lifetime (Basile et al., 2022). According to *The National Intimate Partner and Sexual Violence Survey: 2010 Summary Report*, published by the United States Center for Disease Control and Prevention, more than 90 percent of adult rape and sexual assault victims are female, and 10 percent are male. Men, however, are the perpetrators in the vast majority of sexual assault cases, regardless of the sex of the victim; about 90 percent of the sexual assaults against women and 93 percent of assaults against men are committed by a man (Black et al., 2011).

The numbers support the volume of women-as-victim accounts we hear in the news. Female victims are speaking out, sharing stories of sexual assault perpetrated by men. Some of these women's stories are making the headlines. Male offenders are also making the headlines.

Where are the stories of men who experienced inappropriate behaviors at work as well? Men are also saying "#MeToo," but we rarely hear these stories in the news. These male voices are missing from the discussion about discrimination based on sex.

In November 2019, *CapeTalk*, a news and talk station out of Cape Town, South Africa, dedicated a segment for its global YouTube channel called "Male Survivor of Sexual Abuse Speaks Out." The show's host, Pipa Hudson, opened the interview with the comment, "This is an issue that is just not talked about enough," before she invited the male guest and sexual assault survivor to share his story.

There seems to be a reason we don't hear about these stories as much.

Laura Bradley's 2018 *Vanity Fair* article "#MeToo's Male Accusers, One Year Later" highlighted stories of celebrity men who also came forward about their own sexual assault experiences, sharing accounts of being groped, in some cases, by other men. The article spoke to the "horseplay" stigma that makes it more challenging for male survivors to speak out, meaning that men justify lewd behaviors as simply horseplay.

This is not a new idea either. Back in 2002, reporter Margaret Talbot wrote *The New York Times Magazine* article "Men Behaving Badly," in which she states: "Men's claims of harassment often center on what is considered 'horseplay.'"

What is this horseplay stigma, and how does it prevent men from speaking out about unwanted sexual acts committed against them by other men? The issue is that, among men, potentially inappropriate behavior can be deemed as just "goofing off" instead of a sexual act. A 2021 article by Gold Star Law titled "Hold Your Horses!" said this on the matter:

> *Courts consider "horseplay" to be different from harassment. Horseplay is joking, teasing, bullying, and other such behavior that is not specifically motivated by sex. For example, courts have found instances where one heterosexual male slaps a male coworker on the buttocks to be horseplay, but a heterosexual male doing the same thing to a female coworker could be harassment. The difference is the presumption of whether the behavior is motivated by sex.*

This is where it gets tricky. Who gets to decide whether a behavior is motivated by sex or not? Traditional and, at times, outdated perspectives on male behavior, such as the saying "boys will be boys," can cause people to think inappropriate acts toward another man are normal. As a result, many men may remain silent even when sexual misconduct is directed at them (or another man).

A 2018 Fisher Phillips article titled "'Sexual Horseplay' Or 'Sex Discrimination'? The Half-Million Dollar Question," put it this way:

> *… even if you believe the conduct simply amounts to juvenile horseplay, roughhousing, or locker-room behavior, a jury might one day conclude that the conduct constitutes discrimination [of sex]. Managers commonly overlook inappropriate behavior among workers because they believe the interactions are good-natured. Sometimes the victim even laughs along or dismisses the harassment. But this is no reason to turn a blind eye and neglect your zero-tolerance policy.*

The 2018 *NBC News* story "Some Male Sexual Assault Victims Feel Left Behind by #MeToo" featured music professor Chris Brown, one of several men who accused renowned conductor James Levine of abusing him as a teen (Associated Press, 2018). Brown told the Associated Press there is a double bind for men. "Men are historically considered the bad guys," said Brown, referring to public attitudes. "If some men abuse women, then we all are abusers ourselves ... so, therefore, when it comes to our abuse, we deserve it."

There is another untold angle to the story here too; men who do the right thing.

What about the stories of men who stepped in when they witnessed sexual harassment in the workplace? While some may argue that people should not get media attention for doing the right thing, there is something to be said for role modeling and reinforcing the behaviors we want to see. We do that in chapter eleven.

Where are the stories of men in the office who are in charge, collaborating well with female colleagues and not displaying inappropriate behaviors? The media is not covering their stories, and these men are not speaking out about issues related to gender equity, sexual harassment, work-life balance, pay, opportunities, and more.

These are our Men-in-the-Middle. When I asked, in one-on-one anonymous interviews, men shared stories of doing the right thing. These behaviors did not make headlines. I highlight more of these in the last chapter on reinforcement, but here are a few non-headline moments:

- Phillip stopped a project team meeting to address the topic of respect when one of his engineers made an offhand comment about a female colleague's butt in jeans.
- Tony asked his human resource support team for a report that compared salaries of his male and female employees who worked at the same level. When he saw a gap in

compensation that could not be explained by experience or education differences, he initiated a plan to fix the problem.

- Bud broke the "bro code" and reported what started as a joke among male colleagues ranking the appearance of professional female colleagues. It crossed the line for him when a leader said, "Let's consult the list before picking women for a project team." Bud explained: "Maybe he intended it as a joke, but it was not cool either way."

Somewhere in the spiral of silence, these stories of men speaking up are not audible. Maybe it feels pointless for men to talk about doing the right thing when the majority of conversation in the media exposes men as offenders. Or perhaps they feel it is not their place to speak out when women do the majority of storytelling. It could be that some men feel it is disrespectful to speak out after years of injustice and imbalance between men and women in the office.

The perceived backlash to holding an unpopular opinion may be yet another of many reasons for the silence. Men might avoid the conversation about #MeToo and other gender-related issues in the workplace because they are uncertain of the impact of their words. They may even agree with Jay, who embraces silence on certain topics just in case he could be seen as creepy. Whatever the reason, the spiral of silence is muting the voices of the men in our society on a topic where they can make a difference, influence others, collaborate with female colleagues to innovate for effective solutions, and advocate for change.

Figure 3 below depicts a gender equity spiral of silence visual perspective I created to bring it all together, based on Noelle-Neumann's spiral of silence theory.

Spiral of Silence Applied to Gender-Equity Discussions

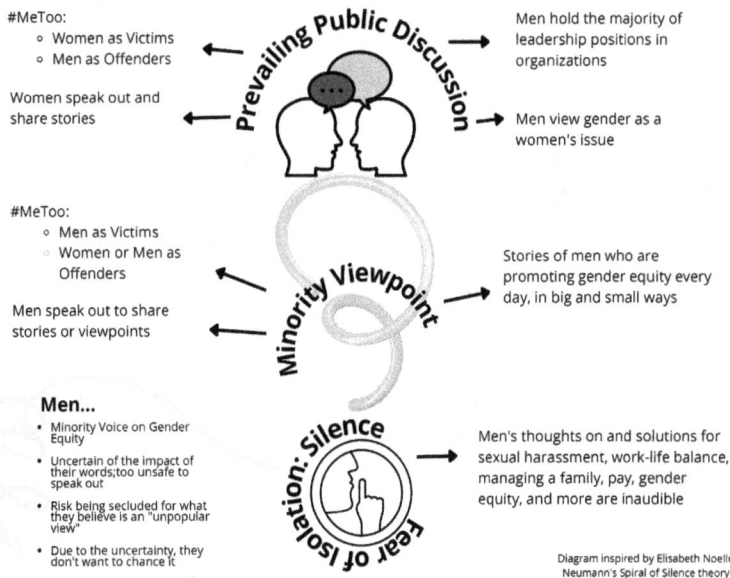

Prevailing Public Discussion

#MeToo:
  o Women as Victims
  o Men as Offenders

Women speak out and share stories

Men hold the majority of leadership positions in organizations

Men view gender as a women's issue

Minority Viewpoint

#MeToo:
  o Men as Victims
  o Women or Men as Offenders

Men speak out to share stories or viewpoints

Stories of men who are promoting gender equity every day, in big and small ways

Silence: Fear of Isolation

Men...
- Minority Voice on Gender Equity
- Uncertain of the impact of their words;too unsafe to speak out
- Risk being secluded for what they believe is an "unpopular view"
- Due to the uncertainty, they don't want to chance it

Men's thoughts on and solutions for sexual harassment, work-life balance, managing a family, pay, gender equity, and more are inaudible

Diagram inspired by Elisabeth Noelle-Neumann's Spiral of Silence theory

Figure 3: Visual depiction of a gender-equity spiral of silence, based on Noelle-Neumann's spiral of silence theory.

At the top, we have the "Prevailing Public Discussion," or rather, the dominant view shared in social and traditional mass media channels. The story coverage elevated and perpetuated a narrative that became the prevailing public opinion; an example of this is that the majority of media stories show women as victims and men as offenders. The case data supports this volume of stories. However, when that is the *only* storyline, and the discourse does not highlight instances of collaboration, mutual respect among genders or strong examples of allyship, the prevailing narrative is that men are seen most often as perpetrators.

The media also promoted a traditional "gender is a women's issue" narrative in 2014 when then *Today* show host Matt Lauer asked General Motor's first female CEO Mary Barra if she got the job because she was a woman and could she balance being a CEO and mom. During that time, I worked for a company closely connected to the automotive industry, and I remember watching that interview and the aftermath on social media. I admired her progress; I had been juggling a career and kids too. *Politico* reporter Kendall Breitman wrote in a June 26, 2014 article titled "Lauer Defends GM Mom Question" that Lauer said he would have asked a male executive the same question too. He had been intrigued by a comment Barra made in a *Forbes* article earlier that year about missing her son's prom due to work.

Imagine the impact if men spoke about work-life balance too, among other issues related to gender equity. Unfortunately, those comments and stories, about men navigating the challenges of work and family, are typically not part of the prevailing public discussion; neither are the conversations about men as victims of sexual assault and harassment or men's role in creating a culture of inclusion promoted as part of the prevailing public discussion. When we include perspectives from men and women, we have the potential to broaden the conversation to address a safe workspace for all that is based on mutual respect. It changes the narrative.

In reference to Noelle-Newman's spiral of silence, men represent the minority when it comes to speaking out for gender equity. The male perspective gets lost as the dominant narrative rises to the top. In the absence of an open dialogue about potentially uncomfortable topics, uneasiness creeps in, accompanied by a fear of doing or saying the wrong thing in mixed-gender interactions. It keeps some men locked in the spiral of silence, promoting the belief that "gender is a women's issue."

When it comes to gender, men are in the majority with regard to roles that can impact change and influence others in the organization. It is men who occupy the most C-suite seats, and their decisions can advance new policies and set the tone for open dialogue and inclusive conversations. Women are doing the majority of speaking up and out about gender-related issues. Still, they are the minority when it comes to positions of power to influence policy and drive change. In short, men hold the majority of potential leverage but don't speak out, while women are in the minority regarding leadership roles but do speak out about gender equity issues.

The proverbial pendulum that swings from one extreme to the other has yet to find balance. In that state of uncertainty and perpetual motion, the silence that lingers on the surface appears to be an acceptance of unacknowledged, unspoken tension.

There is value, however, in embracing the paradoxical mindset about discomfort and conflict as a path to clarity, renewed focus, and a new narrative. In the 2020 *BBC Worklife* article, "Why the 'Paradox Mindset' is the Key to Success," authors Loizos Heracleous and David Robson said successful leaders can simultaneously entertain conflicting or contradictory thoughts. Regarding conflict and competing perspectives, the paradox mindset sees conflict as growth versus a situation to avoid.

The Good Guys: Men-in-the-Middle

The twist in logic is that the conscious ones, like Jay and other Men-in-the-Middle, are most likely not the harassment offenders, according to Kim Elsesser, author of *Sex and the Office* and senior contributor to *Forbes*. She explained it this way:

> *Most men are not going to inadvertently do something like ask a woman to get in the shower with him! The average guy might worry about whether a comment will be misinterpreted, but that has nothing to do with sexual assault and harassment. If you are a guy and you're worried about whether a compliment will be misinterpreted, you've got nothing to worry about.*

Elsesser's quote is in a 2020 book called *Good Guys: How Men Can Be Better Allies for Women in the Workplace* by David G. Smith and W. Brad Johnson, two social scientists and experts on gender in the workplace. They promote the message that men have a crucial role in promoting gender equality in the office as allies and active advocates for women. This is the second book by Smith, a professor at Johns Hopkins University, and Johnson, a professor of psychology at the United States Naval Academy.

The first book, *Athena Rising: How and Why Men Should Mentor Women*, published in 2019, is geared to help men coach and counsel women effectively, supported by evidence that shows women face more barriers than men in securing professional mentors. Johnson and Smith explain that mentoring, allyship, and intentional friendship are key to achieving gender equality in the workplace.

Smith and Johnson also acknowledged that intentional, strategic relationships between men and women can become complicated under conventional gender roles. With the broader awakening and awareness of inappropriate office behaviors under #MeToo, some men viewed one-on-one mentoring of women as dangerous. The authors said men can face a dilemma in the tension between a male wanting to help and develop a junior woman on one level and the competing desire to avoid attraction, intimacy, and the potential complications that can happen when males and females work in proximity. Smith and Johnson wrote in *Athena Rising*:

> *We may have no problem being friends and bros with our male peers, but the prospect of being 'just friends' with women leaves us off-kilter. On the one end of the continuum, we fear sexploitation, perhaps responding to increasing intimacy with sexual overtures. On the other end of the continuum, we anxiously avoid the very intimacy necessary for creating trust, thereby creating sterile and distant relationships.*

I have worked with many men in my career, and I consider a number of these colleagues to be friends. We have met each other's families and had in-depth conversations about current events. I have not had a second thought beyond that platonic, respectful interaction. I can only assume the same from my colleagues. Based on my experience, I thought it absurd that people think men and women can't be in a room alone together until I realized *my* thinking might be outside the norm, the minority.

About eight years ago, a man I had known and trusted for many years asked me to meet him at a local coffee shop. He wanted my advice about an alleged developing intimate office relationship in an organization we both belonged to. He struggled to make sense of the male-female interaction at the center of the office gossip and told me about the reported behaviors between the man and woman.

"Have you ever met with a man at work, alone, and behind closed doors?" he asked me in a serious whisper, his brow furrowed.

I hesitated as I reflected on nearly three decades of work experience, primarily in large, Fortune 500 company environments that spanned the manufacturing floor to corporate headquarters. I thought this was a trick question and hoped he would provide more context about why he asked or what he alleged had been happening behind this closed door. He did not expand on his comments. Instead, he just looked at me, waiting for my response.

"Nearly every day of my career," I responded instinctively with a bit of sarcasm in my voice. "I don't know how I would have done my job if I could not meet with men, often alone."

The reality is that at any point in my career, I worked with men throughout the day. I even traveled with men. In some cases, behind closed doors, I met with male bosses who shared confidential information about the company and leadership decisions I needed to know to do my job. Sometimes, these men reprimanded me, yelling loudly behind a closed door, for a perceived mistake I had made in the process. I have also been in the office alone with a bullish plant manager, nearly in tears as I prepared him to deliver devastating news to employees about the future of a facility and their impending job losses.

I have been in the office alone with a different plant manager who drew me a diagram of a hill and a boulder to remind me that I was at the bottom of it. I joked in a previous meeting that he had made his budget numbers because he shifted an expense to my budget. Even though it was true, and I said my comment in jest, he felt the need to remind me who got to decide. He did it behind a closed door *and* in the next meeting among others. His need to remind me, in front of other leaders, who was in charge was an entirely different phenomenon and a power differential ... but that is for another book and another time.

The friend who asked me to join him for a chat over coffee explained that people involved in this case acted inappropriately—flirting, hugging, and going out for drinks after work hours, along with allegations of other more intimate behaviors. I felt a bit bewildered as he expressed his clear preference for an open-door meeting policy. I respected him, but I also pondered the real need for open-door policy because one man and woman allegedly crossed the line. What implications would that thinking have on work relationships and the work culture?

At about the same time, *The Washington Post* ran an article on the then-United States Second Lady Karen Pence, the wife of Vice President Mike Pence. In the 2017 article, reporter Ashley Parker referenced a comment Pence made when he served as a United States Representative: "In 2002, Mike Pence told *The Hill* [a Washington, D.C. based digital media company] that he never eats alone with a woman other than his wife and that he won't attend events featuring alcohol without her by his side, either." This became known as the "Mike Pence Rule" in popular, mainstream media and created a lot of buzz, sparking conversations.

During my interviews with men, I realized this "rule" permeated well beyond the elected official's expressed viewpoint. At least half of the men I interviewed talked about being intentional when they met alone with a woman in the office or at work-related events. Michael, who has progressed from manager to CEO of a large, multinational company, shared this story: "As a sales manager, I traveled a lot for my job. Two account reps worked for me, one male and one female. Both were great performers, and I knew them both well. When I traveled with the female account rep, I told her, 'You can understand why we can't have dinner one-on-one on the road together, right? It might look bad.' She agreed."

Michael avoided anything that might look potentially scandalous.

After the call, however, I remember contemplating the situation for some time. While I understood his intent, he inadvertently limited "dinner with the boss" as a privilege granted to just one person—the man. This also blocked the potential for sharing business insights that might help her succeed, building business relationships that often link to opportunities like promotions and selection for challenging matrix assignments and mentorships overall.

After the effect of the #MeToo movement, *Good Guys* authors Smith and Johnson shared that data reveals men are even more anxious about engaging with women at work. Their book included a 2019 nationally representative survey by LeanIn—a global organization dedicated to helping women achieve ambitions and work to create an equal world—where 60 percent of male managers admitted that they feel uncomfortable participating in regular work activities with women, including mentoring, working one-on-one, or socializing (Sandberg and Pritchard, 2019).

The *Good Guys* authors suggested that men take a deep breath and reframe the narrative to cure "gynophobia," which is an abnormal fear of women. They said men's claims about women's frequent false accusations of harassment are without evidence. Smith and Johnson spoke directly to male readers:

> *Here's the truth: if you are a well-meaning and admittedly imperfect dude (much like your authors), someone who sometimes makes a mistake but generally wants to get better and be part of the equality solutions at work and in society, then you've got absolutely nothing to fear.*

The authors said the cure for any phobia, including gynophobia, is *exposure therapy*, which requires the diligent practice of the very experience you want to avoid. The first step is acknowledging the discomfort and then working on mastering the skill. In this case, it is about actively and frequently seeking collegial conversations and interactions with women, even when your instinct says to walk away when the topic causes discomfort.

Pushing through the Suck of Discomfort for a New Way

In her 2020 podcast, *Unlocking Us*, Brené Brown, research professor, TEDx speaker, and author known for her work on shame, vulnerability, and leadership, says we need to embrace the FFTs, or "F***ing First Times." In Brown's words, FFTs are strategies to lean into "the suck of trying something new" so that we can normalize it. As much as we'd like to avoid the discomfort, uncertainty, and awkwardness, naming it, working through it, and trying things for the first time is the path to ease and clarity.

There is no workaround or easy button.

The same holds true for conversations we don't want but need to have in the name of progress. For example, think about the first time you had to tell a boss or someone else you respect in your life that you did not agree with their decision. Or take a minute to remember what it was like to do something for the first time that you really did not want to do.

Brown defined vulnerability as uncertainty, risk, and emotional exposure—not as a weakness but as our most accurate measure of courage. She told her podcast listeners: "If there is one thing I know for sure, normalizing discomfort, learning how to stay standing in the midst of feeling unsure and uncertain—that's the foundation of courage" (Brown, 2020).

I heard the concept of embracing discomfort from an experienced corporate leader and Man-in-the-Middle I interviewed. He stated: "There has to be transparency and clear expectations of good and bad behaviors. In that quest for transparency, tension and conflict do exist. The best advice I got in a performance review was that I needed to learn to get comfortable with the uncomfortable—that is when you grow. I think with gender issues today, people are seeking comfort versus embracing the discomfort that leads to clarity and growth."

Brown said rather than let fear, uncertainty, or vulnerability tell us to stop trying anything new, we need to acknowledge the uneasiness, discomfort, and stress and then take the first steps anyway. She also said she has twenty years of research and 400,000 pieces of data in her work that show how naming the feeling and owning hard things gives us the power to affect change. She added that if you don't name the feeling, it will continue to impact you and your ability to be empathetic and see other perspectives (Brown, 2020).

The ability to move forward is what matters.

Two men moving forward are the *Good Guys* authors Smith and Johnson, both with military backgrounds and PhDs, who advocate for men to engage in gender equity conversations. The book is filled with data, resources, and practical tips. After reading their book, I spoke with them about our shared passion for opening the dialogue between men and women.

Smith validated the observation I had drawn from my own interviews, that at the mention of gender, guys check out, believing they don't have a function or role in the gender conversation. "To us, this is where men are the missing ingredient [in gender equity] when it comes to everything, from mentoring to sponsorship and advocacy, which is why we have two books that are focused in particular on how we get men to engage in doing more and being more inclusive in how they do it," Smith explained.

Their works are based on several interviews with both men and women. Johnson added that men "can talk with men very directly, like, 'Dude, here's how you do it,' and we do a lot of sessions with women about male Psychology 101. There is an opportunity, however, to speak about better cross-gender collaboration from both groups, not to add any labor on women to fix anything, but more so for men and women to open a dialogue and establish a relationship of trust."

Earlier in this chapter, I mentioned Lapiano's 2019 *Forbes* article, "Dear Sir—Don't Let #MeToo Make you Afraid of Me." She included a quote from Dr. Arin Reeves, a researcher in workplace leadership and president of employment advisory firm Nextions, that is a possible catalyst for change:

> *We talk about what are the wrong behaviors, but we never as a country, as a culture, talk about what the right behaviors are. Imagine if someone watched you eat for a week and pointed out all the unhealthy stuff but never thought to tell you about what was healthy. You'd be nervous every time you picked up a fork.*

We have an opportunity to change the narrative and prevailing public discussion about what the "right" behavior looks like too (e.g. when men and women work well together). In the process, we can also establish a framework of trust that builds rapport. A culture of trust in the workplace leads to higher productivity and allows people to feel safe and respected (Wooll, 2022). This type of environment creates lasting change and removes the fear of criticism for doing the wrong thing.

So where do we start? We start with conversations, sharing the untold stories too. In a 2022 article on the website BetterUp titled "How to Build Trust in the Workplace: 10 Effective Solutions," author Maggie Wooll identified two of the key trust pillars as "Communicate Effectively" and "Being Vulnerable." Wooll encouraged leaders to ask questions, listen, and be open to share experiences as well as emotions; she also acknowledged that vulnerability is uncomfortable and takes time.

In the context of the spiral of silence, we leave the fear of isolation behind by speaking up and out, sharing the minority viewpoint in a safe space. We practice Brené Brown's "F***ing First Times."

I am not asking people to do anything I wouldn't do myself. In order to write this book, I had to leave my fear behind and embrace a "F***ing First Time." Writing a nonfiction book with detailed proof points, citations, and research-based insights was a first for me, and so was hiring a marketing research professional to help me with a passion project. When I decided to do this, I dove in head-first to understand the issues as well as the stakeholders and present what I hope is a compelling argument to inspire lasting change.

Fueled by my curiosity to answer why men did not speak up about gender equity, I interviewed men and studied the transcripts. I went old school. I transferred the interview insights and quotes to notecards and carried them in a shoe box with dividers separating each category I created in the card-sorting process. My husband got a little jealous of the box and my virtual relationship with these thirty men and their viewpoints.

Now *I* sound creepy!

The notecards ate breakfast with me. They sat on my nightstand when I went to bed and traveled with me on road trips. I went back and forth between the notecards and my computer for additional research. I put some thoughts on paper and then reached out to my network to validate the insights and connect the dots.

After creating a theory of change, I wrote, rewrote, and tested ideas. At times, people agreed with me, and then other times people in my network, including close friends, shot me down for my ideas or said, "Good luck," in a tone that conveyed, "Glad it is you and not me facing the potential backlash." I embraced the discomfort and persisted because I knew it was, and still is, a worthwhile cause.

I am convinced that we have gotten complacent about gender equity. With all the compelling evidence about the benefits of diversity in leadership, there is a better way. This involves both women and men speaking out about gender-related issues in the workplace.

To our Man-in-the-Middle, Jay, if you are worried about being creepy, you probably have nothing to worry about. We need you to embrace the discomfort created by the worry of doing something wrong and speak up and out, maybe even for the first time. Share your views on appropriate conversations in the workplace and create a culture where all feel welcomed and included.

I'll let you in on a little secret about Jay.

When I asked him about gender equity, he had a passion for the idea of equal pay. In his words, "The gap in pay is dumb. It is not right, and I really don't get it." What if Jay could be a disruptor in the field of gender equity and pay, collaborating for good? What if Jay did not have to leave for the bathroom to escape a potentially awkward moment where he didn't know what to say? What if he had something to contribute to the conversation and changed the tone of the "awkward" moment, setting an example for others about appropriate dialogue in the workplace?

When gender equity moves from a women's issue to a leadership issue, we change the narrative. When we see both men and women have a role to play and benefits to gain regarding gender equity, it opens the door for collaboration, the very antidote for fear of isolation.

In the following diagram, we flip the spiral on its side and build momentum through conversations. We start by naming the fear. Next, we move toward the discomfort into the middle and go through the ups and downs of trying something new. Finally, we embrace the power of collaboration for an even better way to work. This process is depicted in Figure 4.

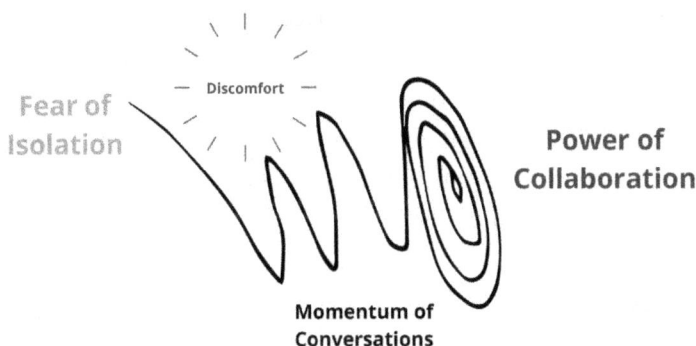

Figure 4: A visual depiction of flipping the spiral on its side to show conversations lead to collaboration.

Men-in-the-Middle have the power to be disruptors of the status quo, to change the narrative, and to collaborate so all boats can rise with the tide. Next, we will look at how men can be disruptors for growth!

Key Takeaways

- In a post-#MeToo era 2018 *Harvard Business Review* article, two corporate training experts wrote about the adverse reactions of the movement. Sixty-five percent of men say it's now less safe to mentor and coach members of the opposite sex.
- Men are uncertain regarding how comments between men and women may be interpreted or misunderstood. This can lead to a spiral of silence, not speaking out due to the fear that going against the majority view will lead to isolation.
- Embracing the paradoxical mindset means challenging the status quo and going against the norm to learn and grow as people.
- As much as we'd like to avoid the discomfort, we can embrace the suck of trying something new to normalize a new way of working that benefits all.
- The path toward gender equity involves men and women talking and working together to build trust and encourage behaviors of mentorship and intentional relationships.

Questions to Discuss or Ponder

1. On a scale of one to ten, one being unbearably uncomfortable and ten being "let's do this every day," where would you rank meeting with a colleague of the opposite sex for a one-on-one conversation at the office? Why did you rate it that way?
2. Has your behavior changed post the #MeToo era in the office? If so, how?
3. What would you need, if you don't already have it today, to feel more comfortable engaging in gender-equity

conversations at work? Be a mentor to a man or woman? Create an allyship for a man or woman?

4. In the spirit of vulnerability, how likely are you to speak out when someone is saying something inappropriate, even if it is a "F***ing First Time"? What might change that for you?

5. What do you recommend to create a safe space for men and women to engage in a conversation about gender equity?

CHAPTER FOUR

DISRUPTORS FOR GROWTH

*Lars has an issue with equality—this idea of all being
equal; he celebrates that men and women are different,
and together we are a formidable force for good.*

Lars spoke with us as both a leader at a national, multi-location
company and an entrepreneur owning his own successful business.
He has seen a lot over the years, and he has a clear picture of what
equality means to him. He explained his perspective: "I believe
men and women are equal, but not the same. We are meant to be
different, not designed to do the same thing, and we are not worse
or better than one another, but together we are awesome."

He also acknowledged the journey to get to this state of awesome
in the office is a bit upside-down at the moment, saying men have
been put in the tumbler and don't know which way is up. "Any
decent guy does not want to be labeled this way (in reference to a
comment he made earlier about the risk of men being seen as jerks),
so when it is confusing, we tend to overcompensate, and that means,
at times, we just don't say anything at all."

He also explained why it is perplexing. "On the one hand, if
women want to be 'one of the guys,' men give each other shit,
and that is part of it. On the other hand, some women skip a
potential conversation with a male offender and go directly to a

guy's manager with a complaint without saying anything to the guy." Lars quickly followed up by saying that he did not fault women and clarified that he was referring to office jokes, not sexual harassment or advances.

His passion came from a place of leveraging the differences between men and women for the benefit of all. He finished our interview with profound comments, disruptive to the status quo and even humorous:

> *The key will be recognizing the difference between men and women, and we have to talk about [gender equity] so we can accommodate and get the best out of all of us. It won't happen by being the same, the very definition of 'equal.' There is a difference between plumbers and electricians, and we need them both. Same is not the same, and equal is not equal—we are not! I, for one, am glad and grateful I am married to a woman— with different skills than me—and not married to myself!*

The men we interviewed consistently stated the importance of embracing diverse perspectives and the value of gender equity in the workplace. Some, like Tom, addressed how accepting both sameness and differences affected him personally:

> *I can play the typical male-centric game of sports talk; you know, the score of last night's game, golf handicaps, who is lifting more at the gym, fantasy football, and more; but after a while, I find it to be incredibly boring. For me, the mix of genders and diverse perspectives on a team changes the dynamic of how we work. I focus on creating that in my work groups. After all, I am a business leader, a dad, a husband, and I have a great dog. I want to talk about a variety of topics, not just last night's game.*

Tom's story reminded me of a time in my career when my husband prepared me on Sunday nights for Monday morning meetings, especially when I was the only female traveling on the company jet with six or seven male colleagues. The plane functioned as an intimate meeting room with the capacity to hold no more than ten people and, most importantly, no way out, at least for the hour or more it took to get from point A to B.

Assimilating to the Status Quo

Back in the late nineties, I got the (then) two kids to bed, prepared for the work week ahead, and packed my bag just as the second round of Sunday Night Football games ended. I asked my husband to fill me in, and not just the high-level facts. I wanted him to train me to speak like one of the guys. This was the assimilation practice that Human Resources did not teach me in new-hire orientation when I chose to work in a manufacturing company with predominantly male employees.

While I worked well with my male colleagues, they offered no advice about the ins and outs of the office politics that came naturally to them, including the hidden rules of corporate plane travel and any company maneuvers that I should be aware of to set me up for success. I do not think they wanted me to fail. They just did not give thought to sharing advice about something that was a part of their routine.

As a side note, I am grateful to my female colleague who instructed me *not* to get on the plane first, as some of these guys, especially the senior leaders, have unassigned but assumed seats in power-hierarchy order. The most senior person got his preferred seat, and the guys "in the know" were wise enough to save it for him, even if the executive was the last one to get on the jet.

"You don't want to get on the plane first and sit in 'his' seat and have him look at you as if you don't know the rules of the game," my female colleague explained to me. She had experience traveling as the only female with this group of men.

"Do you drink coffee?" she asked me.

"No," I responded with a look of confusion on my face, not sure what coffee had to do with company plane travel.

"Good, then this will be easy for you," she said with a look of relief before she continued. If they say, 'Kori, coffee?' you say, 'No, thank you,' and keep your head down as if you are really into the newspaper you are reading."

She explained that often the woman on the plane, regardless of position or title, was the person the men turned to in order to get coffee or beverages for the team. The planes had refreshment areas stocked with sodas, water, and a small coffee bar. When they said, "Coffee?" it didn't mean, "Do you want some?" but "Can you get us some?" My friend added that it's not that we couldn't or wouldn't serve the men when asked; we just didn't want to be seen as servers or taken for granted that way in the office.

Fortunately, company plane travel was not a daily or even weekly event for me. On those Monday mornings that my name was on the corporate jet roster, I did triple-duty preparation in order to:

- be 150 percent ready to manage the crisis at hand—the reason for the business trip
- recall the unwritten rules of the road
- work on my sports lingo to be conversant with my male colleagues

Regarding the last item on the list, my husband, Mike, started his Sunday night training session. "Okay, the two most talked-about quarterbacks from the games today are Brett Favre from the Green Bay Packers and Troy Aikman from the Dallas Cowboys."

After we covered the score and the highlight reel, he taught me some lingo. "It will go something like this: Aikman lit it up again, four touchdowns, three hundred yards passing. He and Emmitt Smith went off last night."

Once he explained Emmitt Smith's position as the running back and how the QB (quarterback) and RB (running back) work together to succeed, he gave me a few more key phrases. "Man, it seemed easy for Favre to find Sterling Sharpe. Sharpe easily had 150 yards receiving, and the Lions had no answer."

I did not want to sit in isolation as the only female. I intentionally sought training to be prepared.

If the conversation came up, I wanted to meet my colleagues where they were in the present moment and say something that showed I was at least conversant in what they had an interest in talking about that morning. I embraced Brené Brown's "F***ing First Times," even before I knew there was a label for it, and worked through the discomfort of trying something new versus avoiding it. I wanted to have a conversation with my colleagues, and I was willing to be vulnerable.

Now, if my colleagues did engage me in sports talk beyond the few sentences I had learned, I no doubt would have shown my true authentic self by saying something like, "Did you see the interview with Brett Favre in *People* magazine? And the wedding pictures with his wife, Brittany Nicole?" I wish I could say I have gotten better at professional sports lingo. Many of my female colleagues are way more conversant in sports than I am. But my point here is that I wanted to get involved and be included in the conversation on the plane.

My husband shared some encouragement, backed by a sobering reality check:

I appreciate that you are working so hard to find common ground, but don't work too hard, Kori. I can guarantee they are not working this hard to figure out how to connect with you, and not because they are bad guys or anything. They just have not had to think about it. We, men, are creatures of habit. We like our beer and our sports, and you can come to the bar and watch the game, but we are not going to work hard to welcome you by intentionally thinking about how to connect with you because this is our safe space, a place to relax, enjoy, and just not think about it.

I got it. The workplace is not a sports bar, but when in company with one another, men may still treat it like their safe space. My husband has been an awesome "manterpreter" over the years, often telling me in a supportive way that I overthink things.

My dad also came to my aid in the best way this man of Scottish and English descent knew how. My mom, the go-to person for emotional support, was out of the country on a pre-planned trip during a particularly stressful time in my career. Before she left, she told Dad that he needed to be there for me, especially since he understood the corporate culture. The day after she left, I called him with a highly emotive situation, and a few hours later I got this voicemail: "Kori, I hired a coach for you. I read about this man in *Fast Company* magazine, and I signed you up for three months. I realize you might feel more comfortable with a woman, but you are working with a lot of men in manufacturing. You need to know how men think and navigate with that perspective."

And that has been my ongoing mantra, much like the approach I took when writing this book. I lead with curiosity to understand a new perspective, go to the source with questions, and ultimately aim to spark a conversation.

In fairness, some of the men I interviewed shared their experiences as the only male on an all-female team:

- "My female boss, much older than me, always said how cute she thought I was. Often, she tried to set me up with one of her daughter's friends. My boss did not make a move on me or anything like that, but the conversation was awkward."
- "A woman slapped me on the ass on the way out of a meeting, as if I had made the winning play on a sports team, in response to me finding a solution that saved us time and money."
- "I had worked with these women for some time, and they felt really comfortable around me. One day, when they were talking about bra fittings, I said, 'I hear you, ladies.' In unison, they shouted back, 'We don't care!' I was not offended, but I can't help to think what it would have been like in reverse, and I was talking about ... the size of jock straps in the office."

Admittedly, more substantive conversations occur at the office than football and bras. When I was on a jet with executives, the situation usually entailed large-scale announcements that caused stress or even conflict. At times, however, *if* the office dialogue goes against the status quo or role-stereotyped, expected norms, those situations can be jarring or even disruptive.

From Status Quo to a Disruption for Growth

Regarding gender equity, we need disruption to the current status quo! Yes, Lars, men are different from women and thank goodness. Yes, Tom, mixed-company conversations, moving from sports to broader topics, change the team dynamics and make the culture more inclusive. You are right, Mike, my husband, men and women look at situations differently. Yes, Dad, working with a male career coach and understanding a different perspective helped me see circumstances in a new light to work through challenging situations for better solutions.

Disruption, however, is not about focusing on what makes us different but on what we have in common and how we can leverage our differences to achieve a common goal. Remember what we learned in chapter two about the March on Washington and the importance of finding common ground? The common ground for people working in corporate America is summed up in one word: growth. In a business setting, growth happens at both the macro and micro levels. In the broadest sense—the macro level—companies measure financial, year-over-year progress. In the individual sense—the micro level—it is about personal growth in the form of professional development and career advancement.

Most of the men I spoke with agree that, at the macro level, diversity leads to growth. Ron, an experienced corporate leader, summarized the Men-in-the-Middle viewpoint about the value of gender equity in the workplace: "You get the right mix of talent to get the optimum collaboration for the absolute best solution. There is no doubt gender diversity and real diversity of all types— race, nationality, gender identities, and much more—help the bottom line."

The business case for diversity, both specific to gender and other traits, is cited by a number of sources. Companies that have a better-balanced representation of women—and diversity of all types—in leadership financially outperform those with less diverse representation. Here are some facts:

1. Companies in the top quartile for gender diversity alone on executive teams were 25 percent more likely to have above-average profitability than companies in the fourth quartile, up 21 percent from 2017 (Dixon-Fyle et al., 2020).

2. A 2022 *Forbes* article by Tomas Chamorro-Premuzic, "The Business Case for Women in Leadership," lists multiple benefits of gender diversity compiled from scientific research in peer-reviewed academic journals. Among the findings:

   a. Women leaders don't just improve financial performance metrics. They also de-risk firm performance and improve corporate social responsibility.

   b. Firms with a higher proportion of women on their boards tend to invest more in innovation and be more innovative. A 10 percent increase in female representation on boards was associated with a 7 percent increase in innovation patents and citations.

   c. "If the gender gaps in participation, hours worked, and productivity were all bridged, the world economy would be $28.4 trillion (or 26 percent) richer" (Madgavkar et al., 2016).

Growth, efficiency, innovation, and urgency are top of mind for nearly every corporate leader I know, especially executive leaders in powerful positions. These same leaders are vulnerable to the king-of-the-mountain-game mentality, where the objective is to stay on top of the hill while rivals work to remove the current leader to become the "new king." In a company setting, unfavorable business outcomes—such as a loss in sales, customers, or a drop in stock value—can cause someone at the top to tumble and lose a job. Stakeholder tolerance for negative impacts on the business is unpredictable and high-risk, pushing leaders to explore every opportunity for growth.

The pressure for continual, year-over-year growth is real.

It would seem then, based on the data cited in chapter three and the above-mentioned *Forbes* article, that leadership would place a high priority on diversity, including women among leadership ranks, to leverage the elevated financial gains and enhanced innovation. In this sense, adding women and diversity in leadership can be seen as a growth lever on par with a new marketing or sales strategy. After all, the annual strategic business plan process is designed to highlight and augment any activity that will improve performance and grow the business.

Despite the strong body of evidence in the business case, however, diversity in the upper ranks usually gets relegated to the human resource team plan and the hiring process. Often, it is not treated with rigor or monitored on a regular basis like the standard metrics of case volume, sales dollars, or customer retention.

From Insights to (In)Action

At the macro level in business, the value of diversity and the case for gender equity is strong. Now, let's look at the micro level, where the individual takes action. Is there really a sense of urgency to pursue every data-backed strategy for growth? I pondered that question when I looked at the 2021 "Missing Pieces Report: A Board Diversity Census of Women and Minorities on Fortune 500 Boards" published in partnership by professional services and consulting firm Deloitte and the Alliance for Board Diversity (ABD), a collaboration among Catalyst, the Executive Leadership Council, the Hispanic Association on Corporate Responsibility, and Leadership Education for Asian Pacifics.

The organizations' research showed there has been progress, but we are decades away from ABD's aspirational goal of 40 percent diversity on each board.

- In 2020, two hundred of the Fortune 500 companies reached 40 percent board diversity. While this number was nearly four times higher than it was in 2010, less than half of the largest companies have reached that goal.

- ABD predicts it will take another fifty-plus years before all the Fortune 500 board seats held by minorities (including women) will reach the goal of 40 percent board representation; growth is less than 0.5 percent per year.
- Linda Akutagawa, Chair of the Alliance for Board Diversity, said, "Despite heightened focus on board diversity the past year, not a single Fortune 500 boardroom is representative of the population of the United States." The latest United States Census Bureau QuickFacts shows women make up 50.8 percent of the population.

In September 2013, Jim Turley, retired Chairman of Ernst & Young and former Chair of the Catalyst Board of Directors, wrote a blog post for Catalyst "Why Business Needs Women" about the business imperative of hiring diverse talent: "Going forward, 70–75 percent of every organization's customers and employees will not be white men. Yet at most companies, over 80 percent of the executive leadership and board of directors are white men. This is not a winning formula for future success." He ended with, "Good leaders don't just talk about inclusive leadership. They get results."

A lot has changed in a decade, but we are far from seeing gender equity as a line item on the annual strategic operating plan that lists the company's growth areas of focus for the coming fiscal year. Here are some highlights from PayScale Inc.'s "2023 Gender Pay Gap Report," an ongoing annual analysis and comparison of pay between women and men:

- The gender wage gap is improving, but not fast enough. The distribution of high-earning, prestigious jobs in society favors men, while the presence of the controlled gender pay gap reveals women are still being paid less than men when doing the same jobs.

- Going into 2023, women earn eighty-three cents for every one dollar men earn when comparing all women to all men.
- When the analysis includes methods that compare similar experiences—job levels, title, education, industry, and hours worked among men and women—the gap narrows significantly. Women's pay is ninety-nine cents for every one dollar.

This *controlled* number led to quite a conversation with a male professional friend of mine, Brandon, who aligns with the 46 percent of men and 30 percent of women who believe the problem of equal pay and gender parity has been "made up to serve a political purpose" (Gebhardt, 2019). Brandon and I both attended a retirement happy hour for a former colleague, and we jumped into a debate like the kind we had when we worked together. The topic remained consistent: equal pay.

"Here is your penny, Kori," he sarcastically said as he slid the copper coin across the table to me. I had just shared the PayScale statistics.

"Oh, I will take your penny, Brandon," I said with a smirk, matching his tone. "But it is not just making a penny less per year. It gets compounded over time. Even if you gave me two million pennies, it would not add up to the big difference in earnings over a lifetime."

"Two million pennies," Brandon looked up as he mentally calculated the number. "That is roughly $20,000. That is not even that much money."

"Okay, Mr. Highly-Educated-White-Man with a degree from one of the best schools in the country," I said. "If your beloved Boston Celtics lost to the Miami Heat by one point, are you going to say, 'close enough' then? Or is your gimme on the golf course a much wider range than mine?" I added, smiling, as I had joked with Brandon in the past about men freely asking for gimme shots after they barely made it onto the putting green.

He laughed.

"I only said two million pennies to illustrate a point, Brandon. You are a smart guy. When a person takes a new job, the offer can be based on earnings history. You already have a leg up there. And what about 401(k), pensions, or other savings plans that build over time based on a percentage of earnings?" I asked.

"It all adds up," I explained. "On a worldwide scale, the World Economic Forum's Global Gender Report 2020 shows it will take another one hundred years to achieve gender equality based on the current rate of progress."

The Call to Action—Men as Gender Equity Disruptors

This gap in equity was exacerbated as women left the workforce at higher rates during the Great Resignation, a 2021 phrase attributed to Professor Anthony Klotz to describe an unprecedented mass exit from the workforce spurred on by COVID-19 (Chugh, 2021). That same year, the United States Bureau of Labor Statistics reported forty-seven million Americans quit their jobs. McKinsey Quarterly's December 2020 report, "The Pandemic's Gender Effect," found one in four women considered leaving the workforce versus one in five men. The greatest disparity came across with parents of kids under ten. The traditional narrative of mom as caregiver put a lot more pressure on working moms during the pandemic. Working moms managed jobs, a household, and a global shutdown that forced in-home schoolrooms.

That is the status quo.

As of 2022, the Society of Human Resources reported nearly two million fewer women in the labor force (Gonzales, 2022). It seems we are moving in the wrong direction to make gender diversity a growth driver. We need some disruption in the name of growth, and you, Men-in-the-Middle, are in the position to do it.

The late Harvard Business Professor Clayton Christensen coined the term "disruptive innovation theory" to describe how industries change over time. The main, dominant market player, the industry incumbent, focuses on the most profitable, largest customer so that it can continue to grow, while the disruptor, with fewer resources, focuses on an overlooked segment at a lower price. Over time, the disruptor builds and changes an industry (Christensen et al., 2015). Think about Airbnb. Who knew people would pay to stay in other people's homes instead of going to a hotel, saving a bit of money in the process?

Today, women are the dominant players when it comes to raising the issues of gender equity and talking about it at work, on social media, and more. As the incumbents, we are focused on where we can have the greatest return. Men can be the disruptors of the gender equity dialogue too. To borrow a phrase from the 1960s television show *Star Trek*'s opening monologue, men can "explore strange new worlds, seek out new life and new civilizations, to boldly go where no man has gone before" (Daniels, 1966; American Rhetoric Speeches, 2020).

Opportunity knocks when we apply the business-world theory of disruptive innovation to gender equity. You, disruptors, can join, and even lead the discussions *and* seek opportunities to make changes in your own networks to normalize the interactions and elevate the gender equity conversation as a growth driver. As a disruptor, you think differently than your peers. In the spirit of growth, you take calculated risks.

Here are some suggestions for disruptive innovation related to gender equity:

1. Get a handful of colleagues to agree to take a female colleague to lunch and **commit to trying some Brené Brown's FFTs**, "F***ing First Times."
   - Ask her questions about her career or life outside of work with the goal of **normalizing these male-female interactions among colleagues** in the workplace.
2. Gather ten colleagues, neighbors, or friends to **start a book club**. The first book out of the gate—well, after reading and working through the questions in this book, of course—can be Eve Rodsky's 2019 *New York Times* bestselling book, *Fair Play: A Game-Changing Solution for When You Have Too Much to Do (and More Life to Live)*.
   - Rodsky has impressively documented all household tasks under the headers of Home, Out, Caregiving, Magic, and Wild Card. She even created playing cards to make the discussion between partners a negotiating game. Set a goal to work through the process and challenge each other to take the lead and equally own household duties.
3. **Create a "safe word" for your team members**, following the lead of one of the men I interviewed.
   - After he got feedback on his 360-degree performance review that he came across as harsh and even sometimes a bit sexist, he had an open dialogue with his team. He asked them to use the word "banana" in a meeting when he came across as close-minded, rude, sexist, talked over someone, or used potentially discriminatory language. It took a bit of time to build the trust and develop a common understanding of the terminology, but after a while, the team had fun with it, as did he, and they all learned in the process.
4. Proactively **talk with your sons and daughters about gender equity** in the workplace and what it looks like.

Role-play a conversation that will lead to a better tomorrow. You can even use the questions at the end of each chapter to prompt a discussion.

5. For men who are single and/or without children, **consider mentoring a group of young professionals**.
   - Better yet, team up with a female colleague and host lunch-and-learn sessions at the office where you jointly facilitate small group discussions about gender-related issues that impact productivity, efficiency, and growth at the office.

6. During Women's History Month in March, get a handful of male colleagues together to **initiate and sponsor a women's celebration event**. Attend the event with the intent to listen, learn, and lead the way to more open dialogue about gender equity in the workplace.

7. When you assign or pick project teams, **be intentional about the diverse makeups of the team members,** looking at gender, age, experiences, and more. Create a reward for teams that generate innovative ideas, from new products to process improvements.

8. At a staff or all-hands-on-deck meeting, **initiate a conversation** about what men and women on the team can do to enhance gender equity at work. Open the floor to ask for ideas and generate a brainstorm list. At the next meeting, engage the team to narrow the list to one or two projects and build an implementation plan.

Through all these efforts and more of your own brilliant ideas, the industry will change from viewing gender as a women's issue to viewing gender as a leadership issue that we want to address to grow successfully and sustainably. In the spirit of Lars, we celebrate that men and women are different, created to complement each other's strengths and bring out the "awesomeness" in each other. We need you, men, to speak out and spark the conversations that will move things faster than if we keep talking alone among ourselves.

You are the disruptors we need to change the industry.

Together, working in collaboration with female colleagues, we can disrupt for greater growth. I understand this might seem risky for some of you. Disruption is not easy. In the next few chapters, we will dive into some of the issues men face, acknowledging the challenges that often go undiscussed. Working through discomfort from a place of empathy can lead to growth, learning opportunities, and embracing a new manner that is even better.

Key Takeaways

- Men and women are equal but not the same.
- The customer demographics are changing. Going forward, 70–75 percent of all organizations' customers and employees will not be white men. Are we ready to lead through that change?
- A 2019 analysis by McKinsey & Company showed that companies in the top quartile for gender diversity alone on executive teams were 25 percent more likely to have above-average profitability than companies in the fourth quartile.
- The 2021 McKinsey & Company *Women in the Workplace* report found more women are leaving the workforce, or at least downsizing their careers, than men.
- Men can be disruptors for good, by initiating, actively participating in, and moving the gender equity conversation forward as a means of growth.

Questions to Discuss or Ponder

1. On a scale of one to seven, one being "no way" and seven being "I already sent the invite," how likely are you to invite a colleague of the opposite sex—or even broader, someone who does not think or look like you—to lunch in a very public place and ask him or her about views and experiences related to gender or gender equity in the workplace?

2. If you are at five or less on the scale above, what would you need to encourage you to move closer to a seven?

3. In alignment with one of the questions in the interview guide, what would you like to see in the future concerning gender equity? Or, if you could wave a magic wand, how would your ideal workplace look a few years from now? What would remain the same? What would be different?

4. In your view, what is the root cause of the slow-to-low progress for getting more diverse leaders in companies when the business case links diversity in leadership to business growth among other benefits?

5. What is your reaction to being invited to be a disruptor for gender equity?

CHAPTER FIVE

FROM ME TO WE

Graham did not identify as an "older, white, Caucasian male," that is, until the audience held the mirror as if to say, "You might not like it, but welcome to a club you did not know you belonged to."

When I spoke with Graham, a senior leader who recently retired from a large Fortune 500 company, he told me about a time someone asked him to speak on a panel at a national diversity conference. Graham had an epiphany when the moderator asked each panelist to indicate how the person identified themselves as part of the introductions.

"The first person said her name and title and described herself as Asian-Pacific. The next person did his introduction, described himself as originally from South Africa, and identified as a black Muslim male. The next panelist described herself as a lesbian white woman. I then shared my normal introduction and said, 'I know you want me to say I am an Irish, German American, Catholic male, but that is not how I see or introduce myself,'" Graham said.

"I remember feeling confused at the thought of being identified as a part of a group, a classification of people, which I think is one of our big societal issues," Graham explained. "I am just a human, a unique person. I just have not thought of myself as a part of a *class* or a separate group."

109

Graham looked in the mirror and saw his perspective of *me*, and the panel opened his eyes to *we*. He saw himself as an individual, while the others saw Graham as part of a group: the white men.

This perspective aligns with research by Bill Proudman, founder of the organization White Men as Full Diversity Partners (WMFDP). The company focuses on diversity and inclusion, specifically engaging white men, the group that holds the volume of leadership positions in companies and, therefore, the most power and influence. WMFDP believes white men, who the organization refers to as the dominant leaders or insiders, are key to driving organizational change (White Men as Full Diversity Partners, 2021).

Eureka! I found a perspective from a man that matched my viewpoint.

We need to engage those who can influence change. This also means making an effort to understand this group and what is going on for them. Are these insiders like Graham discovering how others may see them differently? What else are they saying or not saying that will help us connect for common ground?

A Time-Out to Address Race

Let's take a minute now to address race. Workforce diversity is expansive, including but not limited to age, work experience, socioeconomic status, education, sexual preferences, abilities, and more. Gender and race are discussed most often. Regarding race, companies will track employment numbers for people of color, or POC, as part of an organization's Diversity, Equity, and Inclusion efforts. Commonly referred to by the acronym DE&I, it encompasses efforts the company makes to attract, assimilate, and retain diverse talent, from awareness and education to advocacy.

Unfortunately, progress is slow on all fronts.

In an October 2019 article for *Time* titled "Diversity Has Become a Booming Business. So Where Are the Results?" author Pamela Newkirk wrote: "People of Color—who make up nearly 40 percent of the U.S. population—remain acutely underrepresented in most influential fields." Newkirk, who also wrote the book *Diversity, Inc.: The Failed Promise of a Billion-Dollar Business*, specifically mentioned that nearly three-quarters of company CEOs were white men.

I did not ask the interviewees for race or ethnicity demographics in my interview research. At the outset, I had been uncertain if *any* men would talk with me about gender after the height of #MeToo. So, I only asked about title, size of company, and region of office location to determine if rank, number of employees, or geography impacted answers. Some men we interviewed self-identified as people of color. Data shows, however, that not only are men in the majority of C-suite and CEO positions in corporate America, but the majority also happen to be white men.

As of 2021, 86 percent of Fortune 500 CEOs were white men. This is according to data provided exclusively to the Society of Human Resource Management by emeritus professors Richard L. Zweigenhaft and G. William Domhoff (Wilkie, 2022). In 2018, these experts released a third edition of their book, *Diversity in the Power Elite: Ironies and Unfulfilled Promises,* originally published in 2006. The authors focus on the term "power elite," coined by the late sociologist C. Wright Mills, to refer to those with significant financial or political influence in the United States.

Mills wrote the first edition of his book, *The Power Elite,* in 1956 and updated it in 2000. I share these dates to show that the idea of power and influence among certain groups and not others has been around for some time. Some of us might not have thought about it, acknowledged it, or discussed it until recently, but the idea is not new.

As you read this, you might even relate to Graham's view. You don't see yourself as a member of a group, or you see no advantage to identifying with a group that is criticized for certain viewpoints. If you are a white man reading this and you have the urge to defend yourself, hold on.

This is not a criticism. I set out with the goal of listening. I want to see and hear men out. I want to get to know you—the very people who established the norm. Historically speaking, organizational systems and structures are established around the men who set them up—white men.

This explains why Proudman wrote in his 2019 brief, "The Roots of the White Male Culture," on the WMFDP site that American white men typically don't view themselves as part of a group.

> *The notion of being part of a white male social identity is a strange new proposition —one that is hard to swallow, given the fierce attachment to individual identity. Furthermore, many white men fear a closer look is for the purpose of assigning criticism or blame.*

Similar to my research, Proudman notes that society tends to study and talk about the exceptions to the norm, or rather what falls outside the bell-shaped curve. In a twist on his words with a bit of interpretation, we don't examine what is going on with the Men-in-the-Middle, the norm for corporate American leadership. It goes unstudied because the norm, in the middle, is just the way things are.

In order to engage our Men-in-the-Middle, we also need to understand what is important to them. Over time, Proudman and the WMFDP team condensed the white male culture into six primary characteristics, based on what our American ancestors needed to survive (Morris and Prince, 2019):

1. Rugged Individualism
2. Low Tolerance for Ambiguity and Uncertainty
3. Action Is Valued over Reflection
4. Time Is Linear and Future-Focused
5. Rationality Is Valued over Emotion
6. Status and Rank Are Valued over Connection

It's not that these individual traits are wrong. Most of us know men and women who behave in ways that fit these descriptions. It is important to acknowledge that, as individuals, each of us has leadership traits that span those typically assigned by societal norms to a gender. In a 2023 *Forbes* article, "Feminine and Masculine Workforce Dynamics (Series 2 of 5)," author Nicole Serena Silver wrote: "Men and women both possess masculine and feminine qualities and each person lands within a range on the spectrum. Having the ability to harness both masculine and feminine qualities makes you a stronger leader and a more effective team member." Later in the article, Silver refers to masculine and feminine energies versus assigning them to a gender.

Proudman and the WMFDP team use these traits as a collective list to define a culture, or rather the beliefs and values in an organization that influence work, attitudes, and behaviors of leaders and employees. Work published by Yafang Tsai in the May 2011 issue of the peer-reviewed journal *BMC Health Services*, "Relationship between Organizational Culture, Leadership Behavior and Job Satisfaction," showed how much a culture matters. In his conclusion, he wrote that "organizational cultures were significantly (positively) correlated with leadership behavior and job satisfaction, and leadership behavior was significantly (positively) correlated with job satisfaction."

What happens when the energies in a company are out of balance and there is a preference for one style over the other?

When these six traits permeate an organization's culture and values, stated or unstated, they can be problematic to establishing an inclusive work environment that honors individual strengths. In the "white male culture," as Proudman states, these six traits become a barometer for judging all group or individual behavior. In other words, what works for one group becomes the norm by which we gauge all behaviors. To get even more specific: if I value rationality over emotion, then you should work that way too; if you introduce emotion into my problem-solving, you are seen as weak, less capable, or incompetent at the job.

Proudman wrote in his brief that until white men accept that they are members of a group, as society sees it, the men will not see "how traits of the white male culture affect women, as well as men and women of color, as well as themselves." So, if Graham can't see himself the way others see him, as a white male leader, then it might become a barrier to him when engaging in authentic, empathetic conversations about gender equity in the workplace.

This reminds me of a conversation I had with my friend, Jesse, a hard-working, successful entrepreneur. Jesse had recently interviewed a young female professional for a job at his company. He was impressed by her experience but questioned her commitment to exceed the standard forty-hour work week, an expectation he had for his leadership employees.

"When I was her age, I worked two jobs. I took a clerk job to start, and I volunteered to work weekends, even if it meant missing family events. I was hungry for success, and I showed it," Jesse said, unknowingly referencing the male-culture characteristics.

"Are you hiring your clone, and if so, is that such a great idea?" I asked in a friendly manner. "You told me you want more time away from work and that you are looking for someone to offset your strengths to build the team culture. Who's to say she hasn't made her own sacrifices to get to this point?"

Jesse looked at me with a blank stare and, a moment later, conceded. "I guess I don't know that about her. You could be right."

Self-Awareness and the Capacity for Empathy

In this sense, acknowledging white men as a class is not a condemnation but a tool for showing empathy, enabling men to see and make connections from a new lens—just as we look, for example, at insights that focus on women, women of color, and men of color.

Empathy is understanding and awareness of others' experiences without them having to explicitly say it (Merriam-Webster, 2022). While sympathy is having feelings of pity for someone, empathy is the capacity to imagine oneself in the situation of another, experiencing their emotions (Leading Effectively Staff, 2020). In 2021, the organization Catalyst published research that shows empathetic leadership can increase innovation, retention, and more (Van Bommel, 2021).

If we want people to engage in a conversation they have been avoiding or maybe don't even realize they need to have, it first starts with acknowledging where people are today. Self-awareness, empathy, compassion, and an open mind to see another viewpoint, including how others may see us—even if we don't like it—are traits to be cultivated.

I have worked with men, and women for that matter, who label this soft-skill development as "drama." When I asked a manager what drama meant to him, he said impatiently, "*This*, Kori! Just handle it. I don't have time to think about *why* Ann can't get it done. I just need it done." This is a clear example of "rationality is valued over emotion," one of the primary characteristics of the white male culture mentioned above from the work of WMFDP.

In a manufacturing environment where effectiveness and efficiency are key, time for empathy can seem out of the norm, especially for the "power elite."

Power Elite and Privilege, Oh My!

I realize some of you men reading this book will not identify with Wright's term "power elite," because you, as an individual, may not see yourself as powerful or elite. That is fair. These traits fly in the face of rugged individualism. As a group, however, men—and even more so, white men—hold the most power positions in corporate America and can influence change in systems and structures that advance gender equity.

The phrase "power elite" can elicit the same controversial reactions as "white privilege." Bear with me. I realize these terms create discomfort. Think of this as part of an empathy-building exercise. I understand that the intent of the white privilege discussion is about race and not gender (Wirtschafter, 2021). It is important, however, to look at both issues in similar and distinct contexts.

New York Times bestselling author, psychologist, and former NBA basketball player John Amaechi explained the concept of white privilege in his July 2020 interview on the BBC's *Bitesize* segment. In the video clip, Amaechi said white privilege does not mean your life has been devoid of hard times or suffering. It does mean your skin color has not been the cause of that hardship or suffering. Here is a direct Amaechi quote from the video transcript:

> *Privilege is a hard concept for people to understand because normally when we talk about privilege, we imagine immediate unearned riches and tangible benefits for anyone who has it. But white privilege, and indeed all privilege, is more about the*

absence of inconvenience, that absence of an impediment or challenge, and such when you have it, you really don't notice it, but when it's absent, it affects everything you do.

I appreciated Amaechi's expanded view of the narrative about privilege. My book club read five books on race the year after George Floyd's murder, a time when discussions on race and privilege heightened in the media, at family gatherings, and in organizations. In June 2021, Valerie Wirtschafter, Brooking Institute senior analyst, wrote about this time of elevated race-related talks and online content for the Brookings Tech Stream web page. In her article, "How George Floyd Changed the Online Conversation around Black Lives Matter," Wirtschafter cited it as one of the largest social movements in U.S. history. My book club members wanted to learn more about how one's race may affect the way people are treated by others, especially by those with privilege and power.

Even as a self-described ally of my friends and colleagues who represent people of color, I faced a bit of discomfort at being intentional with the language I chose. I worried about saying the wrong thing. Putting knowledge into practice can be challenging and create more uncertainty.

Likewise, I wanted to learn to understand the Men-in-the-Middle.

By joining the discussion on race and white privilege, I was able to better understand the men who felt it wasn't their place to join a conversation on women's rights. As a white, cisgender woman, I could relate better to our Men-in-the-Middle after talking with them, listening to them, and learning from them. I better understood the reluctance to speak out when you don't want to offend people you care about. Fortunately, I have a great group of people in my network who care about how I am doing and are willing to acknowledge my positive intent. They taught me to see things from a new perspective and encouraged me to ask more questions.

As a way to pay it forward, I want to do that for our Men-in-the-Middle. So, in the next few chapters, we will look at the issues and challenges men face. These often go undiscussed.

Before encouraging men to ask, "How can we help?" we may need to look at and study the issues they are facing. Graham, whose story started this chapter, may not see himself as part of a group, but research, covered in the following chapters, shows this group—men—face their own challenges that go unmentioned. These challenges are so much part of the status quo that men may not see them themselves.

Men-in-the-Middle, We Need You

Now that we—well, me on behalf of women who agree with my viewpoint—have invited you, Men-in-the-Middle, to speak out, it's time to make sure you feel you belong in this conversation. My goal is for you to be seen, heard, and understood.

To do that, we must begin with listening. The International Listening Association credits Dr. Ralph G. Nichols, a former professor from the University of Minnesota, as the Father of the Field of Listening (Bommelje, 2003). In his 1957 book, *Are You Listening? The Science of Improving Your Listening Ability for a Better Understanding of People*, Nichols wrote, "The most basic of all human needs is the need to understand and be understood. The best way to understand people is to listen to them."

To be seen and heard are universal needs, meaning we all share these in common. Experts, from famous speaker and author Tony Robbins to Glenn Geher, a contributor at *Psychology Today*, describe these common needs differently, from love and connection to belonging (Team Tony, 2022; Geher, 2014).

Maslow's Hierarchy of Needs, one of the most well-recognized motivational theories, states that our actions are motivated by certain physiological needs (McLeod, 2020). Love and belonging are in the middle of this five-tier pyramid model that goes from the basic needs of food, water, and shelter at the foundation, the wider base, all the way to the pointed top of self-actualization, achieving one's full potential.

Take a minute to reflect on your feelings about the importance of being seen and heard. That is right, men and women, I did say feelings. It is okay. This is a safe space. Take a minute to read the following scenarios. How do they make you feel?

- You are in a staff meeting, and you raise an idea early on the agenda that seems to go flat, as in no one reacts to your solutions in a good or bad way.
- Your young adult children are in a stressful situation and need advice. You have experience and expertise, but they go right past you and head to their mom.
- You have been the good soldier in the office and put in the time and legwork on a project when your colleague took the easy way out, complained about the assignment, and got the promotion anyway.

It sucks, right?

David Cooperrider, founder of Appreciative Inquiry, a strengths-based approach to change, explained it this way in his research. Every human has the following needs (Hammon, 2013):

- to have a voice and be heard
- to be seen as essential to a group (i.e., "if I were absent, I would be missed")
- to be seen as unique and exceptional

When we make a conscious effort to see and hear the people around us, we increase the communication effectiveness and empower people to be the best version of themselves. That is the magic of DE&I efforts.

When we all have a voice, we have a third option. In the words of Stephen Covey, author of the bestselling book *The 7 Habits of Highly Effective People*, "Win-win is a belief in the Third Alternative. It's not your way or my way; it's a better way, a higher way."

The impacts of listening, connecting, and acknowledging input also align with the work of Roger D'Aprix, a recognized thought leader in organizational communication. I have been a fan of D'Aprix since the early 1990s when I earned a master's degree in Organizational and Interpersonal Communication. I have continued to refer to the concepts in the Manager's Communication Model by Roger D'Aprix for more than two decades, especially when speaking with leadership about how to engage employees. D'Aprix's visual framework, shown in Figure 5, is the foundation I used to teach people management skills to frontline supervisors who work in salt mines and manufacturing plants. The majority of them were men.

D'Aprix outlined a manager's communication responsibilities to create a culture of belonging. He says employees want to know that their manager and, by association, their company cares about them and what they contribute. To engage employees on an emotional level, managers need to answer six key questions that relate to a matching organizational principle.

In 2014, D'Aprix wrote an article titled "Communicating Culture Down the Line" on the website for ROI Communication, an internal communication company that helps leading businesses succeed through inspired communication and engagement. In the article, he depicted the "Manager's Communication Model" as the following chart shows (Figure 5). I obtained permission to use his visual and added the questions in gray to provide more context from an inquiry mindset.

The Manager's Communication Model by Roger D'Aprix

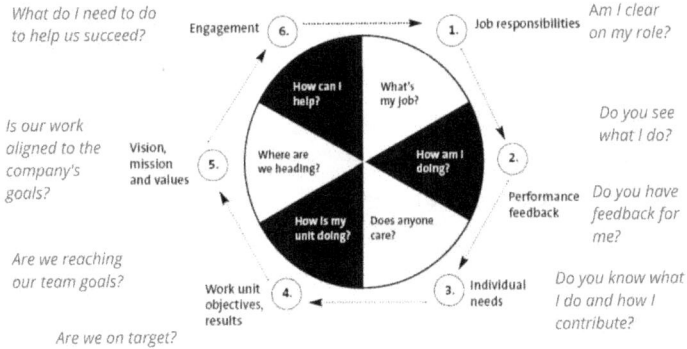

Model Copyright by Roger D'Aprix, All Rights Reserved

Figure 5: The Manager's Communication Model created by Roger D'Aprix, printed with permission. The author added employee mindset questions in gray.

Me Before We for Gender Equity

For me, the essence of the model boils down to this: It is all about *me* before a person can say *we*.

- *We*, the left-hand side of the circle, reflects the desired state of teamwork and collaborative problem-solving. Ultimately, we want team members and stakeholders to ask the following: How is my team or unit doing? Where are we heading? What are the objectives and the company's vision and mission? How can I help us get there?

- Before they ask those questions, it starts with *me*, the right-hand side of the circle: Am I clear on my job role? How am I doing? Does anyone see what I am doing or what is going on with me?

The key to remember is WIFM or WAM—"What's in it for me?" or "What about me?" is always before "How can I help?" Take a minute to think about any change you have gone through or a problem someone asked you to solve. Do you first think about your own perspective? Do you first ask yourself questions like: How will it impact me? How will it impact my job? Does anyone even care about my perspective?

If we are being honest, my guess is you are nodding your head to imply that, yes, this is you. I have been part of a team assigned to communicate major organizational changes—mergers, acquisitions, work stoppages, corporate restructures—and I have even heard senior leaders at planning meetings ask about their own job status first before jumping in with the team to plan for what is next.

I also have firsthand experience seeing the model come to life in my own career.

An opportunity arose for me to change roles and take on a lateral assignment, adding more duties and expanding my skills. I had a clear understanding of why the company needed someone in the open position: to focus on a business challenge that impeded progress and profits at a particular location. I agreed to take the role, but only after I understood the particulars of the job ("What's my job?"); got feedback on my job performance ("How am I doing?"); and was told how it would help round out my experience so that I could grow in the future ("Does anyone care?").

For another job opportunity, where I would be at the center of a large-scale change communication effort to resolve management-union tensions over a proposed work schedule, it required a move halfway across the country for my young, growing family. In this case, the company valued risk and rewarded employees who took it. Turning down an opportunity, even as a then four-month pregnant working professional, meant I might not get offered another chance in the future. With that move, I also had to convince my husband and family that there was something in it for them too.

Since then, I've had many other opportunities to apply Roger D'Aprix's Manager's Communication Model to my career and life. I have also incorporated the model to coach leaders how to work with and influence others. People, including me, think about how something affects us as individuals, the *me*, before we ask how we can help the team, the *we*.

Now, let's apply D'Aprix's model to gender equity.

What is my job? First, let's address role clarity. I am asking men to engage in gender equity in a different way. Some men have told us it is not their job as they see gender equity as a women's issue; however, due to the power men have to make change happen—based on the majority of leadership positions they hold—it *is* most definitely their job. Their job expectations, related to gender equity, have not been clarified. There is ambiguity. The job description has yet to be written, and like explorers, they might have to take some risks to walk in uncharted territory. As mentioned earlier, Proudman and the team from White Men as Full Diversity Partners say a low tolerance for risk is at the top of the list of the male culture characteristics.

How am I doing? Next is a shift from ambiguity to uncertainty. The men I spoke with were unsure what to do or say and didn't want to ask, "How am I doing?" Earlier, I referenced comments from those we interviewed who said they were afraid something they said may be taken out of context or they may be perceived as "creepy." Because of that, many of these men feel there is a chance they might be falsely accused of harassment. There is uncertainty, not only about their role but also others' reactions to their involvement. Brady, a senior leader in market research, said, "I am cautious about how I joke anymore in the office. I am afraid I may say something someone may take out of context." His uncertainty caused some discomfort.

Does anyone care? Uncertainty can turn into a feeling of indifference. Some men may wonder if their perspective matters. This is the "Hidden X," a concept Sandy Linver introduced in her 1994 revision of her book, *Speak and Get Results: The Complete Guide to Speeches and Presentations That Work in Any Business Situation.* Linver explained that all communication has a destination or a point, called the "X," where the speaker wants to take the audience.

For example, as a result of this book, the readers will change their conventional narrative from gender equity as a women's issue to equity as a topic that impacts both men and women. There is also the "Hidden X," which is how we want people to see, think, or feel in response to our communication (i.e., readers feel their viewpoints are seen and heard in the process).

This "Hidden X" is the turning point.

If I want to ask a person or group to help drive a broader vision and value, the first step is to meet people where they are now and acknowledge feelings, both spoken and unspoken. It is about what they say on the surface *and* what they are not saying below the surface.

Yes, Graham, we see you as a white guy *and* a unique person. We care about what you have to say and even what you are not saying that keeps you from engaging in the gender-equity conversation. As a gender stakeholder, I have a role for you when you join the conversation.

It's time to apply empathetic leadership and reframe gender-equity conversations. It's time for us to see it from your perspective too. When you acknowledge that you too are a *me* that is part of a *we,* the rest of us can empathize, see, and connect with the challenges you face too.

Perspective—Taking a New Path

Men face challenges too, and they don't go away or disappear when we avoid discussing them. These issues go beyond the debilitating yet self-perpetuating false narrative that a misinformed joke or accidental touch will lead to harassment charges. This includes the messy emotional stuff that answers the questions: Does anyone care what I am facing as a male in a society that adheres to sex-role stereotypes and gender bias? Does anyone care about my viewpoint as a male related to gender equity issues at the office?

Let's face it: we're often more than willing to share our perspectives but less willing to listen to and benefit from the perspectives of others.

In the world of conflict management, we call this technique "perspective-taking," or "seeing the situation from another point of view." In her September 2013 article titled "Why Perspective Take - Part 1" posted on the website Mediate, author Caryn Cridland wrote: "Perspective-taking may be said to be one of the most important factors in conflict resolution. When we look at a situation from another person's perspective, we are more likely to be able to resolve issues with them, and for the resolution to be sustainable."

You might be thinking, "Hold on, Kori, there is no conflict or drama here."

But most of us have jobs, right? And at work, while we want things to run smoothly, that is not always the case. The Center for Management and Organizational Effectiveness team researched and compiled data and insights from several sources that showed the majority of people not only experience friction with colleagues, but also will disrupt work to avoid the conflict (CMOE Team, 2022):

- 85 percent of individual contributors and leaders agreed they experienced conflict at work.
- 89 percent said they let it escalate.

- 67 percent said they took measures to avoid a colleague with whom they disagreed.
- 12 percent said they'd quit their job before dealing with it.

Conflict can be based on real or perceived differences. Silence or avoiding does not make it go away. When we embrace perspective-taking, we acknowledge the other person has a viewpoint that may differ from ours. We recognize someone else's background, experiences, and beliefs. It is a learned skill to move away from egocentric thinking and put ourselves in someone else's shoes. All of this allows us to influence others more effectively (APA Dictionary of Psychology, 2022).

The topic of gender equity can provoke conflict, especially when we see it only from our perspective.

My spouse and I have had to learn this in couples counseling. After thirty years of marriage, we willingly seek a counselor for husband-wife interaction tune-ups, most importantly when a communication issue keeps surfacing like an annoying sound tape that is caught in a loop of repetition.

The process we learned follows this pattern: the first person brings up an issue, and the person listening has one response, and it is not to get defensive but to say, "So, what I hear you saying is …" The idea is for the listener to validate what the first person is saying to ensure he or she is heard. While my brain might be ready to say, "Heck no, you are way off, you are *so* wrong," my first job as the listener is to say, "Here is what I heard you say." A practiced conversation may look like this:

Husband: "Hey, you did it again. I have asked you a million times not to leave your keys and purse in the car. A slew of break-ins has been reported on Facebook, and your actions put us at risk."

Me: "Okay, what I heard you say is that you don't want me to leave my keys and purse in the car, even in the garage. You believe it is a safety risk. Is that what you are saying?"

Husband: "Yes, I make sure the house is locked up at night to keep us all safe, and you are inviting someone to open the garage and hit the jackpot. That is frustrating for me. That is the last thing I want to happen to my family."

Me: "I hear you say that you are working to keep our family safe, and my actions work against that. That must be frustrating. Thank you for caring."

By leveraging perspective-taking, I shift from my defenses going up in reaction to him harping on me for what seems a trivial thing to see that he is trying to protect the family, something of value for him, something near and dear to his heart. And, as a side note, my husband did agree to share this exchange and tune-up lesson for the good of the cause.

I would like to say it works this smoothly each time, but healthy, effective communication is a lifelong practice. Remember those "F***ing First Times," or FFTs, in reference to Brené Brown's term for the suck of trying something new (Brown, 2020)? Well, it did suck, and at times still does. My point here is not to go all therapist on you.

Perspective-taking is a skill to reduce ambiguity and the discomfort of conflict to get to the heart of the matter. It allows people to be seen and heard, acknowledging hidden fears and feelings that are not directly stated but do exist. The technique helps get below the surface to the root cause of the concern.

Rachael Dailey Goodwin, Ph.D. in Organizational Behavior, is a Harvard Research Fellow with the Women and Public Policy Program and Assistant Professor at the Whitman School of

Management at Syracuse University. She also has some professional experience with conflict resolution. She researches gender issues at work related to power, social cognition, desires to lead, and unethical behaviors (e.g., sexual harassment) that may create barriers for women at work.

During our conversation about her research, she stressed the importance of not putting the onus on women to fix the fear or discomfort that men may face in the post-#MeToo era. She said people don't realize that alleging victims of sexual harassment are often penalized when their alleged perpetrators remain silent or when people in positions of power deny the conversation they are trying to bring to the table. She also suggested shifting the narrative to be about something we solve together:

> I think some of the discomfort toward these difficult conversations could be eliminated with just a greater emphasis on perspective-taking. They need to understand where we are coming from, and we need to understand where they are coming from. Even from a feminist perspective, to understand all the underlying causes of gender oppression, we also need to understand the perspectives of men who may be hesitant to address the gender equity conversation. It's a complex problem. We need to work together to understand one another's perspectives, and to collaborate on solutions together.

Graham, we see you and appreciate that you spoke up on the public panel about your own aha moment and how others see you. You didn't see yourself as an "Irish, German American, Catholic male," and you certainly do not talk about it; however, you are a stakeholder in gender equity. We hear you, what you are saying, and what you are not saying with regard to gender-related issues.

Self-awareness, listening, empathy, and perspective-taking open new conversations.

Yes, we need men to engage in the discussions and solutions to address gender equity. Before we get men to say *we*, we need to acknowledge the *me* in men. Men face their own challenges that could be a barrier to moving the conversation forward toward greater progress for all.

It's a matter of working *from-through-to*. In order to move *from* the undiscussed rigid gender expectations, we must work *through* the often-uncomfortable communication *to* achieve a transformation.

These next few chapters are about perspective-taking, not to *fix* anyone or tell someone they are wrong, but to unearth conversations that allow people to be themselves and feel seen and heard. These are the conversations we need to have to make change but often go undiscussed.

Key Takeaways

- Increasing self-awareness and effective communication in the form of empathy are important leadership skills. Empathy is about understanding others' experiences without them having to say it. This skill can increase innovation and retention.
- Roger D'Aprix's Manager's Communication Model frames up an employee's motivation to fully engage. It's all about *me*—as in "What's in it for me?"—before a person thinks of the *we*. Before people ask, "How can I help drive change?" they first need to know, "What's my role, how am I doing, and does anyone care?"
- When people communicate an intention, there is both a stated goal and a hidden one. The "X" is what we want people to understand, i.e., gender equity is a leadership issue.

The "Hidden X" is how I want to be perceived, as an expert or empathetic champion. It is important to *see* the hidden too.

- Perspective-taking is the ability to put ourselves in someone else's shoes while recognizing that person's point of view, experiences, and beliefs. We're often more than willing to share our perspectives but less willing to listen to and benefit from the perspectives of others.
- It takes men and women working together to understand one another's perspectives and collaborate on solutions.

Questions to Discuss or Ponder

1. How have you seen D'Aprix Manager's Communication Model come to life in your own organization, especially in the case of communicating change?
2. What do you think about Sandy Linver's idea that purposeful communication has a stated goal, the "X," and a hidden one, the "Hidden X?" How might acknowledging the "Hidden X," how we want people to see, think, or feel about us, impact the way you interact with others?
3. Are you familiar with the concept of perspective-taking as a conflict management tool? Can you share a time when you saw a situation from another person's viewpoint and it changed your perspective?
4. How can perspective-taking help set the tone for increasing gender equity conversations among men and women?
5. Can you name two-to-three people from the opposite sex who might create a safe space to have conversations about gender equity? Set up a meeting or lunch and ask questions to test out your perspective-taking skills.

CHAPTER SIX

PERSPECTIVES AND THE PARADOX

In his formative years, Bob had a great sense of certainty and pride seeing his single mom succeed in her company career. Now, however, he finds it risky to meet with a female colleague alone.

"Seeing a female as a barrier-breaker in business was normal for me as I grew up. My mom had been the first female at many different things, and she instilled in me a foundational understanding of gender equality," said Bob, a mid-level leader with more than twenty years of tenure with his company.

Bob spoke with a sense of assuredness as he confided to me that a single mom raised him and simultaneously succeeded at the office. He saw how hard she worked and the sacrifices she made. That was his lived experience.

Post the height of the #MeToo viral social media activity, however, Bob's perspective on gender equity did not change, but his actions did. He admitted he treated men and women differently in work-related social interactions, even if the context of the conversation related to the job.

"If a guy asked me to go have drinks after work, I would not hesitate. In the past, I would do the same for a female colleague, but now that is a different story," Bob said. "I am more nervous now about being on my own, one-on-one, at business or social events with a woman. It is risky. These days, you are guilty until proven innocent, so I try to be very cautious and make sure I have a mixed group around me," he explained. This perspective, the way he sees work-social interactions now, changes how he interacts with others—and it's all based on their gender.

As a result, his female colleagues and employees are missing out.

Andrew Marder wrote in a 2017 blog, "How After-Hours Events Can Make Your Business Stronger" for business software support company Capterra, explaining that social activities such as workplace happy hours can foster colleague camaraderie. He cited a 1995 study by Christine Riordan and Rodger Griffeth in the "Journal of Business and Psychology" titled "The Opportunity for Friendship in the Workplace: An Unexpected Construct." The researchers found that employees' perceptions of friendship opportunities impact job involvement, satisfaction, and, ultimately, job turnover. A 2018 *Forbes* article by Alan Kohll backed those findings, adding that social activities at work can foster a sense of belonging, lower burnout, reduce stress, and improve health.

In my experience, at business-related social activities, leaders and colleagues also tend to share information that might get lost in the daily high stress of back-to-back scheduled business meetings in an office setting. When they have room to think and process in a different setting, leaders may provide more context or clarify any confusion on the spot. These discussions may be about office politics, late-breaking developments, a change in circumstances, etc. In these out-of-office social settings, the value of time spent goes beyond camaraderie to impact business decisions, as the better information you have, the better decisions you make.

In a social setting, I may learn that information changed since our morning meeting, or about an office political landmine between two colleagues I previously had not been in tune with (i.e., a dispute over a customer relationship, project ownership, or a difference in leadership). In each instance, this "new" information could influence my recommendation and when the conflict involves people senior to me, the better-informed decision could impact my career trajectory, selection for a special assignment, or even a promotion.

Bob might even know all of this, yet it is not enough to sway him from avoiding meeting with a particular gender one-on-one—or being extremely cautious when he does. "I had a younger female employee who wanted me to mentor her. She asked me to meet her for lunch. I thought twice about it. I intentionally directed her to pick a public place, but the risk was still on my mind."

Bob defined gender equality as "everybody has the same opportunity to achieve the same thing and ... to speak up and be heard." At the same time, he did not hesitate to accept a request from a male colleague or employee to meet for a work-related lunch or after-work drink, but often declined invitations from female colleagues or employees if it was in a one-on-one setting.

While Bob supports gender equality, he won't treat men and women in a similar way regarding work-social events like meeting over drinks or dinner. He perceives there is a potential risk of a false accusation, especially when, in a one-on-one setting, it would be his word against hers. This theme of avoiding "what could be" came up a few times in my interviews. This is all the more reason to get men's concerns, perspectives, fears, and feelings of uncertainty out in the open and learn to talk about them in a productive way.

A verbal expression of support for gender equity and, at the same time, actions that seem incongruous to that belief reflect a social complexity we face today. Bob believes in equality but treats men and women differently. Researchers call this cognitive dissonance, the mental discomfort that results from holding two conflicting beliefs, values, or attitudes (Cherry, 2022). It can be an opportunity for learning and growth if a person is willing to live in the discomfort, lean into it, and stay open to new perspectives; however, at times, people relieve this tension of incongruence by rejecting or avoiding new information. In the avoidance, they stay silent.

Whose Perspective is it Anyway?

In the analysis of the interviews, I became intrigued by the say-do gap, which is a business term meaning "practice what you preach" or even "do what I say and not what I do." In short, it signifies our stated intent and actions or behaviors do not align. The men said they saw the power of diverse and inclusive teams and the positive impacts on the business. Yet, at the same time, like Bob, they avoided some equitable behaviors.

One of the men let me in on a secret.

"Sure, at the macro level, I agree that diversity in leadership is good for the business. I have no doubt about it. But at a micro level, I don't know how this will impact me," explained a Man-in-the-Middle interviewee. Due to this uncertainty and ambiguity of outcomes, he does not engage in gender-equity conversations. As a reminder, low tolerance for ambiguity is a male culture characteristic mentioned in chapter five.

Some interpret silence or reticence to speak out as not caring. Another perspective, however, is that silence reflects the uncertainty of not knowing what to say or even what to do.

As the men got more comfortable during the interview process, a few shared other experiences that influenced their way of looking at things. "I had been up for a position and did not get the promotion," a Man-in-the-Middle explained. "My boss told me the female candidate got the job. Then he said to me, as if to explain it or soften the blow, 'You know, at all of these leadership team meetings, we track retention for women and people of color, not the guy who has been loyal to the company for ten or fifteen years.'"

Some men also raised the issue of the "mommy track," the idea that some women take extended time away to raise kids, which impacts career advancement. "If I took extended time off, even if for good, solid reasons to raise kids, I would not be promoted either," explained an experienced senior director from a company in the Southwest.

While I will address this point more in chapter eight, working parents do face a researched but often undiscussed "parent penalty" at the office for de-prioritizing work in favor of family. Writer and editor Chris Morris reported on the job impacts for working parents in a 2019 *CNBC* article, "Disconnecting to Spend Time with Your Kids Could Sabotage Your Career." Citing a recent study by the charitable organization Working Families, parents who work part-time have a 21 percent chance of being promoted in the next three years, compared to a 45 percent chance for their full-time counterparts. Working Families also reported that the average mother waits two years longer for a promotion than the average father. Morris acknowledged that Working Families is a charity based in the United Kingdom, but the organization said the results transcend boundaries.

Men face penalties at work too.

In his 2019 Harvard Business Review article, "To Make the Case for Paternity Leave, Dads Will Have to Work Together," the global expert on dads at work, Josh Levs, acknowledged that the penalty for men is real. He collected several anecdotes and stories for his book, *All In,* including these excerpts that he mentioned in his article: "A lawyer in Florida recently told me that his boss said to him, 'We have six weeks of paternity leave, but you're not taking any.' A public relations executive in California told me her husband's boss criticized him [when he requested leave], asking, 'Why isn't your wife doing that?'" I share more about Levs's story in chapter eight.

During the interviews, I stayed in researcher mode, listening and taking notes, not commenting or judging. After the interviews, I tested ideas with people in my network to learn about other perspectives. In these conversations, I could push back, probe, and poke the bear, all in the name of perspective-taking.

I wanted to hear their viewpoints, even if and *especially* if they were different from mine. In the potential discomfort of facing a difference of opinion, I could learn to be an ally for change.

Acknowledging the Paradox

In 2020, Coqual, a global think tank dedicated to workplace diversity, equity, and inclusion, released the report, "What Majority Men Really Think About D&I (And How to Engage Them in It)," compiled by lead researcher Julia Taylor Kennedy and team. Just a reminder that D&I stands for "Diversity & Inclusion." The report is a compilation of survey questions and in-depth interviews with full-time, working professionals with at least a bachelor's degree.

The Coqual team wrote that to engage "majority men," it is important to understand men's attitudes toward diversity and inclusion at work. This majority-men group is defined as white, straight, cisgender men—95 percent of the group. As a reminder, "cis" means their gender identity aligns with their sex at birth. The other 5 percent of majority men were non-white straight cis men and worked mostly with white men.

Half of the men interviewed agreed that diverse teams lead to more innovation; yet, here are the men's responses when Coqual asked about the importance of D&I at work:

- 10 percent said it is not important at all.
- 42 percent said it is very/extremely important.
- 48 percent said it is *not* very or somewhat important.

So, about half of the men appear to be apathetic or indifferent to the importance of D&I. I found this insight intriguing, especially when the business case for diversity is strong. The direct benefits of gender-diverse teams, according to various sources (Hunt et al., 2018; Turban et al., 2019; Lorenzo et al., 2018) are:

- higher profitability
- higher productivity
- improved innovation

D&I can be a growth lever, as I also cited the business case in chapter four, impacting the lead measures of profitability, productivity, and innovation, which any male leader will tell you he is 100 percent behind. At the same time, the majority of men do not appear to be very interested in D&I.

It's a paradox when two things are true and contradict one another in the same statement.

We've briefly touched on this before, but there is so much to say about this phenomenon. My friend, Pam S. Harper, author of the 2003 book *Preventing Strategic Gridlock*® and host of the podcast *Growth Igniters*® *Radio,* is passionate about acknowledging the intersection of paradoxes in the workplace.

In a 2021 article for Financial Executives International titled "How Financial Executives Can Achieve Long-Term Performance in a Short-Term World," Harper identified three *Growth Igniters*® Paradoxes that are constantly at play with one another in an organization that is pushing to accelerate game-changing growth in the face of uncertainty and ambiguity:

- **The Visionary's Paradox:** The bolder the vision, the stronger the pushback.

- **The Success Paradox:** The stronger the push toward new paths to growth, the stronger the pull of the status quo.
- **The Momentum Paradox:** The organization that accelerates momentum for growth creates friction.

In other words, opposing forces are at play. Could it be a male-gender perspective paradox? If we parallel Harper's Success Paradox, the logic would follow:

- **Male-Gender Perspective Paradox:** The stronger the push for gender equity, the stronger the pull toward the status quo.

Even if the business case for gender equity is solid, a man may not actively push for progress. In a state of uncertainty about the impacts of equity on his own career or how he may come across in mixed company if he speaks out, he pulls back his support. With so much ambiguity about his role in creating a more gender-equitable workplace, he may even wonder if his perspective matters to anyone. Does this sound familiar? In chapter five, D'Aprix's Manager's Communication Model showed that before a person will ask, "How can I help?"—*the we*—he has to answer if anyone cares—*the me*.

The push-pull of the paradox creates internalized or expressed tension. By nature, we are creatures of habit and like comfort. While growth can happen in the discomfort, as addressed earlier, it is not our favorite place to be. Therefore, Harper also says we need to recognize signs of "the orbit of status quo" that can lurk in the organization, which is our tendency to revert to what we know.

More importantly, she states that if these uncomfortable issues are not openly discussed, they can become destructive elephants in the room. "We see this happen when the *formal culture*, the words on the wall—vision, mission, values—if you will, clashes with the *informal culture*, the way things really get done." Harper elaborates: "Ideally, the formal and informal cultures align in a positive direction, but when they don't, it is important to embrace the *Growth Igniters®* Paradoxes and get these diverse perspectives out in the open. New conversations are essential to break the orbit of the status quo and accelerate momentum for growth" (Harper, 2021).

In a parallel thought process, the formal culture says gender equity is good for business and the right thing to do. The informal culture shows the sense of urgency or actions don't match. The informal culture goes undiscussed.

In 2015, the global communication agency, Weber Shandwick, surveyed executives in fifty-five global markets and published the report, "Gender Equality in the Executive Ranks: A Paradox — The Journey to 2030." The paradox, in a similar context to the above, refers to the push-pull: the case that supports gender equity and the advancement of women, pushing toward a better way, and, at the same time, what tugs or pulls back to the status quo.

One factor that caught my attention was the finding that nearly half of the male executives and 39 percent of the female executives agreed with the statement: "The media is too focused on equality for women and neglects men's career issues."

Both men and women feel we are not addressing the challenges they face. Hold onto that thought.

Getting Perspectives Out in the Open

In Bob's case, the post-#MeToo era has him worried about a false accusation of harassment if he meets alone with a woman, specifically at dinner or over drinks, even if it is related to work. Some other men face ambiguity about how attracting and hiring women and people of color impacts them. Others lack clarity on how managing differences and pushing for equality works, especially in cases when a person is absent from work for family or medical leave while the rest of the team picks up the extra critical work.

This last example represents the unwritten and undiscussed impacts of the parenthood penalty, where one employee may be working extra time to prioritize the added workload while the other person is perceived as prioritizing family, even if the person is on medical leave for childbirth. We can agree that the physical and medical impacts of childbirth are limited to one gender.

When we acknowledge—without judgment—the elephant in the room, sharing these perspectives creates an opportunity to open a new dialogue. In that dialogue, we can address strategies and tactics to manage the fear of sharing perspectives in the first place.

Silence will not get us there.

Here is what silence or ignoring the issues looks like in the face of discomfort. Picture an elephant in the corner of a room that, despite its size, only Bob can see. This elephant is wearing a T-shirt that bears all the words and expressions that cause angst for Bob and other Men-in-the-Middle: "Harassment," "False Accusations," "Saying the Wrong Thing," "What Were You Thinking?" "You Are Fired," "Lawsuits," "Jail Time," and more.

A female colleague is standing right in front of the elephant that is invisible to her and says, "Are you okay, Bob?"

Bob looks at her, and, directly behind her, in his line of sight, he sees the elephant looming tall in the corner. As sweat drips from his furrowed brow, he says, "Everything is just great."

If we don't see it from the other's viewpoint, we can't address the discomfort. If we can't address the discomfort, the orbit of the status quo returns. Men-in-the-Middle remain silent and see gender equity as a women's issue and not their conversation to have. This gets even more complicated when one group is socialized not to share authentic feelings—in some cases, fear and uncertainty—even if they can't articulate why they feel that way.

Just to illustrate the importance of perspective-taking and sharing, my husband agreed to let me share this recent story about our perspective blindness and the impacts on a decision.

My husband, Mike, and I share an Apple ID. He set up the account, so, of course, he set it up to meet his needs. He was not selfish. He just didn't think about it, and we were both anxious to get our devices up and running—so much so that we did not think about impacts down the road.

Fast-forward to a time when the setup did not work for both of us. I habitually call him for forgotten passwords; after all, he is our family IT person. Well, one day, he reached the end of his tolerance.

"I am right in the middle of something. Come on, Kori, how hard is it to press the password key and have it auto-populated?" he said with an air of annoyance at my fourth call that week.

"Umm, *hello*, it might auto-populate with your information but not my account information," I said, matching his tone of annoyance. And then I attempted to "business-splain"—my version of "mansplaining"—my view of this problem.

"You don't see my user experience," I said to him smugly, as if I were on the phone with an IT-help-desk person who was both unsympathetic to my view of the screen and sure it was a human error causing my problem.

He paused for a minute, matched my tone of smugness, and raised the volume one turn to the right. "What did you just say? A password key pops up on my phone's screen, and I just punch it. Do you see it in the bottom left corner?"

I raised my voice to match his escalation. "Yes, I see it, but when it populates, it says, 'Not *recognized* on this device.'"

He reacted in silence on his end, as he still couldn't quite register the problem, especially when his phone was working smoothly. In his defense, I had experienced this issue for months prior to this call, and I had just reached my own tolerance limit at that point.

Neither of us took the time to look at the situation from the other's perspective. He judged my ineptness, and I judged his arrogance. The situation escalated and ended with a truce, hence the tune-up, marriage-communication counseling I mentioned earlier.

And just for closure on this story, when I went to the Apple Genius Bar to see what I could do, Mr. Apple Genius assigned to my case gave me some sound relationship advice. "You could separate your Apple ID, but it would be like getting a divorce. You know, you will have to decide who gets custody of the Netflix movie download, who gets the Apple Podcast account, etc."

Admittedly, I avoided the discomfort of deciding who gets access to what, and I decided to work within the system, for now.

You see, my husband leveraged the power of the Apple ID setup, a system that benefited him when his information auto-populated with ease at the push of a button. He did not even realize his "privilege" in having that set up until he virtually stepped away from his phone and saw that mine did not respond the same way. Those with perceived privilege, or, in my case, those who leveraged the power of the Apple ID setup, might not even realize their privilege. It is like the proverbial old tale: when you ask a fish to describe water, the fish might say, what is water? When my husband wasn't experiencing the same problem I was, he kept thinking, "I don't see what the problem is."

And that is the form of privilege referred to in chapter five; it is the absence of an inconvenience or challenge because a system or process has been designed around the needs of an individual or a group. The privilege, in this case, is not having to think about or see the challenges at all. Mike is not from a "privileged class" in that he got his phone handed to him on a silver platter; he worked for it, and it worked for him.

Similarly, the privilege associated with being male in a corporation is not an indictment of a man's personal work ethic but an acknowledgment that men may have an advantage over others who might not have the same "user experience."

If men only gauge privilege by how hard a person works for something, versus the perspective of an absence of challenges others face, they may lack the empathy to see equity from a different angle.

Perspective-Taking: A Rethink Tool

Michael Welp, in his 2017 TEDxBend talk, "White Men: Time to Discover Your Cultural Blind Spots," explained that men—in this case, white men—are fish in water who rarely have to leave their environments because the male-established culture permeates most of where they go. Welp is the co-founder of White Men as Full Diversity Partners (WMFDP) with Bill Proudman, whom I mentioned in chapter five.

Welp did not present this view as a criticism or an excuse; what he meant is that there are times when men don't know others experience the world differently than they do until they step out of their own environment. Most likely, we have all experienced an "oh wow" moment of discovery. It's an awakening where the world looks different from another person's perspective.

The diagram below, Figure 6, illustrates that we can look at the same thing from different angles and life experiences and see it in our own way. Each expression of what the two people see in the middle of them is correct from their viewpoint—one sees "wow" and one sees "mom." Neither one is wrong.

What do you see?

It depends on your perspective.

Figure 6: Illustration to show the concept of perspective-taking.

The discomfort happens when we verbalize our view to the other person, and they look at us and react like we are wrong. I share this next embarrassing story just to illustrate this point. At a dinner out with friends, I ordered a steak.

"How would you like that cooked?" the waitress asked.

"Raw," I answered.

"Ma'am, could you repeat that? How would you like it cooked?" she asked me again, looking confused.

I said "raw" again, with a little annoyance in my voice at the shocked look on her face when she asked a second and third time.

A friend piped into this exchange with, "Kori, are you a cannibal or something?"

It finally clicked for me. I totally had the word "rare" in my brain, but I said "raw"—and not just once but at least three times. She was right to look at me with concern and confusion. The ability to take someone else's viewpoint into account, especially when there is tension and discomfort, opens a new opportunity for conversation.

P.S. The apology for my contrite behavior came in the form of a big tip. As a communication professional, the word "sorry" seemed light for my moment of enlightenment.

Male Perspective: Sameness/Difference Paradox

Welp dove deep into the male perspective in his 2016 book *Four Days to Change: Twelve Radical Habits to Overcome Bias and Thrive in a Diverse World.* The narrative follows a group of four men embarking on the White Men's Caucus, facilitated by Welp and Proudman. In the book, Welp acknowledged the challenge of calling it a White Man's Caucus. He explained that the point is to gather men, not men of color, to do perspective-sharing about diversity. It's not about exclusion but awakening a group of men who are typically accused of exclusion, the white men.

The book invites the reader to go on the path of discovery with four men, whom Welp described as a compilation of men they have met over the years doing the caucus. Over a four-day period, the men's eyes opened to the water—as in a fish that jumped out of the water and observed its habitat before diving back in the tank—and, maybe even for the first time, the men saw the world from a diverse, more inclusive perspective. The caucus format proved to be effective.

The organization Catalyst published the report "Calling All White Men: Can Training Help Create Inclusive Workplaces?" which included an analysis of pre-and post-survey responses from men who attended the caucus or a "White Men and Allies Learning Lab," as well as feedback from colleagues of the participants (Prime et al., 2012). Researchers reported significant positive changes related to the five behaviors that are important to being inclusive:

- showing critical thinking about different experiences of social groups

- taking responsibility for being inclusive
- inquiring across differences
- listening empathetically
- addressing difficult issues related to differences

In addition to self-reporting, coworkers of the participants said that, four months after the training, participants demonstrated greater interest in learning about people with different perspectives and worldviews.

As I read the book, at times I asked myself, "Seriously? Is this how men share feelings with one another?" At other times, I felt moved by the vulnerable perspectives men shared about parenting moments or even childhood beliefs that influenced them as adults.

Welp also introduced his own set of leadership paradoxes, one being the "Sameness/Difference Paradox," the challenge of recognizing commonality while, at the same time, acknowledging differences. When I read about this paradox, I immediately thought of a plant manager I worked for early in my career as a professional at a manufacturing plant. He yelled at me a lot. Much later in my career progression, I saw him at the headquarters office, and he told me he thought highly of me. He said he was tough on me to help me grow. I laughed and said, "Oh, I grew all right!"

I distinctly recall a time when he called me to his office to ask my perspective and coach me on how to handle a situation.

"I called you here, Kori, because your communication committee members have really screwed you over," he said. "They have twisted your words, setting a series of events in motion. You should call them down to your office and chew them out for screwing you over!"

As I walked back to my office, I contemplated my next move, admittedly rattled that this team had violated a confidence outlined in our meeting protocol. Due to that violation and twisting of words, I found myself up shit's creek with another manager on the leadership team. It was not good.

I called an emergency committee meeting in my office.

"Okay, team, Robert [our plant manager] just informed me that what we discussed in our meeting got back to him within five minutes of the meeting's end," I said in a calm voice. Then I addressed the problem directly, asking what happened, reviewing the protocol, and aligning on a new process.

Next, I apologized to the senior leader whose work was impacted by the information leak. He needed an outlet to express his frustration over a decision that had been made above my pay grade. I took accountability, and he expressed a viewpoint of anger and disappointment in very colorful language. I told him I heard him and had put practices in place to ensure it did not happen again.

That afternoon, Robert called me back to his office again. "I hope you yelled at them for putting you in this shitty spot," he said with a little venom in his voice.

"I did not yell," I explained. "I addressed the issue directly and put a process in place for how we will work going forward. I also walked up to Dick and apologized. He had no mercy. I took accountability."

"You are *way* too nice. Not yelling at them was a big mistake," he said, raising his voice at me. "You are in danger of letting them walk all over you. You need to show them who is in charge, especially when their decision impacted your operations and, worse, your reputation."

"Thanks, Robert," I replied. "I had to be authentic to my way of working, and yelling at people is not the way I work. I take other approaches to deal with conflict head-on. I did not shy away from it. I just handled it differently than maybe you would have handled it."

I had ascribed to my own view of effective conflict management, acknowledging the situation, asking to hear the team's perspective, and then putting a solution in place to correct the action that led to the problem in the first place. I got downgraded on my performance review that year, not for the leak but specifically for not holding the group accountable—in essence, for not yelling at them the way my boss expected me to do.

The example I shared was intended to illustrate the sameness/difference paradox. The difference in perspectives is okay; the potential danger happens when we judge others for not doing it our way. Welp explained how the majority of men—in this case, white men—often focus on treating everyone the same in order to be fair and equal, but the impact is that others don't feel the same. The standard of sameness is defined from one perspective: the majority male.

At the end of each chapter in his 2016 book, *Four Days to Change*, Welp included one of twelve new mindsets to thrive in a diverse world. Mindset #2 is simple yet profound:

> *Incorporate multiple perspectives, even if they are contradictory. They give you a more intricate view of the world. Seeing the world from only one perspective gives an incomplete view.*

Regarding gender equity, men have a perspective too.

It may be contradictory or even surprisingly similar. When we invited Men-in-the-Middle and asked them about gender equity, a potential for new conversations emerged. Whether you interview and speak to men directly like I did or read the books *Four Days to Change, Good Guys*, or others I mention, it is an opportunity to incorporate multiple perspectives and grow (Welp, 2016; Smith and Johnson, 2020).

The ability to view issues and situations from both your own and another's perspective makes it easier to find mutually beneficial solutions, according to David W. Johnson, co-director of the

Cooperative Learning Center at the University of Minnesota. In 2019, Johnson wrote an article for *Psychology Today*, "The Importance of Taking the Perspective of Others," where he asked why it is difficult to find solutions to problems that satisfy everyone. Perspective-taking also communicates that one really understands their thoughts, feelings, and needs.

It is usually easier to jointly solve a problem when the other people feel understood and respected," Johnson explained. This includes feeling heard. When people feel heard, they are more apt to be open to new ideas and take action, including speaking out.

A Catalyst report titled "When Managers Are Open, Men Feel Heard and Interrupt Sexism" stated: 61 percent of men who feel more heard say that they would likely directly interrupt a sexist comment, compared to 35 percent of men who feel less heard (Sattari et al., 2021). The action or inaction men may take to engage in gender-equity conversations or interrupt inappropriate behaviors, ranging from sexist remarks to speaking over a female colleague, directly relates to whether they feel heard.

Perspective-Taking and Psychological Safety

Although men and women have different perspectives, they share a concern for what is called "psychological safety" when it comes to gender equity and gender-related issues in the workplace. The Center for Creative Leadership describes psychological safety as a shared belief held by members of a team that others on the team will not embarrass, reject, or punish them for speaking up (Leading Effectively Staff, 2022).

A lack of psychological safety means people feel unsafe speaking up or out. For women, who represent less than 20 percent of C-suite positions, the lack of psychological safety is due to the power and influence men have over their careers. For men, it is about the ambiguity, ambivalence, and uncertainty of their role and the perceived risk of saying or doing the wrong thing.

This includes Bob, who, at the start of this chapter, said he has no issues meeting with male colleagues for conversations after work, but he is more cautious about meeting with female colleagues alone, even though the purpose of the meetings is about happenings at the office or work-related events. He still believes in gender equity and, at the same time, has restricted one gender from a conversation or perspective-taking in the process.

On the surface, gender equity within a company is a complicated issue, requiring multiple tasks and steps to track parity, regarding status and pay, at different levels in the organization. It is also complex, exacerbated by the emotions of psychological safety and the deeply ingrained biases that often go undiscussed, especially for and by men. In the next few chapters, let's dig into those items that we don't discuss: sex-role stereotypes, maleness, and the biases that impact men, which keep them from sharing their perspectives.

Key Takeaways

- Perspective-taking is the ability to put ourselves in someone else's place while recognizing their point of view, experiences, and beliefs, which creates a basis of understanding between two people.
- Perspective-taking is a learned skill that, with practice, can reduce ambiguity and the discomfort of conflict to get at the heart of the matter.
- In his TEDx Talk, "White Men: Time to Discover Your Cultural Blind Spots," Michael Welp, PhD, explains that men, in particular white men, might not be aware of their bias or that others have a different experience because the male culture permeates most places they go.

- On the path toward gender equity, leaders can face a number of paradoxes, leading to the coexistence of contradictory ideas. Men-in-the-Middle verbally supported the push for a workplace where men and women are equal, but in the state of uncertainty and ambiguity about game-changing behaviors, the culture pulls the organization toward the status quo.
- The idea is not to blame or shame men or women but to acknowledge there is more than one perspective. Sharing those perspectives can open a new conversation for change among all.

Questions to Discuss or Ponder

1. Do you recall a time when your perspective and another person's perspective were so different that you learned something new in the process?
2. How can you encourage perspective-taking among your team or colleagues or in your next meeting?
3. Have you thought about men, and in particular white men, as a culture? How would you describe that culture? If you are a white male, do your characteristics match those traits? If not, what traits or characteristics would you list or add?
4. What does a sense of belonging look like at your organization? And, as a follow-up question, what can you do to increase a sense of belonging in your own organization? Brainstorm a list.
5. Do you agree that men face a threat of psychological safety at work? If yes, how can we change that? If no, why not?

CHAPTER SEVEN

WHAT LURKS IN THE BUMMOCK?

Thomas was eager to have a conversation about #MeToo and gender equity in the office. Then a question reminded him of a recent meeting with his boss and other higher-ranking company executives. He hesitated to share more ...

"I have been looking forward to this call!" Thomas exclaimed after I identified myself for our scheduled phone interview. Thomas is a fast-rising leader at a Fortune 500 company. He often finds himself presenting to, learning from, and observing the behaviors of C-suite executives.

"I have been thinking about this for the last year and a half, and it is relevant to my life," he continued. "And no one has asked me about it yet, so let's start."

I did not need to do much prompting for this interview. After following the introductory protocol, he told me this story:

> *Most of the senior executives at the company are white men, much older than me. When it's just guys in the meeting, it is the usual guy-to-guy ribbing about something, you know, like ...*

> *Allen's report was late. He will have to man up and hang with us at the office past 6 p.m. Or even Jordan will have to grow a pair and confront Ken on missing the deadline.*
>
> *Then, my female colleague attended, and it was different. [The men] apologized for swearing and said they did not mean to do this or that. They abdicated decision-making when they would usually bark orders.*
>
> *After the meeting, my female colleague asked me for advice. She started our meeting by saying, 'Why was he talking to me like that? It was so patronizing.'*

Thomas shared the story with me as if he were a fish that jumped out of the water and made an observation before he dove back into the tank.

In that "out of the water" experience, he also looked forward to sharing with me a tip he thought could benefit other women. He sent me an article as a follow-up so I could share it with others. In a 2016 article for *The Cut*, a site for women including the latest fashion trends and takes on timely issues, author Claire Landsbaum wrote about a technique deployed in the Obama White House to promote equity:

> *Female staffers adopted a meeting strategy they called amplification: When a woman made a key point, other women would repeat it, giving credit to its author. This forced the men in the room to recognize the contribution—and denied them the chance to claim the idea as their own.*

Thomas followed this by telling me that early in his career, he learned he was not always right and to take in all perspectives first before taking action or reacting. I made an observation near the end of our call.

"Thomas, you have many great ideas, and I can tell you are really engaged in this call. Thank you," I said, setting up my next question. "You have a solid and rather unique perspective on gender equity. Why did you wait a year and a half to have this conversation, as you said at the beginning of the call?"

He hesitated and then said, "I guess no one asked me."

I unpacked that after the call, following up with additional research. Thomas did not know he had a role to play in the #MeToo, #TimesUp, and gender equity conversations. Turns out he had a lot to say *after* I asked him.

As with most of the other interviews, an important nugget came at the end of the call. At that point, typically, the men felt more relaxed. I had reassured them at least twice that their identities would be anonymous in the book. I even let them pick their fictitious names if they wanted to be part of that. Then I asked the magic question: "Would you like to share anything else?" Most of the time, the men revealed an insight that intrigued me even more.

In Thomas' case, when I asked him the question, there was an abrupt change in the tone and pace of his speaking. He even told me he was uncomfortable sharing this, and I had to reassure him a third time that his name and identity would be protected. His voice became almost a whisper as if he did not want anyone to hear what he was about to say. Looking back now, I realize this was likely a lack of psychological safety at play. I listened as Thomas picked his words carefully:

> *We have done business with many smart, successful women, some even growing their own companies from a start-up mom-and-pop business to a significant size. I have been in the room and, at times, appalled at the way the senior leaders talk about these women when they are not there. These are men I trust and who have helped guide and drive my career. With a guy, they might*

> *say he's an idiot or a moron, but the vitriol about the women is more prominent. It's not a question of her business results. It is a question of her character they talk about, like how she is terrible to work with. I've got to believe that is something inherent, like, I don't like 'her being in charge of me.'*

Thomas could be articulating the symptoms of an Australian-originated concept called "Tall Poppy Syndrome" (TPS), defined as times when people are attacked, denigrated, or cut down due to their achievement or success (Meyer, 2022). High-achieving men and women can be TPS victims in sports, celebrity status, and in the workplace. In March 2023, Dr. Rumeet Billan, CEO of Women of Influence+, led international research and published the white paper, "The Tallest Poppy: How the Workforce is Cutting Ambitious Women Down," regarding the impacts on women and the culture at work. Almost 90 percent of respondents—including thousands of working women across demographics and professions from 103 countries—said they experienced TPS at work. These behaviors ranged from downplaying or dismissing women's achievements to leaving women out of discussions and taking credit for others' ideas. The consequences are costly to the bottom line:

- **Retention:** Almost 70 percent of women reported they looked for a new job.
- **Productivity:** 75 percent agreed that TPS impacted their work efficiency.
- **Culture:** Almost 80 percent said it created an atmosphere of distrust.

The study also showed that when participants shared their experiences, only 20 percent were encouraged to do something, like confront the person, seek counsel from Human Resources, or report it to a senior leader. More than 40 percent of women said they did not get suggestions or advice to take action, and 23 percent of women said they were encouraged to keep any "complaints" to themselves.

Perhaps if we socialize, name, and talk about the Tall Poppy Syndrome, we can stop the impacts for both men and women, as Dr. Billan suggested in her white paper. Naming it could have helped Thomas too.

When I asked him what he said to the men and how he handled it, he confided he had not thought about their behaviors as a gender equity issue until we started talking. He had not said anything at the time and had not shared that story with anyone before our conversation. He realized our conversation prompted him to look at it differently.

Psychological Safety and Implicit Bias

Perspective-taking, addressed in chapters five and six, is an effective technique for minimizing discomfort and even conflicts in a social situation, but it is not easy to see things from another person's perspective. If it was, we would see a lot more empathy in the world. Perspective-taking can also reveal the impacts of implicit biases and harmful sex stereotypes, including those about masculinity. In 2017, The Perception Institute, a consortium dedicated to reducing bias and promoting belonging, wrote on its web page, "Thoughts and feelings are 'implicit' if we are unaware of them or we are mistaken about their intent." The Institute defines implicit bias as when we have attitudes toward people or associate stereotypes with them without our conscious knowledge.

Perspective-taking is hard because we are fighting our subconscious minds, where the bias and deeply ingrained stereotypes live. Most of us know the idiom, "Before you judge a man, walk a mile in his shoes." In other words, before we form an opinion or speculate, work to understand a person's experiences, challenges, and thought processes. What if, due to implicit bias—those deep subconscious attitudes—and rigid gender stereotypes, our shoes are on the wrong feet? It affects our ability to walk in someone's shoes.

To take it a step further, what if the uncertainty of the *subconscious,* implicit thoughts, and the unspoken but often *conscious* role expectations create a culture where people don't feel safe speaking out?

My conversation with Thomas inspired me to look at the intersection of all these concepts.

To be clear, Thomas did not use the words "psychological safety"—introduced at the end of chapter six—or "implicit bias" in our interview. But let's explore how both of these likely came into play. First, he had ideas to improve gender equity. For example, the news story about amplification but chose not to speak up until asked.

Next, when I prompted him, he found himself uncomfortable as he recalled a story that did seem to highlight an example of inequity. When he raised concerns about the behaviors of men in power and influence in his career, he dropped his tone as if he did not want anyone else to hear what he said. Could both be forms of a psychologically unsafe setting from two different angles?

- The women could reject his idea-sharing as a form of "mansplaining," the term used when a man explains something, typically to a woman, in a manner regarded as condescending or patronizing (Merriam-Webster, 2018).
- If he told the men in power that he was appalled by their comments, he might worry they would reject him and even stop supporting his career.

I practiced perspective-taking. I listened to Thomas and worked to see the situation through his eyes. I approached the interviews like an anthropologist, attempting to understand why the majority of men did not proactively speak up or out about gender equity.

My methodology included qualitative interviews backed by secondary research.

As a female, I can't and don't speak for men. But I studied what the men said to see the situation—the quest for gender equity and an observation that men seemed to be quiet and disengaged—from their experiences and beliefs. The challenge is that since we all have implicit bias, or subconscious beliefs about various social and identity groups, I had to acknowledge that I might be influenced based on the experiences I've had with men in my network. Digging deep, I could see the subconscious bias and the fear of speaking out at play in my own work, just like in the perspectives of the Men-in-the-Middle.

And before I felt I could share the insights I learned, I did extra research to back up my points and those of the men I interviewed. I put the work into finding credible sources from well-established organizations and trustworthy experts, not just at my editor's request but also to connect the readers to people with different perspectives and experiences to encourage them to look at it from all angles. And most importantly, the intent behind my research was to demonstrate that this is a universal concern and that I am not alone in my passion to create a sense of urgency and pursue lasting change within the issues that relate to gender equity.

With degrees in journalism and communication and a proclivity for continual learning, I study things like resolving conflict through perspective-taking, the way an architect looks at floor plans or a mechanical engineer examines a machine. Seeing things from another perspective can reduce bias and stereotypes that often lead to conflict (Galinsky and Moskowitz, 2000; Devine et al., 2012).

Unfortunately, fear can also get in the way of conflict.

In a 2019 article for *OR Today Magazine* titled "The Role of Fear in Conflict Resolution," Daniel Bobinski wrote about the five universal fears:

- fear of criticism
- fear of failure
- fear of rejection
- fear of not getting what you want
- fear of losing what you have

We have all experienced at least one of these causes for fear, if not multiple at the same time. Allow me to be vulnerable and share my fears of criticism, failure, and rejection, backed by some evidence.

When I first had the idea to write this book, I knew I wanted to offer a way forward to gain momentum on an issue I deeply care about. I had a goal to build a compelling case to engage men in addressing gender equity, but I couldn't ignore all the other issues that got tangled up in the messiness of culture, politics, and emotions. I had to address the discomfort of change and emotional uncertainty within a "cancel culture"—the latter meaning withdrawal of support from public figures or celebrities who have done things that are not socially acceptable today (Merriam-Webster, 2023).

In today's society, this has extended beyond celebrities. There is little tolerance, empathy, or grace for misspoken words or mistakes. This also heightens the fear of isolation for going against the status quo that we addressed in chapter three, regarding the spiral of silence.

I stepped out of my own shoes to take on the perspectives of the men I interviewed, acknowledging their experiences and beliefs and getting clear on where their concerns lie. At times, listening to their stories triggered memories from my own career when I had experienced inequitable treatment.

Here are a few examples: a male boss offered me less than the starting salary range for the position; a male leader told me it would be too expensive to send my family on a foreign assignment but then picked a man with a family to go; a male executive, known for his angry outbursts at meetings, told me I needed to keep my emotions in check and tone down my passion.

The height of the #MeToo viral activity spotlighted, for me, a missing voice on gender issues—the perspectives of men. With men holding the majority of leadership roles in corporations today and the data that indicates that will not change soon, we need men to be allies for gender equity and positive, sustainable change in behaviors and policies.

My curiosity led to an inquiry. I asked men about it, listened, analyzed, and researched insights. Even though the logic is solid and I understand how elevating male voices from the silent sidelines of the issue can help bring about change in the case for gender equity, I had my own fears about sharing my message. While writing this book, with every well-researched source and each finished chapter, I still felt uncertain about how people would respond. I had already witnessed intense reactions based on conversations I had after the initial interviews.

Here is the evidence of my fear from the lens of my older sister, who has known me my entire life. She is now a tenured professor of business at a university, and I respect the way she weaved a successful corporate career as she pursued her master's degree in business and then ultimately a doctorate degree before winning numerous awards as a teacher. With her title as "sister," she had the credibility to call me out; her credentials just add to the integrity.

She told me, "I can tell when you are uncertain. You barrel down and research the heck out of an issue. You find enough data to even outweigh your own opinion as if you have to prove to yourself that your intuition is right." Well, sister, check out my bibliography. This is not a dissertation or an academic paper, but I have read enough journals now to see that every point has to be backed by evidence.

161

And, to give my brother—who has successfully worked many years in large organizations—a shout-out too, the man of few words told me that it's "an important issue to acknowledge that there are fears for men too."

Based on the interviews I did and the insights I gathered for this book, I looked at the intersection of all of these ideas: bias, fear, and perspective-taking. This involved a deeper examination of the impacts of psychological safety and implicit bias on perspective-taking in the context of conversations—especially when these discussions were between men and women and focused on gender equity.

I created some visuals to explain how I connected the elements in this chapter. Figure 7 below builds on Figure 5 from the previous chapter.

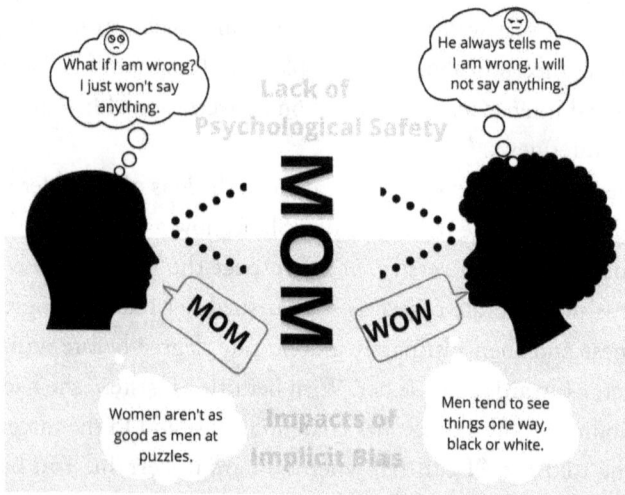

Figure 7: An illustration to show how both Implicit Bias and a lack of Psychological Safety impact perspective-taking.

When practicing perspective-taking, keep in mind that two people can look at the same thing from different angles and see it in a distinct way (e.g., the word "MOM" or the word "WOW").

Our perspectives are also influenced by other forces, including psychological safety and implicit bias.

The top of the chart represents the influence of psychological safety, or, rather, a lack of it. Each individual may fear negative consequences of speaking up, including a decrease in self-image, status, or career. In the article "Psychological Safety in a Speak-up Culture," international accounting firm Grant Thornton's 2020 Women in Business study showed that less than half of senior leaders believe it's mostly true that different points of view are encouraged in business meetings.

Amy Edmondson, a professor at Harvard Business School, is credited with coining the term "psychological safety" in reference to work culture. In her *Harvard Business Review* podcast interview, she said that too often, the culture is to not rock the boat (Edmondson, 2019). "No one ever got fired for silence," she said. "Learning is great, but not in front of people."

When avoiding conflict to feel safe, people miss out on the opportunity to be heard and make a difference.

The bottom portion of Figure 7 reflects the impacts of implicit bias, which can also influence perspectives. These stereotypes exist in subconscious awareness. It is like the time I saw a picture of young kids on a senior executive's desk and said, "Cute grandkids!" He was older than me, and the kids were younger than my kids. It turned out, those were his kids from a second marriage. *Oops!*

Introducing the Bummock

Implicit bias, unspoken concerns, and confusion about men's roles in promoting gender equity exist in the bummock. The bummock, in the British-English Dictionary, is the portion of the iceberg below the water. On average, 90 percent of the iceberg is submerged (Collins English Dictionary, 2022); see

Figure 8 below. The Iceberg Model of Change Management explains that leaders tend to focus on the issues they see at the "tip of the iceberg" (Abbas, 2021). The part of the berg below the water, the bummock, is more complex and potentially even more damaging if not recognized or managed. What lurks below the surface in the bummock are those topics and unexpressed emotions or feelings that often go undiscussed and might impede collaboration.

Remember the Titanic? The crew visually spotted the tip of the iceberg above the surface, but, at that point, it was too late; the ship had already hit the much larger portion of the iceberg below water.

In the case of Thomas, he buried the discomfort of the experience with his executive team until I prompted him with a question that brought it to the surface.

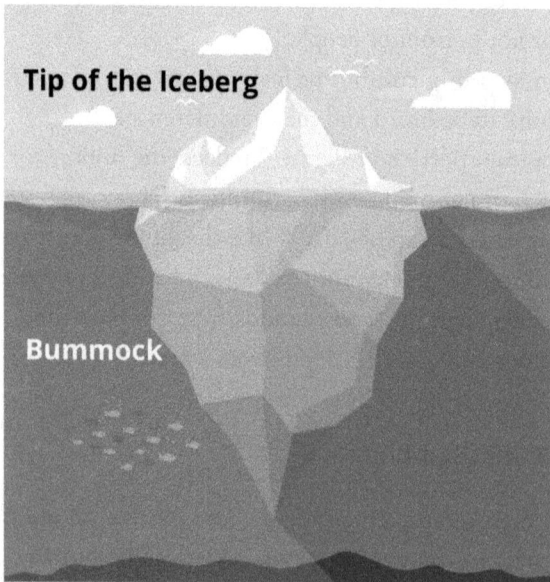

Figure: 8: A visual to illustrate the Iceberg Theory of Change Management and the concept of "The Bummock."

As we covered in the previous chapter, at the surface, there is agreement among genders about the importance of gender equity and the positive impacts of having a more diverse workforce, including women. At the tip of the iceberg is where some people pitch the flag and make the claim, "I don't see color or gender, and I certainly do not claim to be *privileged* or *the power elite* by any means."

When people look out into the world from the top, they may take great pride in the climb and even celebrate their efforts to be inclusive. The climber may be so focused on achieving the task at hand that they don't see the head start they got over peers, even if they did not ask for it. That perceived advantage could be based on the opportunities and experiences related to color or gender alone.

We have talked about the impacts of uncertainty and ambiguity. Now let's look at some of those concerns that lurk deeper in the bummock and threaten to sink gender-equity conversations.

What's lingering below the surface?

- A 2020 Pew Research Center study showed both women and men acknowledge progress has been made in gender equality; however, three in ten male respondents say this progress has come at the expense of men (Horowitz and Igielnik, 2020).

- A 2018 study in the *Journal of Social Issues*, "Zero-Sum Thinking and the Masculinity Contest," found men, not women, reduced support for gender-fair workplace policies when there was a perceived threat [e.g., career loss, judgment, exclusion from a group, etc.] impacted by an increase in their zero-sum thinking (Kuchynka et al., 2018).

- A 2022 Catalyst report by Geoffrey Kerr and Alix Pollack titled "Engaging Men: Barriers and Gender Norms" found that "even when men have the best intentions to support gender equity, opposing forces undermine progress." Following are some findings from survey research:

- 74 percent said that apathy toward issues of gender equity is a factor in men's lack of action; they were unconcerned or saw no compelling reason to engage.
- 51 percent said men don't act due to perceived or actual ignorance; they are ill-equipped to advocate for gender equity simply because they are men.
- 74 percent of men also said fear is a barrier for three main reasons: 1) loss of career status as women progress; 2) making a mistake when trying to reduce gender bias; and 3) judgment from other men.

I recall a time in the office ten years ago when a male colleague, Bruno, explained the logic behind his "fear" to me, in his own terms. I led a project that required working with experts across the company, and I had the approval from the bosses of the virtual team members to work with them before the project started.

Bruno's boss gave Bruno the assignment to work with me on the project. Bruno had also been blowing off my emails. When I asked him to meet, he finally responded and surprisingly agreed. As soon as we sat down, Bruno explained why he had not been responding to my attempts to communicate. "Look," he said. "I could help you, but I am not willing to jeopardize my family to help you out."

I admit I was taken aback by the comment. I rifled through my memories, trying to capture a moment when I might have said or done something that would concern his family or family status. Before my mental search could complete, he continued, not waiting for me to speak: "You see, if I help you, then it looks like I have time. And if it looks like I have extra time to help someone from your team, then that will reflect on my job review that I did not use the time to help my own team to succeed. In turn, that will lead me to get downgraded on my performance review. If I am downgraded on my performance review, then I will not get my bonus. If I don't get my bonus, then I can't take my family on a vacation that I promised; therefore, it will hurt my family."

I looked at him, a little dumbfounded.

After all, he laid out a clear, complicated logic model, and it took me a minute to process the complexity below the surface. A minute later, still baffled, I responded, "I would never want to hurt your family."

After a few more attempts to convince Bruno we would all win if this business case worked, I had mentally decided to work around him. I would not go to his boss, as I might need Bruno's allyship later. I would go to one of his colleagues, whom I had a relationship with, and ask him to teach me how to do Bruno's job and my own. Bruno thought helping me on a project would cause him to get a poor performance review, even though he was aware his boss had assigned him to work with me on a cross-matrix project that would benefit both of us professionally, as well as our departments and the company.

While I did not agree with Bruno's decision and it created a lot of extra work for me, I appreciate to this day that he shared the root cause of his silence. After I consulted with a peer who knew him well, I discovered the size of the bummock I had been up against. A rumor had spread that I was after his job; even though it was untrue, he had already made up his mind—helping me was out of the question.

Fear is a bummock behavior.

Bruno outwardly expressed concern that he was afraid helping me would impact his compensation. Thomas indirectly expressed fear when he lowered his voice to describe appalling behaviors in the office.

When we get to the root cause behind the silence—fear, concern for reputation or facing judgment, uncertainty about impacts, and more—we can address the problem and continue on our journey toward gender equity. Staying in the bummock can lead to other issues. One example is toxic masculinity, another form of bias that impacts both women and men.

Toxic Masculinity and the Masculine Culture

In the 2020 article "What Is Toxic Masculinity?", *Verywell Mind* Editor-in-Chief Amy Morin wrote that toxic masculinity, the idea of "maleness," puts cultural pressures on men to behave in a certain way. She added that it affects all boys and men in some fashion.

Citing a 1986 study, "The Structure of Male Role Norms" by Edward Thompson and Joseph Pleck, Morin wrote that many definitions of toxic masculinity appear in research and pop culture, but there are three core components:

1. **Toughness:** This is the notion that men should be physically strong, emotionally callous, and behaviorally aggressive.
2. **Anti-femininity:** This involves the idea that men should reject anything considered to be feminine, such as showing emotion or accepting help.
3. **Power:** This is the assumption that men must work toward obtaining power and status (social and financial) so they can gain the respect of others.

Toxic masculinity is described as the cultural ideal of maleness or manliness, applauding strength, penalizing emotions, and, in some cases, measuring manliness by sex, violence, and power. It does *not* mean all men are inherently toxic; it is an ideology that confines men to one set of extreme behaviors by which they are judged as men. It leaves no room for qualities like fairness, gentleness, or cooperativeness.

The irony is that the narrow list of manly traits weakens the masculine identity. Four professors, three male and one female, who collaborated on research and the 2023 *Harvard Business Review* article "What Fragile Masculinity Looks like at Work," wrote: "A wealth of research has shown that masculinity is among the most fragile of identities, so precarious that even seemingly minor threats can push otherwise-ethical men to lie, cheat, harass, and even commit assault, all in an attempt to prove they are 'real men'" (Kouchaki et al, 2023).

The results of their research showed that when men perceived experiences as threats to their masculinity, they were more likely to engage in behaviors that are obstacles to collaboration, including withholding help, mistreating coworkers, and lying for personal gain.

Below the surface, lingering in the bummock of topics that go undiscussed, is the impact among men who don't fit this one-dimensional view of what it means to be male. In the absence of a conversation that elevates the value of both masculine and feminine energy and approaches, conventional ideas prevail, including man as breadwinner, "The Bro Code," or even male sexual bravado.

Here are a few examples that male advisers in my network, including my husband, shared with me:

- An unwritten rule on the golf course states that men who don't hit the ball past the ladies' tee are supposed to golf with their pants down the rest of the hole (I've not seen it, but I have heard men say it).
- When men cry, other guys will say, "Don't be a pussy!"
- If a man has difficulty lifting something, their male peers might say, "C'mon man, my mom can lift more than that."
- If a man is uncertain about accepting an invitation from other men, the guys might say, "What is wrong with you? Do you need to check with your wife first?"

- When a man is vulnerable and opens up about how an experience impacted him, he is met with a comment like, "The ladies meeting is down the hall."
- Treating a comment like "grab them by the pussy" as simple locker-room banter, as in the 2016 apology of then-United States presidential candidate Donald Trump, when 2005 audio footage leaked of him saying that about women (Burns, et al., 2016).

As a mom of two sons, I agree with Mark Greene's 2018 Medium article called "Why Calling It 'Toxic Masculinity' Isn't Helping." After all, masculinity itself is not toxic. When all men and male behaviors are judged based on these limited, defined male norms, these "manly" behaviors create a box or mold that men are expected to fit in. That is not inclusive. Greene, an editor at the Good Men Project®, explained how "toxic masculinity" blames and shames, while a "culture of masculinity" invites men and women to look at the impact of "Man Box" culture.

The focus of the negative association is on the culture in which people ascribe these behaviors to men, versus calling all masculinity toxic. In short, "Man Box" culture refers to the rigid set of expectations and behaviors society deems manly and imposes on men.

Even the Harvard professors mentioned above, who researched and wrote about fragile masculinity, suggested we broaden the definition of masculinity to idealize "good men" instead of focusing on "real men" defined by traits in the "Man Box" culture.

In Figure 9 below, we see how the narrow definition of the "Man Box" or Masculine Culture impacts perspective-taking (which is already compounded by a lack of psychological safety and implicit bias, as reflected in Figure 8). Figure 9 depicts the impacts of toxic masculinity, referred to in this book as the "Man Box" or Masculine Culture.

This rain cloud of traits can drown out gender-equity conversations, especially for men.

When we don't talk about those issues—toughness, power, and anti-femininity—they remain in the bummock. Conversations and perspective-taking can serve as a waterproof umbrella and help shield the damaging impacts of the "Man Box" culture. As Greene said, putting the focus on and discussing a culture of masculinity invites men and women to look at, study, and talk about the impact of "Man Box" culture as a way to move forward.

In other words, we embrace a formula of *from-through-to*; we move from rigid expectations through open and authentic communication to transform the narrative about gender equity.

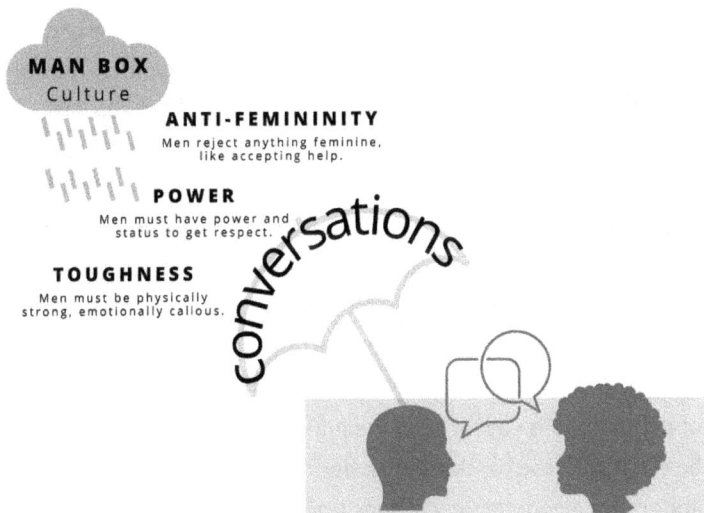

MAN BOX
Culture

ANTI-FEMININITY
Men reject anything feminine, like accepting help.

POWER
Men must have power and status to get respect.

TOUGHNESS
Men must be physically strong, emotionally callous.

conversations

Figure 9: An illustration to show how conversations can create a protective shield against the impacts of the "Man Box" culture.

The masculine "Man Box" culture impacts women and men. Something important to note is how this rigid, narrow view of the masculine identity may prevent men from seeking help when they need it most. The nonprofit Mental Health America's "Five Minutes to Men's Mental Health" showed that six million men in the United States are affected by depression, and they are 3.5 times more likely than women to die by suicide (Pappas, 2019).

Men who bought into traditional notions of masculinity had more negative attitudes about seeking mental health services (Yousaf et al., 2015). Recognizing the need, the American Psychological Association created, for the first time in 2018, new guidelines to support men, acknowledging that the rules of the "Man Box" culture do more harm than good (Fortin, 2019; APA, 2018).

New York Times reporter Jacey Fortin wrote about the guidelines in her 2019 article "Traditional Masculinity Can Hurt Boys, Say New A.P.A. Guidelines," where she quoted Dr. Judy Chu, professor of psychosocial development at Stanford University: "When boys and men challenge patriarchal constructions of gender, they're at risk of being perceived as failures or as weak," Dr. Chu said. But she added that when women, girls, and nonbinary people criticized the patriarchal systems that oppressed them, another idea began to take shape. "Maybe those systems hurt men too, even as they conferred certain privileges. It brought to light overlooked issues because there was a taboo against talking about it."

The idea here is to take the "Man Box" culture out of the bummock. Dealing with the damaging effects of this limited view of masculinity is part of gender-equity conversations too. This could be the root cause blocking men and women from talking together about how gender-related issues impact them in the office, and it may even impede company performance. It is time to dismantle preconceived ideas based on outdated stereotypes that bind us in order to advance gender equity for all.

Authentic conversations that address gender-related issues from both male and female perspectives are opportunities for a new narrative that leads to sustainable, equitable change. Thinking outside of the box, people—men and women—can demonstrate both masculine and feminine traits. A woman can be both a nurturing leader and an assertive negotiator, and a man can be a powerful influencer and a caring boss and humanitarian. People are not one-dimensional, but complex beings, often managing and transitioning from one role to the next (i.e., employee to parent, colleague to caretaker, or executive to volunteer).

In the absence of conversations that elevate and normalize that characteristic traits are not necessarily gender-specific, or at least an awareness that personal strengths and preferences might differ from work culture expectations, people can face a conundrum. For example, a person who values winning, individual victories, and a competitive environment—typically assigned to male traits—may struggle when incentives are based on collaboration within a team or division performance.

Avoiding these discussions or responding with silence does not promote the change that people want to see. A 2020 Catalyst study, "Interrupting Silence at Work: How Men Respond in a Climate of Silence," found that in organizations where men are silent, men are 50 percent less likely to be committed to interrupting sexist behavior at work and 40 percent less confident in their ability to address other people who engage in sexist behavior (Shaffer et al., 2020).

Providing men with opportunities to discuss issues of gender in majority-men groups may reduce men's concerns about making mistakes or being judged as sexist. In Thomas's story at the start of this chapter, he wanted to talk, and our conversation sparked idea-sharing as well as discovery.

That is a step toward progress.

Perspective-taking can help us embrace conflict in a healthier way, but it can be blocked by the negative stigma endorsed in the masculine culture. When the issues men face remain in the dark, below the surface in the bummock, men can experience an internal tug-of-war; for example, if I speak out about gender equity, will I be seen as pro-feminine and open myself up to teasing by my male colleagues? When men choose silence over verbalizing concerns, they also miss an opportunity to influence positive changes in policy and culture.

Greene, the champion of shifting from the phrase "toxic masculinity" to a "culture of masculinity," said a message of compassion toward men is the way to benefit the women and children of the world. "If we are going to win this battle, we must condemn the culture of toxicity while showing compassion for the men and women trapped in it, as we work hard to create culture change," he said.

In my conversation with Professor Rachael Dailey Goodwin, whom I mentioned at the end of chapter five, she explained men can be socialized to put on a masculine front and to avoid or not acknowledge that they care deeply about these issues, even if they really do. For example, she said men may think they can't talk openly about sexual harassment or other gendered issues and still be able to fit in with the "boys' club." When these issues go undiscussed because people avoid them out of discomfort, it can send a false signal that this conversation is not important enough to address.

This makes getting involved in gender equity discussions or engaging in gender-related issues an unsafe space for men.

But we can change that.

Experts like Dr. Robert Blum say to change that, we also need to shift the narrative on gender to include both the way it impacts women and girls as well as men and boys (Blum, 2019). Blum is a professor at Johns Hopkins who specializes in adolescent health with a focus on gender socialization and how it shapes wellness. He contends that gender inequality also harms men and boys, in part due to ingrained sex-role stereotypes that start at a young age, such as boys are aggressors and girls are physically weak. He refers to these in research as "gender straightjackets."

In the next chapter, let's look at gender issues related to boys and men and practice raising them from the bummock, below the surface, to the tip, where discussion happens. When we acknowledge gender socialization, sex-role stereotypes, and work-life balance from the male perspective, we open the potential to engage in new conversations about gender equity that are more inclusive and have the potential to lead to even better outcomes.

Thomas, your view matters. Please speak out.

Key Takeaways

- Psychological safety is about your ability to speak up and share your authentic viewpoints without fear of negative consequences to your self-image, status, or career.
- Implicit bias is when we unknowingly have attitudes toward people or associate stereotypes with them.
- The iceberg is a metaphor that illustrates the challenge of a culture change. The largest part of an iceberg is the bummock, which is the part we can't see that exists below the surface. It represents the unstated assumptions or topics we don't discuss, and these often create bigger obstacles and prevent progress.
- The masculine culture assigns traits to men that they must meet or they are not deemed "manly." This can be damaging to men's mental health.
- Engaging men to share input and participate in gender-related conversations is important; involving them is not a zero-sum game for gender equity but a win-win for men and women.

Questions to Discuss or Ponder

1. What did you observe about the exchange with Thomas at the beginning of this chapter? Do you identify with any of his comments? Why or why not?

2. Do you see gender equity from the lens of the iceberg analogy? What lurks below the surface for you in the bummock?

3. Have you seen the impacts of the masculine culture in your workplace? If so, describe what it looks like from your perspective.

4. Take a look at Figures 7 and 8. Can you recall a time when you experienced any of these elements? Saw the same situation differently? Had a concern for psychological safety or implicit bias?

5. What is one thing you could do in the next thirty days to reframe gender conversations in your organization?

CHAPTER EIGHT

CAN MEN REALLY HAVE IT ALL?

Blake struggled with the phrase "fair but equal,"
saying equality is essential and will happen when
we acknowledge that men face challenges too.

Blake, a corporate leader from a West Coast-based U.S. company, focused the attention on work-family balance during our interview. Like Thomas from chapter seven, Blake said he had been looking forward to our call; he had a lot to say and had not really spoken about his views with anyone. The interview request email had triggered some thoughts, and, during the call, he verbalized those.

"There is a perceived double standard that men face an unspoken penalty for being a 'family guy.' If my colleague, Jane, leaves early to pick up her kid from school, that is expected. If I want to leave early to attend my kid's soccer game, I am questioned for putting my kid and family first over loyalty to the company. That is just the way it is," Blake explained.

"Families are not so much of a women's problem but a family one, and men can't bring this issue into the workplace. If we are going to treat everyone fairly, this needs to be addressed too," Blake said, his conviction getting stronger each time he referred to the ideas of fairness and family for both men and women.

When Blake says he can't bring this issue up, it is not that a policy prevents him from doing so. As an exempt corporate employee who gets a flat salary, he has a bit of flexibility in his schedule. For men, it is akin to the feeling of passing the offering plate at church and people watching to see if you put something in or not.

The pressure is real. The penalties for men may be real too.

I wrote briefly about the "parenthood penalty" in chapter six to address a comment from one of our Men-in-the-Middle about the impacts of prioritizing family over work for both men and women. He approached it from a point of difference, alluding to women's absence from work as a barrier to career growth.

I circled back here in chapter eight to address work-family or work-life balance from a different angle. Here, Blake is stating that family and work-life balance associated with interests outside of work is something men and women have in common. Raising a family, however, is not just a women's issue, but a source of common ground, a shared value that men and women experience differently.

Once again, there are double standards for men and women. The intentions and penalties aren't necessarily declared out loud, but the data tells the story that prowls in the bummock.

On the one hand, the "motherhood penalty" and the "fatherhood bonus" exist, referring to research by Sociology Professor Michelle Budig, who found that on average, men's earnings increased by more than 6 percent if, when they had children, they lived with them, and women's decreased by 4 percent for each child (Miller, 2014).

On the other hand, men face penalties too for putting family over work, despite increased societal expectations around parental involvement:

- Men who leave the workforce for family reasons can expect to earn 26.4 percent less later in their careers than they would have had they not left the workforce (Coltrane et al., 2013).

- Men who ask for family leave are "feminized" or, rather, judged as weaker, uncertain, and less competitive (Rudman and Mescher, 2013).

- Caregiver fathers were judged as not tough enough and excluded more than "traditional" fathers, dads who worked full-time with at-home spouses. Mothers, on the other hand, face more harassment and mistreatment when they spend less time on caregiving (Berdahl and Moon, 2013).

- Fathers who were highly involved in childcare reported the greatest levels of harassment compared to other men in the sample, in particular fathers who provided minimal childcare (Harrington et al., 2015).

- Literature calls it the "wimp penalty" when men are committed to sharing household chores, childcare, and building up and supporting women. These "family-engaged men" are perceived as less competent and less masculine, especially by their male peers (Johnson and Smith, 2018).

The Boston College Report, "The New Dad, A Portrait of Today's Father," noted fathers who are heavily involved in caregiving could be subject to informal and formal professional sanctions (Harrington et al., 2015). These same researchers also found that 99 percent of working fathers believe their supervisor expects no change to occur to their work patterns after becoming parents.

Society has raised the flag, and rightfully so, on the unhealthy messages and stereotypes that hold girls and women back. It is also time to elevate conversations about the unhealthy messages that impact boys and men. As Blake said, if we are going to address gender equity, inclusive of a broad range of topics from pay to work-life balance, we need to acknowledge that men face challenges too.

In this chapter, I will name a few of these workplace issues to raise them from the bummock to the tip of the iceberg so that we can talk about them to heighten awareness and bring them into focus. These are the research-backed insights that are, at times, counterintuitive to the way society talks about work-family balance and conflicts.

The way to normalize something is through conversation— raising awareness of the issue and talking about it, even if it goes against the norm. If we don't label these potential concerns, then we are susceptible to "the orbit of status quo" that can lurk in the organization. In chapter six, I mentioned this concept from Pam S. Harper: the idea that when we face discomfort and don't talk about it, we are likely to revert to the norm, the conventional idea, or how things stand with little to no change.

In this case, deeply ingrained sex-role stereotypes, a masculine culture defined by rigid expectations of male behaviors, and gender socialization can hurt men too. If we don't validate Blake's expression of unfairness and talk about issues that men face, the orbit of the status quo will continue holding us in a perpetual, circular motion of inequity. We miss an opportunity to engage the very men who are in influential positions and can make a difference in the culture.

Work-Life Balance Impacts Men Too

As a matter of fact, research supports Blake's observation of a double standard, at least in the way working mothers and fathers behave when it comes to managing family events and workloads. Findings from Bright Horizon's 2020 "Sixth Annual Modern Family Index" showed:

- Working fathers are more likely than working mothers to miss family events (65 percent versus 58 percent) and family dinners (38 percent versus 29 percent) because of work.

- Working fathers feel the need to tiptoe around their colleagues even more than working mothers, with 59 percent admitting they have snuck out of work to take care of their family because they couldn't be upfront with their colleagues, compared to 42 percent of working mothers.

In alignment with Blake's comments, the above research shows that men do feel like they can't bring up family issues at work. What's interesting to note is that research shows men are more involved in their children's lives today than previous generations (Petts, et al., 2018). Perhaps, to be better fathers, men are *sneaking* out of work at a more frequent rate, hiding the true motivation for leaving. In turn, that makes the work-life conflict for men immensely complicated, and we can explore, through awareness and conversations, how to change that. Not talking about it perpetuates the very narrative we are trying to break and rebuild for men and families.

In a 1994 (updated in 2005) *Tampa Bay Times* article titled "Men in Dual-Career Families May Face 'Daddy Penalty,'" writer Tamar Lewin quoted Professor Linda Stroh: "There's a definite daddy penalty, but it's only on the dads in dual-career families. I think it's a new diversity issue for companies to think about, the diversity of family type."

Except this isn't a new issue.

The article above is from almost three decades ago, and we still haven't learned how to talk about work-life balance from the male perspective. We've since talked about the income gap or about women juggling careers and motherhood, and those are real and important issues; for the most part, however, we've stayed mum when it comes to the "daddy penalty," despite men being impacted too.

It turns out that desires and challenges regarding work-family balance are similar among men and women. For both mothers and fathers, the stress associated with missing events and time spent at home with their children has remained steady since 1986 (Bright Horizons Family Solutions LLC, 2020). Two decades later, in 2017, Kristen Shockley, lead researcher and assistant professor at the University of Georgia, and a team of others conducted a global meta-analysis of gender differences in work-family conflict from more than 350 studies that also included more than 250,000 people. Shockley and team found that men struggle with work-family balance just as much as women do, regardless of the levels of gender equality in their own country.

This study was referenced in a 2017 news article titled "Men Struggle as Much as Women to Maintain Work-Life Balance," where staff writers for the Indian English-language business-focused daily newspaper *The Economics Times* shared a thought-provoking statement by Kristen Shockley:

> *We essentially found very little evidence of differences between women and men as far as the level of work-family conflict they report. Women hear that other women are struggling with this issue, so they expect they will experience greater work-family conflict. There also is some socialisation for it being OK for women to talk more about it than men.*

Why is that the case? Why is it considered okay for women but not men?

The article explained that "men often do not feel comfortable discussing work-family concerns because of fears of being stigmatised, threats to their masculinity or negative career repercussions." Shockley explained that women are socialized to talk about work and family, but men are not, and they don't, at least at work. Shockley also stated: "I do think it's harming men, who are silently struggling and are experiencing the same amount of work-family conflict, but no one is acknowledging it." Once again, we see the impacts of the spiral of silence from chapter three.

"Women are a generation ahead," Rich Dorment, editor in chief of *Men's Health* magazine, told Reed Tucker in an interview for his 2020 *New York Post* article, "Men Can't Have It All Either, Struggle with Work-Life Balance." Dorment explained: "There was the rush into the workplace in the seventies and eighties among women. That's when they felt the competing demands between work and [family] life. Men were much later to face those same pressures."

Women have been balancing work-family conflicts for some time and still struggle, carrying the bulk of household responsibilities, cooking, cleaning, and childcare, to name a few (Bright Horizons Family Solutions LLC, 2022). We have built networks to share advice and tips on how to do it better, but we are still not there. It is newer for men, and they don't share their struggles or ask for tips or establish networks of support. Society is more likely to accept when women ask for advice, counsel, or ideas to try a new approach.

I am a champion for men and women meeting together in mixed company to form a Work-Life Balance Employee Resource Group at the office. Employee Resource Groups, or ERGs, are voluntary, employee-led groups where participants share characteristics, gender, ethnicity, and lifestyle interests (Hastwell, 2020). The groups provide support for personal or career development and create a safe space for members to be themselves. At times, allies are also invited. Allies are people who might not share the affinity—race, gender, heritage, etc.—but have an interest in supporting it.

Later in this chapter, I examine the ways men socialize, which makes this a bit of a challenge. However, I want to catalyze new conversations and help be a part of the solution. This includes reaching into and raising issues from the bummock, disrupting the spiral of silence, and acknowledging the "me" issues before we get to "we."

Family and Having It All

Engrossed in Dorment's comment, I ran into my girlfriend Gail and spoke with her about his perspective on men being new to work-life struggles. I asked her to listen to my logic about the challenges men face, their silence about them, and the need for men to be part of the gender-equity dialogue to drive change.

She drew the line at a man support group.

"Give me a break, Kori," she said. "I just worked a full day, picked up two kids from after-school activities, helped them with homework, dealt with the dog who decided to barf on the carpet from who knows what, vacuumed the crumbs in the kitchen that probably made the dog sick, and my husband walked in from work and said, 'What's for dinner?' Men have had the advantage for years in terms of wages, managing household duties, childcare, and more. They are the definition of having it all."

"Okay, Gail, I get it. Give me a little rope here," I pleaded. "We read in mainstream media all the time about, 'Can women have it all?' And yes, you and I, as working moms, have shared our challenges over the years. I have always said it is about getting clear on the *it* and the *all* in that sentence. Do we really know what men are facing and what our sons will be facing if they decide to have families?"

"Okay, girlfriend," Gail said, partly in jest. "Just be careful, or I will have to pull your feminist-equity-advocate card if you go too far."

I am not naive to the intent of a headline that asks, 'Can Women Have It All?' I just think we need to reframe and clarify the question. By one standard, "it all" could mean financial wealth, an influential position, a great marriage, and smart, happy kids. By another standard, "all" could mean time, the freedom to come and go as you please, or work when you please so you can pursue your own interests. Perhaps we can change the narrative to a better question: "Can we feel enough today at work and at home?"

This applies to both men and women.

Some days run smoothly, and some have more bumps in the road. Rather than focus on where we fall short based on society's expectations of having or doing it all, can we say, "Today I have done the best I can do"? Ultimately, it is about being the best version of yourself at work and home—*being* and *feeling* enough—in the present moment, even when it seems the chaos of life, more specifically the clash of work priorities and goals outside of work, surrounds you.

In a 2002 *Harvard Business Review* article, "Executive Women and the Myth of Having It All," author Sylvia Ann Hewlett shared findings from a research project she did with Harris Interactive and the National Parenting Association to explore the balance of personal and professional lives of highly educated, high-earning women.

The survey focused primarily on two age groups: women aged forty-one to fifty-five and their younger peers, ages twenty-eight to forty. Overall, thirty years into the women's movement, Hewlett wrote that "the brutal demands of ambitious careers, the asymmetries of male-female relationships, and the difficulties of bearing children late in life conspire to crowd out the possibility of having children." The survey results showed that 42 percent of high-achieving women in corporate were childless, yet the vast majority of those women wanted children and a successful career.

Hewlett's data from 2002 showed the obstacles that exist for women to "have it all." More than twenty years later, as I wrote this book, a quick Google search of "work-life and having it all" revealed a long list of articles on the challenges working moms continue to face.

Workplaces remain in the fallacy of the *ideal* worker, a person who does not have to manage unpredictable, complex family dynamics; this reflects the breadwinner-homemaker model that dates back to the Industrial Revolution (Williams, 2020). In reference to fathers missing family events, the data shows there is a stigma in the workplace in general—for both men and women— associated with having a family (Bright Horizons Family Solutions LLC, 2022).

Early in my career, I took great pride in concealing my own working-mom status in the office; truth be told, my at-home spouse allowed me to do that effectively. Under the motherhood penalty and fatherhood bonus, referring to Budig's research shared earlier that women's earnings decrease when they have children but men's earnings increase, I uniquely had a foot in both proverbial shoes; I was the primary breadwinner, similar to many fathers who are rewarded the fatherhood bonus, and, as working mom who gave birth to four kids, I "qualified" for the motherhood penalty.

My husband and I chose that path. He gave up his marketing career before the birth of our second child, while I changed jobs, and we moved halfway across the county. He became the at-home, full-time parent, and I became the sole provider, a lifestyle we lived for more than two decades. We wrote about that in our 2017 book, *ZagZig Parenting: (Mis)Adventures of a Career-Driven Mom and Stay-at-Home Dad.*

The intent of the message behind "zagzig" was not about discussing the "right way," but to challenge the conventional narrative and create conversations about deeply ingrained, rigid gender stereotypes that bind us to one way, limiting authenticity in the process. I am not a man and can't speak for men, aside from what the men I have interviewed told me. I shared their stories anonymously with permission. I can, however, relate to being the breadwinner, working sixty-hour weeks, traveling for business a lot, and feeling the tug-of-war between family and work. I enjoy working, managing challenges, and practicing creative problem-solving with smart people. I also love my family and know the ups and downs of parenting. It is a blessing, and one I don't take for granted—the opportunity to collaborate with a smart, compassionate partner in order to make both career and family work.

My partner at home just happened to be a man.

I can relate to returning home after a tough day at the office and taking on homework duty as soon as I walked in the door, or going on a late-night grocery store run for the snack a child had to bring to school the next day, or starting a load of laundry at 9 p.m. because a child needed a uniform for a game.

I know that "having it all" is challenging for men *and* women. Again, I say you have to get clear on the "it" and "all." My husband rolls his eyes at "having it all." He says trade-offs always exist.

It goes back to perspectives.

I interviewed a lot of men for this book and spoke with many people in my network as I processed remarks and themes that surfaced in the analysis part of the research. During one follow-up conversation, a particular man expressed his sentiment on the idea of "having it all." Chandler told me that no woman would give me credit for the struggle of having it all because I had help at home.

"You should really write about men who are super champions, or these pro-women men, and what they do to accelerate gender equity," he said, explaining that he considered himself a pro-women man. "Your husband is one of them. He elevated you and your career, and he was brave and secure enough to be an at-home spouse."

Later, I thought about how that line itself had so many twists in it, like a fresh, new coil spring on a trampoline that has yet to be stretched and squeaks in the process of breaking it in. I appreciate my husband and our "role reversal" lifestyle that we lived for many years. But my experience is not too different from Chandler's. He had help at home too. I can only hope he describes his wife's work at home as part of elevating his career and applauds her bravery for being an at-home spouse in today's world.

Wouldn't it be lovely if we described at-home moms and dads that way? Even better, what if we celebrated and supported the commitment to manage both work and "family"—including children, parents, or other situations outside of the office—as well as we can, regardless of family structure, whether there is one working spouse, a dual-working couple, or a single-parent head of household? Imagine if we honored each other for the roles we play in our respective homes and families, not just in the workplace.

"I already wrote a book about that and included his perspective," I responded to his comment, referring to *ZagZig*.

"Yes, well, no one has really read that book," Chandler responded. "It will be much harder to tell a woman how to have and manage it all when you had a stay-at-home spouse to help you. You will not get much empathy. You might do better off writing about pro-women men and saying how you benefited from one."

As I processed that discussion, I reminded myself that feedback is a gift. In this sense, I got a different perspective that made me think about it from another angle. I value a diverse set of inputs that help me reexamine possibilities through the eyes of another person. It often creates a more complete picture, even if it makes me pause and rethink my own position.

I shared his comments with my "pro-woman man" as I processed this information, and he said, "I think he missed the point. Yes, you had help, but you also actively helped in and around the house as your second job. Take it as a perspective, a start of a new conversation. That is why you interviewed men, to understand how our brains think or don't think. So, don't overthink it."

Seeding a New Conversation for Change

Perhaps these quotes from the men I interviewed confirm men can't have it all when it comes to work-family conflict. When I asked the men about any regrets, the senior leaders typically put it in the context of work interfering with family:

- "I gave up a lot on the personal side to get where I did; most of the impact being on my family, and that was difficult. I wish I could have balanced it more." —Former CEO who worked his way from a brand manager to the top of the company

- "If I had my druthers, I probably would have taken more time off work to hang with the kids. I did a lot, but sometimes I think, you know, I could have spent more time with them." —Former senior executive who progressed from a manager to a C-suite executive at a large company

- "Looking back now, I regret that I got caught up in the mentality that work comes first. I thought that was how I provided the best for my family, as in, the better I performed, the more sales I did. The more sales I did, the more money I could spend on family trips or expenses. You know, provide more. However, that meant I told my kids, 'one more phone call,' 'one more business trip,' 'one more night in the office.'" —Senior leader of a large company and dad of now three grown children

These sentiments are a testimony that the fallacy of the ideal worker still exists and that Blake has a point—we need to look at the issues men face too. Back in 2013, well before the height of #MeToo, the *Journal of Social Issues* published a special issue called "The Flexibility Stigma." The compilation of articles focused on why employees don't take advantage of policies like flexible work schedules; in some cases, the decision is driven by fear of wage penalties, lower performance evaluations, and fewer promotions. The authors wrote that women don't want to be "mommy-tracked," and men worry about being seen as feminine, which is directly related to the "wimp penalty" (Williams et al., 2013).

In a 2019 *New York Times* article, "Men Say They Want Paid Leave but Then Don't Use All of It. What Stops Them?", reporter Claire Cain Miller wrote:

> *Just as women have for decades, men are finding it hard to balance career and family in the ways they want. When the difficulties come to a head, both men and women tend to resort to traditional roles, even if it's not what they'd planned or hoped to do: Women take a step back at work to prioritize family needs, and men do less at home to prioritize work.*

In her article, Miller referenced two studies that point out how, even today, the stickiness of traditional gender roles is hard to overcome. One suggestion, researchers say, is for workplaces to change the way they talk about fathers and include fathers in parenting groups.

Josh Levs, the expert on modern dads at work I briefly mentioned in chapter six, is raising the dialogue on fatherhood in the workplace. Levs, a two-decade CNN and NPR journalist, wrote an award-winning book in 2015 about his own journey taking legal action against Time Warner (CNN's then-parent company) for fair paternal leave so he could care for his preemie daughter and sick wife. His book, *All In: How Our Work-First Culture Fails Dad, Families, and Businesses—And How We Can Fix It Together,* is full of facts and case studies for support.

At the time of the case, biological fathers were allowed only two weeks of paid leave, while mothers and parents caring for a child who was adopted or born through surrogacy had the option of ten weeks of paid parental leave. Levs advocated for including dads like him. As a result of the case, Time Warner changed its leave policy, and fathers got six weeks of paid leave.

The double standard for men continues. In 2020, the policy discrepancy remained a challenge for men and gender equity overall. Steven van Soeren, a product designer for Disney's streaming service, got fired after returning from two weeks of paternity leave (LeBlanc, 2021). When he sued his former employer, a federal court dismissed his case and ruled the firing could not be unlawful discrimination because van Soeren had not been pregnant. The American Civil Liberties Union said some local and state laws, like in New York, for example, add protections against discrimination for caregivers regardless of gender, but existing federal law falls short. Sex roles are changing, and laws are not keeping up.

Levs credits women for speaking out about work-life balance and encourages men to speak out too, among each other and with female colleagues and women in their lives. I appreciate Blake for acknowledging that it is also time to elevate male issues on gender equity.

There is one difference, however, between men and women that might make it a little more challenging to create a two-way discussion and normalize that males and the issues men face are part of the gender conversation too. There is variation in the way men and women socialize.

Face-To-Face vs. Side-To-Side Contact

While men and women both form relationships for the same reason—shared interest, support, and companionship—there is a difference in how genders interact (Bates-Duford, 2018).

- Females tend to be relationship-oriented, depending on **face-to-face** contact; they communicate and share thoughts and feelings in face-to-face communication.
- Men tend to prefer activity-based engagements, characterized as **side-to-side** contact, valuing shared activities; the conversations are less intimate and more transactional.

Conversations can look and be valued very differently in a face-to-face vs. side-to-side interaction, especially when men and women are talking together.

More than twenty years ago, when my at-home spouse took our first child to dance class during the day, he was often the only man in the parent waiting room and the only parent away from the observation window.

"The moms are constantly chatting at the crowded watch-your-kid window, talking about life while they *ooh* and *aah* as their kids perform," he said. "This morning, I got Z in class and was feeding the baby when one of the moms started asking me a few questions. Another one came over and said it was her first time meeting an at-home dad. That was weird."

I thought it was just a conversation starter for women. Then he told me a heartbreaking story.

"Most of the moms go for ice cream after class, but we don't get included. Usually, Z is okay with that, but today she asked me why she could not go," he said. "I didn't have the heart to tell her that we did not get invited. I guess I should have tried to talk at the window."

The next week, I had a day off. I took our daughter to dance, and one of the moms and I quickly struck up a very intimate conversation about a range of topics, from kids to shopping and date nights; yes, we did get invited to ice cream to continue the conversation. While my husband had been amazed at how much I learned in a short span of time, he had no intention of asking his fellow dance parents, in this case, the moms, about date night or any other social activity when he returned.

On the other hand, my husband has maintained relationships with a bunch of men he met in elementary school through college. Each year, these friends get together for a guy's weekend, and every year, without fail, upon his return, I ask about wives and kids, jobs, moves, and life changes.

He consistently responds with, "I don't know, Kori. We just don't talk about that."

It took me a while and a lot of research to realize that he is not being a self-absorbed jerk with his friends—none of them ask about family during that sport-related, bonding weekend. But this tradition has gone on for thirty years, and these friendships are lasting. They are quick to forgive a "bonehead" move and are there for each other when someone needs help. It turns out they know the most important parts about each other's lives, but they squeeze in those comments over sports talks and a few beers.

This experience with my husband, backed by research about the ways men and women socialize, piqued my curiosity about how to engage men and women together. I decided to try a different approach.

Can we move from face-to-face or side-to-side to a hybrid version based on mutual interests? Can we meet Men-in-the-Middle and women where they are today and create a new path? After all, the world's challenges are too big to let gender-limiting beliefs get in the way of collaborating for limitless ideas and possibilities to better ourselves, our families, and our communities.

Any time I envision a "from-to" scenario and find myself moving from a current way of working to a new one, years of change management training kick into high gear. Now that we have invited men to break the silence on gender equity and speak out, and we have acknowledged that men face issues too, let's look at a framework for sustainable change. Imagine the possibility of men and women talking together about work-life balance issues as a path forward to equity for all.

Key Takeaways

- Both men and women care about work-family or work-life balance, but it impacts them differently. Women are socialized to talk about acknowledging this issue and getting tips and ideas from each other. Men are less likely to talk about it or ask for time away to support their family due to informal sanctions like the "wimp penalty."
  - This is related to other research that shows men and women interact in different ways too. Women communicate face-to-face, sharing thoughts and feelings. Men tend to be less intimate and more transactional, sharing side-to-side.
- The 2020 Modern Family Index shows dads are still more likely than moms to miss family events and dinners because of work. Yet, the stress associated with missing the events for working moms and dads has remained equal and steady since 1986, related to the fallacy of the ideal worker.
- Contrary to popular belief, men can't "have it all" either, as both men and women face balancing work-family conflict from different angles. With time demands on all professionals, men and women, maybe it is time to shift the conversation from "Can we have it all?" to "Are we the best version of ourselves at work and at home?"
- The intersection of men, family, and work-life balance is not talked about in the workplace, and it can be perceived as risky for men to raise the conversation about their struggles; women, on the other hand, are socialized to share and discuss work and family.

- Sex and stereotyped roles are slowly changing, yet some laws and policies are not keeping up. Among forty-one nations, the United States is the only country that does not mandate any paid leave for new parents (Livingston and Thomas, 2020).

Questions to Discuss or Ponder

1. How do you respond to Blake's comments at the beginning of the chapter that, when it comes to family and work-life conflict, there are some topics that men can't talk about at work?
2. Does it surprise you that men and women have the same desires and challenges with regard to work-life balance?
3. Have you looked at the policies in your own organization for work-family leave? Are they equal, or do they create opportunities to address gender equity in your organization?
4. Have you seen a shift in the gender roles for household management? Is there more balance or less? How has that changed over time?
5. What can you do to create a safe space for men to openly discuss work-life balance issues?

CHAPTER NINE

ADDRESSING THE AWKWARD

*Alex saw the barriers to the problem as avoiding and ignoring,
and he wanted to fix that. However, he also acknowledged the
uncertainty and complexity we encounter on the path to change.*

Alex is a senior leader with more than twenty years of experience in
multinational organizations, and he specializes in getting leaders
to perform better together. He manages a majority-female team.

"Post the height of the viral movements #MeToo and #TimesUp,
it is uncomfortable to generate any gender-related conversations in
the office among men, especially for those who have been in the
workplace for some time. I worry we are ignoring that demographic,
and they are walking on eggshells," Alex explained.

"Some tension is good," he continued. "Too much is detrimental,
but it could flip. They are avoiding; they are not engaging or
interacting. I think it is a problem. I don't know if, eventually, the
pendulum will swing to the middle."

Here we circle back to chapter one, where Robert described
gender equity as energy in motion in the form of a pendulum. The
swing back and forth, from one extreme to the next, is the essential
first step before the pendulum settles in harmony at the center.

In the swing is also the chaos of uncertainty, ambiguity, and
complexity. Uncertainty itself is a paradox. On the one hand, we

tend to avoid the unknown; on the other hand, taking risks in a moment of discomfort can lead to some of the most fulfilling moments of our lives. Bill Eckstrom took it a step further in his 2017 TEDxNevada Talk, "Why Comfort Will Ruin Your Life," saying, "What makes you comfortable can ruin you, and what makes you uncomfortable is the only way to grow." In 2019, Eckstrom and his co-author Sarah Wirth wrote their book, *The Coaching Effect,* about embracing discomfort as a path to change and growth.

As they flipped the narrative from manager to coach, I thought of my own coaches, especially the ones I worked extra hard for or ran a little faster for in my youth. Early in the first chapter of their book, Eckstrom and Wirth introduced the concept of discretionary effort, that willingness to go beyond the minimum. Likewise, I want our Men-in-the-Middle to move from the safety of silence through the discomfort to embrace a new framework for progress. I want them to exert their discretionary effort to gain momentum toward attaining gender equity.

Alex and I also shared a common viewpoint.

"Put me in, Coach," he said. "I wanted to participate in this project because I want more men to engage in these conversations too. The sooner that men and women can talk together about gender-related issues and get these concerns out in the open, the sooner we get rid of the awkwardness. When these conversations become the norm, that's when it becomes real, and we see true progress," explained Alex.

The desire is there, but the solutions are still puzzling.

Alex is motivated and not just to alleviate the discomfort of the gender-related social anxiety at work. The practicality of a business challenge drives him to engage in the conversation. "I feel like we are putting together the puzzle, and I am not sure we'll ever solve it, but we have to work toward it. We will not be able to fill all of the open positions we have today if we are not *comfortable* with more than half of the population," Alex said in reference to a talent pool where the United States population is 51.1 percent female and 48.9 percent male (Statista, 2022).

I got excited when the comments of the men weaved together, connecting the dots to paint a picture of a perspective or two. Even as I refined my writing and reexamined the men's stories, a theme emerged. The men found themselves caught between an emotion, perhaps in the bummock, and logic that sat on the surface. In Alex's case, there is a practical problem to solve: we have open positions to fill, and we need to look at the entire talent in the pool, including women, who are the majority in population numbers.

At the same time, for some men, engaging more than half of that talent pool can create discomfort in the office due to the uncertainty and complexity of one-on-one, male-female interactions that potentially lead them to feel like they are walking on eggshells.

Hiring people can be complicated, especially in a dynamic, changing world, but there is a process to doing it well. The uncertainty of how a person will work with a group of people or push through an uncomfortable situation is unknown, and that makes it complex.

My friend, Amy Segami, stated that the key to solving the puzzle is to differentiate complicated issues from complex ones. An engineer turned artist, Segami is an international speaker who tells crowds to stop using the concepts of complex and complicated interchangeably. It can cloud the problem-solving process. She explained:

> *The 'T' in complicated stands for 'tasks.' It is a series of step-by-step processes, like the assembly of a sandwich or even a Tesla. Each requires a series of multiple, step-by-step moves to create the finished product. The 'X' in complex, however, stands for the 'X factor' or uncertainty. 'X' in any math problem represents the unknown factor.*

Segami calls Alex's description of awkwardness the turbulence that is a source of change and innovation. "You can't have anything happen in life to improve or get better without turbulence," she said in her 2020 TEDxWilmetteWomen Talk, "Everything New Emerges from Turbulence."

Uncertainty is part of the turbulence, so let's jump in and get these concerns out in the open so that we can make progress.

The Turbulence of Emotions

To our male readers, allow me, as a friend and ally, to let you in on a little secret: emotions, including the potential for embarrassment, fear, and uncertainty, impact your decision-making. But don't worry. I promise I will not call you "dramatic" when you bring those into a meeting with you. I know it is just a natural part of who we are.

Over the years, my job has put me at the front line of communicating large-scale organizational change, from mergers and acquisitions to closing locations, as well as exiting and replacing leaders. At times, organizational leaders have labeled me "dramatic" or asked me "to leave the drama at the door" when I explained to them how their decisions could or would impact the lives of people on the manufacturing floor.

I don't think these men were heartless; they had to make a tough call. We learned in chapter five that a characteristic of the white male culture is a preference for rationality over emotion. In a masculine culture, it is easier not to address emotions or feelings. It is easier to explain the logic of a decision, right?

Well, logic and emotion are not "either/or"—they are connected.

Research from global analytics firm Gallup showed that about 70 percent of customer brand preference decisions are based on emotional factors and 30 percent on rational factors (Pendell, 2022). The influence of emotions, in the form of risk, uncertainty, and intuition, remains true even in the case of financial decisions, according to Daniel Kahneman, the first psychologist to win the Nobel Prize for economics in 2002 (Smith, 2002). Without going into the lengthy details of his work, he is credited as the father of economic behavior for demonstrating and validating that the intuitive, subconscious part of the brain works fast to make judgments and come to conclusions, while the deliberate, rational-thinking part is much slower and not at the forefront of our decisions (Groenewegen, 2022).

This might seem counterintuitive. We are taught from an early age that sound decisions come from a methodological decision process versus an emotional one (Morse, 2006); however, neurologists found that patients who experienced damage to the prefrontal cortex, where emotions are processed, struggled to make even routine decisions.

In a 2006 *Harvard Business Review* article titled "Decision and Desire," Gardiner Morse urged readers to change the narrative on the logic of decision-making, whether negotiating an acquisition, granting a loan, or trusting a partner, the brain is busy assessing the situation with its own agenda.

Now, let's look at how this emotion-logic brain processing plays out with regard to leadership and gender. In 2015, the Pew Research Center published a report called "Women in Leadership: Public Says Women Are Equally Qualified, but Barriers Persist." Pew is a think tank that conducts public opinion polls and demographic research about issues, attitudes, and trends shaping the world.

Chapter two of the report specifically addressed the questions, "What makes a good leader? Does gender matter?" When it comes to key leadership traits, including intelligence and capacity for innovation, respondents ranked men and women about equal. They did give more credit to women for their compassion and organization. About 40 percent of those who answered the survey, however, also said that a double standard existed for women seeking to advance compared to their male counterparts; about half believed men will continue to hold more top executive positions in the future.

Following the "if-then" statement in *logic*, if the data shows people believe men and women are equally qualified in terms of leadership traits, then why don't they believe men and women would hold an equal amount of leadership positions? The double standard is related to "emotional reasoning"—described as the basis for a belief influenced by emotions—that people apply to that information.

Author and speaker Anthony Metivier offered a possible explanation for why that is in his June 2022 blog on the website Magnetic Memory Method called "Logical vs Rational Thinking: What's the Difference?" Metivier wrote, "The problem is that many people reason things out [based on their own beliefs] *without* using logic. We bring in experiences, context, emotions, personal values, convictions, ethics, and other things that make us human."

Based on that logic, the half of Pew Research Center survey respondents who believed men will continue to hold more top executive positions in the future—even though they also believe men and women show equal leadership traits—are bringing other contexts into logic, including experiences and emotions like fear, anxiety caused by uncertainty, or even confusion.

Emotions influence decisions and are part of change. In 2018, Kandi Wiens and Darin Rowell published the *Harvard Business Review* article "How to Embrace Change Using Emotional Intelligence." The authors acknowledged the emotion in the room where change happens:

> *Changes at work can be emotionally intense, sparking confusion, fear, anxiety, frustration, and helplessness. Experts have even said the experience of going through change at work can mimic*

that of people who are suffering from grief over the loss of a
loved one. Because change can be so physically and emotionally
draining, it often leads to burnout and puts into motion an
insidious cycle that leads to even greater resistance to change.

The field of studying the impacts of emotions on decision-making is growing and raises questions about logic in the context of human behavior (Lerner et al., 2015). Neuroscientists found evidence of differences when men and women are under stress, which could be the result of high-risk decision-making, trying something new, or facing change. When men are under stress, they take more risks, bigger than they would ordinarily choose, while women take more time to weigh the options (Mather and Lighthall, 2012).

While my goal is not to add stress to the gender equity conversations, there could be a benefit from the healthy tensions between emotions and logic, in particular for men. Congratulations, Men-in-the-Middle, you are well-equipped to take risks in the face of stress, and this could pave the way forward in the gender equity conversation. As stressful as change is and as uncomfortable as solving the puzzle of gender equity may be, men, you are cut out for this—your brain is wired for it! Take the risk of trying the new, nerve-racking thing you've never done before and see where it leads. Start speaking out about gender equity with male and female colleagues.

You can be part of the solution. Women, as we weigh the options, we can look at men as influential partners to build the momentum to disrupt the current state of gender equity and get there faster than the data projects to date—which is years from now and, in some cases, not even in our generation. Collaborative conversations between men and women can help us gain momentum and get us there much faster. Working together, we may see the pendulum stop swinging and, finally, land right in the middle.

Let's look at what it might take to get our Men-in-the-Middle to move the gender equity conversation forward in partnership with female colleagues. Despite advances in technology, fashion, manufacturing, research, space exploration, and more, the dynamics of gender equity and the related gender-role stereotypes remain caught in a deep-seated narrative: the "dad is the breadwinner and the mom is the caretaker" paradigm. I want to change the narrative or at least add a fresh perspective to the current dialogue. Why not? The pendulum is in motion anyway.

Gender Dynamics and Assimilation Right at Home

That pendulum was swinging back and forth even in my own home when all four kids lived with us. My husband and I had created an environment of equal sides for a healthy debate. With two daughters and two sons, the dinner table was a lively place for food, fun, and facing off on various topics, especially as the kids got older and shared their own perspectives. They spent their formative years in a home where gender and sex-typed roles had been different from a number of their friends, and I had hoped that might contribute to their well-rounded thinking and perspective-taking abilities.

In 2014, our family consisted of two sons in junior high and two daughters in high school. On a rare night when we all made it to the table at the same time, the conversation took an interesting twist.

"I had a noteworthy experience today," I said. "Doug, a male leader at work, called me 'demanding' when I held a vendor accountable to contract terms. I had seen Doug negotiate contracts and instill accountability with business partners a number of times. Apparently, Doug thought when I did it, I was being too harsh and demanding and put the male vendor in a bad spot."

"Mom," my third child pitched in, "should we send a video to Doug of how demanding you are with us? Maybe we will get some sympathy." He had to add his trademark sense of humor to any situation and ate it up when his siblings laughed too. After a few more jokes and laughs, the conversation shifted.

"Mom, we don't want to be pro-women, anti-men feminists like you," my oldest child said. "What if we want to have babies and stay home with the kids when we grow up?"

Talk about emotions and logic working hand-in-hand. I had encouraged the kids to use their own voices and speak their truth, but I have to admit the question gave me pause. We raised her in a home that broke rigid gender stereotypes, but, at that age, she had been drawn to the traditional paradigm of working dad, at-home mom. That is okay with me. She will make her own choices in life. I felt intrigued, not bothered. What did concern me, however, as I looked into my boys' eyes, was if they perceived me as pro-women and not pro-men. I want my boys and the men in my life to succeed too.

I looked at my girls and calmly said, "First, you can be who you want to be. My story is not your story. You are just starting to form your own path, and that is great."

Turning to my boys, I said, "Next, I am pro-women, and I am pro-men. I am a champion for you boys too! True feminism, to me, is a belief that together we can be the rising tide that lifts all boats. We don't have to compete. We can all benefit. It is possible to make room for everyone when we change our mindset and invest in each other, and we don't let rigid gender stereotypes define who we are or the choices we make. By stereotypes, I mean what society says men or women "*should* be" based on their gender. If you want to work outside the home or be a stay-at-home dad, you can, and if your sisters want to be a professional working mom or an at-home mom, they can too."

The boys, both about eleven and thirteen years old at the time, stared back at me in a moment of silence.

"What if I want no kids or I want to be an elk, grazing in Colorado? Will you support me too, Mom?" asked our family comedian, child number three, as a way to break the silence.

As I reflect now on that moment, one thing stands out to me: the insinuation of a zero-sum game, where one wins and one loses, the mentality of being pro-women at the expense of men.

Through the eyes of my daughters and sons, and at the encouragement of my spouse, I had the desire to become more aware of multiple perspectives and influence conversations for the better from a new angle, one that shifts from gender-limiting beliefs to uniting to advance limitless possibilities. I asked myself the following questions:

- Why can't women be described as assertive and men as emotional?
- Who says that strengths, whether athletics or aesthetics, technical expertise or creative expression, problem solver or people optimizer, are gender specific?
- How can we embrace a *non* zero-sum game for a win-win?
- What will it take to get to a strength-based narrative for leadership?
- How can we engage men to speak out, innovate, and problem-solve this together?

The Emotions of Change in a VUCA World

As the world changes, we expect to see social changes in our environment. In the post-#MeToo era, has gender reached VUCA status? VUCA is an acronym first introduced by the United States Army War College following the 9/11 attacks in 2001 and later adapted for business (VUCA-World, 2023). The letters in the acronym stand for:

- **Volatile:** Change is rapid and unpredictable in its nature and extent.

- **Uncertain:** The present is unclear, and the future is uncertain.
- **Complex:** Many different, interconnected factors come into play with the potential to cause chaos and confusion.
- **Ambiguous:** There is a lack of clarity or awareness about situations.

According to the Mind Tools Content Team, an online toolkit and resource for professional development, one of the biggest challenges of managing a VUCA situation is resistance to change. It is easier and safer to stick with the tested methods than try something new. Does this sound familiar? Said another way, we are back to Harper's lurk of the "orbit of status quo" from chapter six.

Any part of the VUCA acronym—volatile, uncertain, complex, and ambiguous—can lead to an imbalance. Combined, these disruptions add intensity to a problem-solving perspective. VUCA environments can make people anxious, take a toll on the internal culture, overwhelm individuals, and even jeopardize innovation (VUCA-World, 2023). Let's look at VUCA as it relates to gender and gender equity from the perspective of the men we interviewed:

- **Volatile:** The candidate pool has changed. Today, women represent the majority of the United States population and account for the majority of undergraduate and graduate degrees (Fry, 2019). While men continue to hold the majority of leadership roles in organizations, some perceive an unpredictable aspect to one-on-one interactions with women in the workplace. Whether it is real or perceived, the discomfort exists.
- **Uncertain:** The men are uncertain about crossing the line between an innocent comment and a harassment complaint and, more broadly, what change related to gender equity means for them.

- **Complex**: The men know and outwardly agree on the value of diverse teams and the importance of including many voices for better problem-solving; however, lurking below sea level and posing a perceived threat is the perception of a zero-sum game and the strong stereotypes of the "Man Box" culture. This causes a say-do gap.
- **Ambiguous**: Many men think gender and gender equity are female issues; they are not sure what their role is in the conversation, and there is no clear path to get there.

As unnerving as it is to be going through something volatile, uncertain, complex, and ambiguous, there are benefits to the changes a VUCA environment can lead to. First, let's acknowledge that change, whether it is perceived as good or bad, can be challenging. Tanya J. Peterson wrote in the August 2022 article for the website Healthy Place "Why Is Even Good Change Sometimes So Hard?" that "positive change can feel negative because the stress wreaks havoc on our mental health."

Embracing discomfort not only opens our minds to new ideas, but perceiving a "negative" experience as a *sign of progress* is motivating, especially when the positive benefit for that change is delayed (Woolley and Fishbach, 2022).

VUCA situations demand that you avoid traditional approaches to leadership and make vision, understanding, and clarity your guiding principles. The best leadership tactics for VUCA are collaboration, participation, debate, and accepting change. They are *messier* in that they may create discomfort, like addressing conflict, getting team members to align on a common framework, or managing the emotions of change. At the same time, these leadership tactics allow the group to be flexible and take action quickly.

Sometimes change takes time, and we can only appreciate it when we look back to see how far we have come. Change is also complex due to uncertainty, unpredictability, and obstacles that get in the way when something is hard or we don't know what to do.

In her 2018 book, *That's What She Said: What Men Need to Know (and Women Need to Tell Them) About Working Together*, Joanne Lipman, journalist and former *USA Today* editor in chief, acknowledged another aspect of complexity that we have yet to touch on here: women sometimes put up an obstacle to open dialogue and progress.

What is the obstacle?

Among data-driven research, personal experiences, stories, and twelve tips and takeaways to move the gender conversation forward, Lipman, in a moment of perspective-taking regarding the power of gender stereotypes, points to times when men advocate for women, and women are often surprised and even annoyed with their actions.

One of the men I interviewed shared his observation: "Look, you women don't help each other out either. I have seen more women cut each other down behind other women's backs than I have seen men do to each other." While I focus on the male-female dynamic, it is important to at least acknowledge that complexity as another place to explore for further research. In the Man Box Culture, discussed in chapter seven, a competitive, zero-sum game can impact behaviors of men and women who are looking to progress in the company. Embracing the change from a win-lose to a *rising tide lifts all boats* mentality, women and men can encourage one another.

For a visual perspective on that future state and an example of change amidst office politics, onboarding, and acceptance, I follow the lead of the 2020 book *Good Guys* by Smith and Johnson and suggest people watch *Purl*, a nine-minute animated film directed by Kristen Lester and released by Pixar in 2019. It follows lead character Purl's journey from day one on the job as her authentic self, through the process of her adaptation to the company's "masculine" culture, her temptation to exclude someone new like her, and then her path back to authenticity. The desire for assimilation and belonging can lead us to take on behaviors that seem counter to what is natural.

Leading Over "Shoulding" with a Change Mindset

Change can be uncomfortable. Change can lead to growth. Change that lasts has the support of a process that considers both the technical and the people sides of change. For example, it's one thing to build a technology program that enables increased data accuracy for better decision-making. It is another to get people on board to use it, especially if it requires a different way to enter the data. Anything that requires people to do something differently would benefit from change management.

Nicole Braley, a *Forbes* Communication Council member, wrote in a November 2021 *Forbes* article that change management is one of the most essential leadership skills. Vanessa Boris of Harvard Business Publishing Corporate Learning said in 2020 that leaders at all levels in the organization are involved in change management, from senior leaders working toward serving markets better to frontline supervisors helping to improve how teams work.

Despite the benefits, change can be difficult for all, especially men, according to Jamie Logie of The Good Men Project®, an online site for conversations about what masculinity looks like today. Logie wrote in his 2015 post "Why Change Can Be Difficult for Men":

> *Change in life is inevitable, but that doesn't make it any easier to face. I think when we acknowledge, instead of ignoring it, we become better equipped to handle it each and every time it comes.*

The path forward to gender equity includes men. This holds true even if, according to a 2019 *Time* magazine poll, men and women agreed gender inequality exists in the United States, yet a quarter of the men surveyed said the country does not need to take action steps to fight gender inequality (Barone, 2019). It can be hard to build a movement to address a problem when several stakeholders don't believe there is a problem.

It would be most effective if we could clearly state the problem as well as our shared vision for the future and then focus solely on moving in a linear fashion, from awareness to reinforcement, at both an individual level and a cultural level. We know, however, that larger challenges exist below the surface in the bummock. I have already addressed a few at length: silence amid the uncertainty, ambiguity related to role clarity in gender-related conversations, sex-role stereotypes, psychological safety, fear, vulnerability, and more.

A change mindset requires a tilt toward being open to a new approach through asking, listening, and letting your curiosity lead. Michael Welp, of White Men as Full Diversity Partners (WMFDP), explains it as a shift from advocacy, defending your position or territory, to inquiry, being open to listen, learn, and shift (TEDxBend, 2017). The idea here is to leave the judgmental side we all have in us at home in time-out. That allows us to be curious, inquisitive, and open to change.

I also like the idea expressed in Chris Thurman's 2021 book, *Stop Shoulding All Over Yourself: Making the Journey from Condemnation to Compassion*. I would like to extend that to say, "Stop letting sex stereotypes tell you who you should be, and stop relying on stereotypes and bias to tell others who they should be."

I say this because I was once caught "shoulding" in public.

Over lunch, a former colleague, who happens to be male, heard me go on a tirade about what a person in my life should have been doing, and his words have stuck with me ever since.

"Kori," he said, "in the past five minutes, I have heard you use the word "should" at least five times to describe what someone else should be doing because you didn't like it. Tell me this. What should *you* be doing differently to change the situation?" asked my wise friend, who continues to reach out and check in with me on my well-being and my "shoulds".

Dear reader, I need to come clean. I am not above judgment. I have done my fair share of dissing certain male traits, even in my own husband, who is a super good guy. Everyone makes mistakes, everyone has biases, and all of us resist change at some point in our lives. It is part of being human.

Creighton University Professor Erika L. Dakin Kirby is an expert in workplace communication, specifically in the area of gender structure and work-life balance. We spoke about this project over coffee, and she put it all in perspective for me: "People are going to fuck up—say or emphasize the wrong thing. In some ways, speaking things aloud is how we learn, so, hopefully, we can grant grace when someone who seems well-intentioned through all other communication cues has a misstep."

I'm learning, and I continue to do so. I know I am not alone. I hope more will join in, leading with curiosity, a willingness to ask questions, and an open mind to listen. I am aware of the biases, both conscious and subconscious, and I have a desire to change those through knowledge, research, and practice. As Professor Kirby said, I may mess up, but my intent is on the right track. It's taken me my entire life thus far to figure out how to disregard traditional sex-role expectations and not be affected by judgment for going against the status quo. I'm finally in a place where I feel I can share what I've learned without telling others what they should or shouldn't do.

My "shoulds" are now in order, for the most part.

Avoiding the shoulds, relying on my own experience, and acknowledging the different perspectives among men and women compelled me to suspend accusations or assumptions and lead with curiosity. My main goal now is to create a new path for open conversations for the current generation and for my own sons and daughters.

Post the height of the #MeToo viral movement, I reached out to ask men about their views on gender to listen and learn. I never told them what their perspective should be or what they should say to me to make this book happen. I let them be themselves, and I turned that into a book. And my call to action is also not a "should". It's not that we *should all do this,* and we *should all want this to happen as a result.*

I think we all know that there's an imbalance; people don't know what to do about it, and perhaps some guidance would help us. You do you and do what you think we need to do to make progress, but, in case you're stuck, here are some insights from a group we don't typically hear from and tips to move forward and build momentum.

Now that we're all in agreement that things need to change, I want to share a change model that's helped me out many times in life.

ADKAR®: A Model and Path for Change

A common problem is that people don't always know where to begin and how to maintain change. Prosci®, a recognized leader in change, defines change management as the application of a structured process and set of tools for leading the people side of change to achieve the desired outcome. It focuses on how to help people engage, adopt, and use change in their day-to-day work.

Prosci® is known for its ADKAR® change management model, which is an acronym that encompasses the following steps of the process:

- **Awareness** of the need for change
- **Desire** to participate and support the change
- **Knowledge** on how to change
- **Ability** to implement required skills and behaviors
- **Reinforcement** to sustain the change

I studied and even earned a certification in this Prosci® ADKAR® process; therefore, it has informed and provided a contextual model for the way I structured and wrote this book. I reached out to Prosci, Inc. for permission to refer to the model. I do need to note, per my agreement, however, that Prosci, Inc. is not affiliated with and does not endorse the content of this publication. I refer to it here because I am a fan of the framework it provides to explain change. At this point, I invite you, the reader, into the process to see how we can apply it together to solve the gender equity puzzle today. After all, we need to undergo a change to move forward, forging a new path and diffusing the ideas and actions to attain gender equity in the workplace and beyond.

When we look at gender equity as not just a women's issue but a leadership issue, we can learn from new, unexpected sources of knowledge—the men—to help us navigate and leverage insights and get in alignment for a path forward.

In the following diagram, Figure 10, I added the element of conversation to the model based on a mindset of being curious, cultivating the ability to proactively inquire, and applying listening techniques. That is how I found our Men-in-the-Middle.

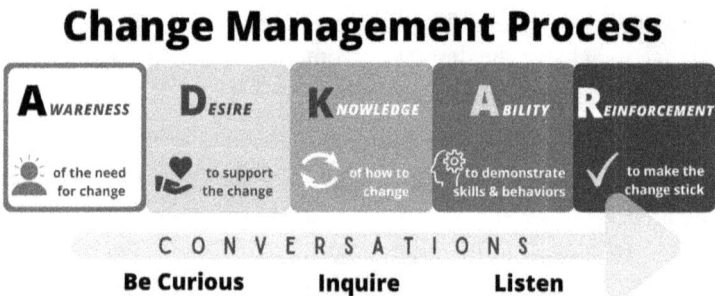

Change Management Process

AWARENESS	**D**ESIRE	**K**NOWLEDGE	**A**BILITY	**R**EINFORCEMENT
of the need for change	to support the change	of how to change	to demonstrate skills & behaviors	to make the change stick

C O N V E R S A T I O N S

Be Curious   **Inquire**   **Listen**

The author created this graphic to visually represent the tenets of the PROSCI®, ADKAR®, and AWARENESS DESIRE KNOWLEDGE ABILITY REINFORCEMENT® registered trademark of Prosci, Inc. The concepts are used with permission. Prosci, Inc. is not affiliated with and does not endorse the content of this publication.

Figure 10: A Visual Representation of the Prosci® ADKAR® Tenets

Let's study and apply the AWARENESS DESIRE KNOWLEDGE ABILITY REINFORCEMENT® model to gender equity. The *awareness* piece in this book is about the role men have in moving this business case for gender equity forward to action. Men, who today hold the majority of power positions and influence in corporate America, have the opportunity to be change disruptors if they speak out. You, Men-in-the-Middle, are a key part, the missing ingredient to create a sense of urgency around gender equity as a business issue to ignite growth.

The *desire* is trickier and requires a shift in thinking from a zero-sum game to a vision of abundance. Leading with a lens of curiosity allows us to first acknowledge, see, and hear what is below the surface, in the bummock, that keeps men silent. For some, it is a fear of the unknown, of being isolated, of saying the wrong thing. We need to acknowledge that before we invite men into the conversation.

It is not an either-or but a yes-and.

Yes, gender inequality exists in the workplace. Yes, some men have harassed and even oppressed women in the workplace. Yes, the majority, the Men-in-the-Middle, the ones who can influence gender equity, have remained silent in fear of perceived repercussions, ranging from false accusations to criticism from other men and the risk of a loss of belonging that is key to inclusion.

Despite all of this, we do have 1) a strong, evidence-based business case for change; 2) the opportunity to shift mindsets to see that discussing gender issues can benefit men and women; and 3) the power to forge a new path, working together, to make gender equity attainable for all.

Do we all, men and women, have a desire for perspective-taking that will improve our chances of working together to create a better tomorrow? I am hopeful this is a yes!

In terms of *knowledge*, the know-how—the third step in the ADKAR® model—I have referenced several resources I respect and have learned from throughout this book. Here are a few examples:

- Catalyst, the website for the global nonprofit that offers a number of well-researched articles and tools to spark conversations about gender equity and invites men to participate in Men Advocating Real Change (MARC) in the workplace.
- *Good Guys* authors Smith and Johnson champion and guide men toward mentorships and allyships, backed by research, interviews, and examples.
- Proudman and Welp from WMFDP have done extensive diversity training targeted toward the majority male. The website also links to thought-leadership articles and other tools.

Given the work in this field and the resources that exist, I am opting not to reinvent the wheel on how to do this or that but to take a slightly different angle to raise the issues out of the bummock. I continue to use the words of the men I interviewed to promote new perspectives in hopes of provoking more dialogue among men and women in the workplace.

In the next chapter, we will focus on *ability*, the fourth step in the ADKAR® model, specifically one core, relevant ability regarding communication and conversations. Afterwards, we will round out the book with ADKAR®'s fifth step of *reinforcement*, where I share examples, both obvious and subtle, using the words of the Men-in-the-Middle I interviewed about what they are doing right. The last chapter will end our journey together by reinforcing the good things men don't talk about as a springboard for more conversations.

Now, let's build our ability.

Key Takeaways

- The fear of uncertainty, ambiguity, isolation, and a list of other obstacles impact decision-making for men and women and our ability to adapt to change. Acknowledging the emotional part helps normalize our concerns and removes the awkwardness.

- VUCA describes dealing with volatile, uncertain, complex, and ambiguous conditions. When we look below the surface, gender equity meets the VUCA criteria.

- The best leadership tactics for VUCA are collaboration, participation, and debate, as well as accepting change.

- Change management is a process that acknowledges the people side of change, and presents a potential formula to engage men in gender equity conversation, shifting from a position of silence to speaking out in the form of advocacy.

- ADKAR® is a recognized change management model that stands for *awareness, desire, knowledge, ability,* and *reinforcement.* It can be a road map to progress, both inside organizations and in life.

Questions to Discuss or Ponder

1. In your own words and experiences, how would you apply VUCA to gender equity conversations?

2. When have you been involved in a change management experience at your workplace? Can you share a time when people focused on the process of change but not the people side of change?

3. Based on the previous chapters, do you have an awareness of the challenges we face engaging men in gender equity

solutions? How would you explain it to others in your own words?

4. The fear of uncertainty and ambiguity can hold people back from jumping into a conversation. What do you need to engage members of the opposite sex in a conversation about gender equity? What would you say to other men to get them to discuss gender equity issues?

5. List the top three takeaways you have learned from reading this book so far. What do you need to take the next step? Or do you have your own framework or idea to move the conversation forward? What could you do in the next 30/60/90 days?

CHAPTER TEN

ABILITY IN MOTION

Kirk and Rob described having gender-equity conversations with women as an awkward dance. They both hope that we learn to navigate that discussion and ditch the discomfort.

Kirk has been around for a while. He is a senior director with experience at a few large companies in the banking and consulting industries. Before that, he was an entrepreneur. Rod, on the other hand, spent his entire career in the consumer industry, progressing higher and higher. In my respective interviews with them, both referenced dance as a metaphor for conversations between men and women and the potential to be as smooth as two professional ballroom dancers despite the present state of clumsiness.

Kirk: "It's awkward right now. We speak with women every day, but we are not asking them to dance in the gender equity conversation. Perhaps it is because we have two left feet or our minds have gone blank. We are not sure what to say or how far to go in the conversation."

Rod: "It's an awkward deal on both sides, and people don't know how to dance around that yet—like a junior high school dance. When conversations become a bit more normal, that is when it becomes real."

219

Rod worked for and with many women throughout his career and did not ascribe to the awkward feeling himself but did concede he heard far more stories of discomfort post the #MeToo movement than he had before.

"There is a heightened sense of awareness that, for the most part, is good," he explained. "At some point, it will have to come back to more of a happy medium for men to feel comfortable that they don't have to be dancing on eggshells around women. The key for me is to use your common sense and show respect for everybody."

Rod may be right—most people do know the basics of respect. But walking on eggshells doesn't allow people to put that knowledge into play and test their abilities in real life, where the reaction is unpredictable or uncertain.

Ability: From Knowledge to Skill in Practice

The fourth step in the ADKAR® model, *ability,* is the propensity to perform based on the knowledge you have gained. This is true of any new skill, from playing a sport to delivering a presentation to your boss. It is one thing to watch a basketball game and study the moves of a point guard; it's another to be in the game on the court with the defense in your face trying to get the ball away from you with a shot clock ticking down and the fans yelling for or against your team. If sports are not your thing, think about the cooking shows that are popular on television. Watching a chef make a gourmet spread and seeing the plated meal at the end of the show looks incredibly appealing. However, even after reading the recipe, watching a YouTube video, and rewinding it a few times, your version of that gourmet dish may look like a Sunday night leftover casserole.

Fostering an ability requires practice, time, coaching, access to tools, and feedback. My friend, Dr. Deanne De Vries, embodies a willingness to try a new ability, practice it, and embrace humility. An advocate for the continent of Africa and international best-selling author of the 2022 book *Africa: Open for Business,* De Vries shared a story about visiting an African country.

"I knew this country spoke Portuguese. I speak a number of languages, including Swahili, but I had not mastered Portuguese," De Vries told me regarding her trip. "I believe in being on the ground and experiencing the culture firsthand, so when I approached the two immigration officers, I gave it my best shot to greet them in Portuguese," she continued. "Speaking in Swahili, one worker turned to the other and said, 'Her Portuguese sucks.'" De Vries laughed. "Then in Swahili, I said, 'That's a relief; let's talk in Swahili.' After their initial shock, we all laughed, and I made two new friends who helped me navigate the immigration process with ease."

De Vries, known for her use and promotion of authentic African sayings and artifacts to share her wisdom, offered this Swahili proverb from eastern Africa: "You cannot know the extent of waters you have not been to."

When I told her about this project and my passion to build momentum for gender equity conversations, advocate for change, and create a new narrative, she shared another one: "A sugarcane is sweetest at the joint." She explained that sugarcane is a very hands-on, labor-intensive plant to grow and harvest, and the joint, which has a high-level concentration of sugar, is the toughest, hardest, and sweetest part. This cultural wisdom from Africa is uttered to remind people that good things may appear difficult to achieve, but, in the end, it is worth it.

Take a minute to reflect on a time when something was really hard, but once you mastered it, you reaped the benefits of that work. It could even involve a *conflict,* in the broadest definition of the term, spanning beyond a clash between opposing groups or individuals to include:

- a disagreement about something important
- opposition between two simultaneous but incompatible feelings (Vocabulary.com, 2023)
- a mental struggle arising from opposing demands (Dictionary.com, 2023)

The last two are often referred to as internal conflicts, and we heard examples of these from our Men-in-the-Middle. The men said they believed in the value of a diverse workforce, and yet they were conflicted about what to say or do because they were uncertain how gender equity would impact them. The men had a lot to say about gender equity in one-on-one anonymous conversations, but other concerns rendered them silent in the office.

In their silence, the issues and the conflicts, whether internal or with people of the opposite gender, did not go away.

For some people, conflict is like the stalk of the sugar cane at the joint; it is too hard or uncomfortable to work through and takes up too much time in a work environment that values efficiency and effectiveness. For others in the company, facing conflict is seen as beneficial, leading to early problem identification, better problem-solving, healthy relationships, improved productivity, and early growth (Boyle, 2017).

Conflict, in this sense, is like a dance where each partner takes turns stepping forward and backward, navigating nonverbal cues, and pivoting in motion, sometimes to the same melody (a common goal) and other times dancing to music only they can hear (implicit bias and other subconscious thoughts). Whether we are living in Kirk's junior high dance world or Rod's comparison to dancing on eggshells, challenges involving conflict almost always start with discomfort before you master the tango or foxtrot.

The benefits come with the *ability* to try something new and work through the discomfort of the conflict for a better way. Do our Men-in-the-Middle and their female co-workers have the ability to speak out amidst the discomfort of gender-equity-related issues?

Translating Knowledge to Ability

At about the midpoint in my career, I worked on a project that took a three-year cycle from concept to payout. I had taken a risk on a lateral position and a physical move to a new location. The job required learning a new skill set and working with partners across the enterprise—talk about change management! About one year into the role, I could no longer claim "new" status, as in the time when your colleagues give you a grace period and help you out; that was over.

During year two, I hit a snag with a dysfunctional team that not only resisted collaboration but also blocked progress when the team members assumed I intentionally encroached on their territory for my personal gain. When I sought advice from my boss, the very person who recruited me and sold me on this opportunity, she met my plea for help with a "good luck," saying that team would most likely never cooperate with me. The team had a reputation for not cooperating with any *outsiders*.

About nine months later, my boss offered me a different job in the department so that I would not have to work with that team. I told her I appreciated the offer and turned it down. I had been working the sugarcane joint, and I saw some progress. When I had been up against a rock and a hard place, I found a person I could trust. We worked well on a previous project, and even more importantly, it appeared to me that she worked well with my nemesis team. I asked her to lunch.

"Samantha, thanks for meeting with me. I hope you can give me some counsel. I have seen that you work really well with Dominic's team, and I need advice," I explained, unsure how she would react.

"Oh, they are special, all right," she responded with a smile and a laugh, much to my relief. "Can you show me how you present information to them and what you are asking them to do?"

I came prepared and, over the next twenty minutes, walked her through my presentation deck and the ask of the team. She listened and took mental notes. When I paused for a breath, she had a light bulb moment.

"I see," she said. "We have a communication issue. You are not speaking their language or even presenting information in the way they are used to seeing it."

Over the following twenty minutes, between bites from lunch and slurps of water, she asked me questions, probed, and then took two of the slides and walked me through how the team would actually present the data. Her take included a complete shift in mindset for me. After lunch, she sent me follow-up items to continue my learning.

I gained confidence that my logic had been on track and my business case had been solid. I had just been using different business terminology and was missing data that the marketing team relied on for decision-making. I had not been aware that the data even existed!

Samantha agreed to meet with me to practice my new business language, and I developed other relationships with finance and the market research team to help hone my ability to speak the craft and deliver the right slice of data. The time came, and the apparent nemesis team listened to me and said, "Okay. This makes sense."

They agreed to my case.

It might not sound like a resounding endorsement, especially for all of the effort I put into it, but it was the encouragement I needed to forge ahead. This small victory led to a series of events that got the project off the ground. Three years after the concept, the project delivered sales growth, increased brand reputation, and opened doors for other customer relationship-building opportunities.

Working on company-wide enterprise projects created a treasure trove of opportunities to speak a different "language," new to me but not to my colleagues.

Another time, I worked with an IT professional who constantly said "no," but then he came back to me twenty-four hours later with a "yes" solution. Out of frustration and a desire to change the pattern, I reached out to another peer coach, who became an IT mentor for me.

"Kori, Brad has been a programmer, and a good one, that has transitioned to an analyst role," she explained. "Analysts translate technology solutions to people like you, business people who are not IT experts. The strength of a programmer is to be behind the curtain and not talk to anyone. He will say 'no' to most of your requests, but give him time to process, and he will deliver the solution."

She was right! I worked the sugar cane joint again. In both cases, in the face of conflict situations, I did the work to figure out what I needed to know and, most importantly, which ability I needed to put in practice to get better results.

Whether it is an external conflict with other team members or an internal struggle related to emotions like uncertainty, competing demands, or proposed organizational changes, working through the discomfort of potential conflict is an ability that will lead to open communication and an opportunity to address the changes we want to see.

Think about this mantra: *from-through-to*: from discomfort, through communication, to a better, more productive way.

If the discomfort of facing conflict, either interpersonal or among peers, still holds you back from working through challenging issues, then let's look at another motivator to build your ability to address obstacles for positive change—the cost.

Avoiding Conflict is Costly

Conflicts at work and the associated discomfort related to projects that require meaningful yet challenging conversations to resolve competing priorities are inevitable. I shared two examples of how I worked through those challenges. In order to change the trajectory of a project, gain role clarity within a team, and collaborate with peers from another department, I had to develop and hone my ability to perspective-take, initiate a conversation, and work through it.

Equally, however, I could have shared stories where I spent inefficient, unproductive work time kibitzing about a colleague who threw me under the bus, took credit for my idea, spoke over me in a meeting, or mansplained a concept. Can you relate?

The Center for Creative Leadership, a center of excellence on leadership and executive education, said conflict incompetence by leaders costs money in terms of lost productivity time as well as other indirect costs including absenteeism, broken trust, quality of working relationships, and more (Leading Effectively Staff, 2021).

It often boils down to a willingness to have a conversation. The organization Crucial Learning calls these "crucial conversations," based on the book *Crucial Conversations: Tools for Talking When Stakes Are High* (Grenny et al., 2021). A crucial conversation is defined as a discussion between two or more people that meets the following criteria:

- the stakes are high
- opinions differ
- emotions run strong
- the outcomes significantly impacts the lives of participants
- there is a risk of negative consequences

Crucial Learning offers training courses to build this conversation *ability* in leaders. The company also attempted to quantify the costs when people avoid uncomfortable and potential conflict-causing situations. Under the former name of VitalSmarts, Crucial Learning published a 2010 research summary called "The Cost of Conflict Avoidance." The survey results showed that up to 95 percent of a company's workforce struggled to speak up to their colleagues about their concerns, and employees wasted an average of $1,500 and an eight-hour workday for every crucial conversation they avoided.

Joseph Grenny, one of the authors of the *Crucial Conversations* book, wrote a blog on the Crucial Learning website titled "Avoiding Conflict is Killing Your Bottom Line." He made another reference to the survey results that showed "8 percent of employees estimate their inability to deal with conflict costs their company more than $10,000, and 20 percent say the drawn-out silent conflict can remain a problem for more than six months."

The cost of conflict adds up. CPP, Inc., a global organizational development company and the exclusive publisher of the Myers-Briggs® assessment, reported that workplace conflicts cost U.S. companies $359 billion a year. In 2008, the company conducted an extensive study on workplace conflict. I pulled these highlights from the data-heavy report:

- 85 percent of people at all levels experienced conflict at some point in their work life; 29 percent of respondents indicated that conflict in the job is almost constant.
- One in twenty respondents estimate that over the course of a drawn-out silent conflict, they waste time ruminating about the problem for more than six months.
- Nearly 50 percent of all participants attribute personality clashes and warring egos as a primary cause of workplace conflict.
- On average, employees spend 2.1 hours every week—approximately one day a month—dealing with conflict in some way (e.g., being involved in a disagreement, managing a conflict between coworkers, etc.).

If you are a research skeptic or a methodology guru, cut that number in half, thirds, or even quarters. It is still a lot of time and money lost.

Let's look at this through the lens of gender equity, when conflict, in the form of silence, avoidance, or lawsuits, is costly. Could we be more efficient if both men and women actively engaged in conversations to learn, grow, and improve the ability to manage conflicts and raise the crucial conversations related to gender equity in the workplace? This includes both internally motivated discomfort—unsure what to do or how to handle a situation—and conversations between two or more people.

The authors of *Crucial Conversations* said the remedy for conflict is transparency in the form of open, honest communication. That means having talks about what is not working and why. It is not fun in the short term, but the outcome gets the team to a better place (Grenny et al., 2021). As we have seen above, that could translate to bottom-line cost savings.

My husband swears I love conflict and says a healthy debate is as much fun for me as a kid playing Candyland. He, on the other hand, would rather have a double root canal than embrace conflict. What I know about the benefits of working through conflict gives me joy.

As *Forbes* contributor Ann Latham wrote in her 2015 article, "Don't Deal with Conflict, Eliminate It with a Culture of Clarity," 95 percent of conflict is caused by a lack of clarity. I love the outcomes of conversations that involve conflict if they lead to clarity in the context of job roles, objectives, project deliverables, perspective, and more. That is my "why." For that reason, I am willing to face the discomfort of conflict-related conversation and continue to hone my ability—it adds to more clarity.

Clarity is one of the benefits of dealing with conflict. The Strategy and Design consulting firm ThoughtForm shared a blog post on its website titled "Four Business Benefits of Clear Communication." These benefits are as follows:

- Removes ambiguity: A clear, strong foundation for progress is void of jargon and explains terms and concepts that are not intuitive.
- Increases actionability: Clarity removes barriers to action and creates a path forward.
- Avoids bunny trails: Clear communication keeps the audience on track and out of rabbit holes that detract from the purpose.
- Demonstrates accountability and confidence: Clarity removes the fluff and creates a clear, persuasive argument to show the value in an idea.

With all of these benefits, let's build our ability to handle the discomfort of conflicting ideas, perspectives, or feelings. Let's put our ability to manage conflict in a new, positive light.

Managing conflict and ambiguity are two of the thirty-eight global competencies in the Korn Ferry Leadership Architect™ Global Competency Framework. Korn Ferry, a global consulting firm advising clients on all aspects of human talent, is known for its work in competencies, defined as measurable skills and behaviors that lead people to success at work. Korn Ferry published a book called *FYI: For Your Improvement - Competencies Development Guide* that includes a write-up on each skill and corresponding assignments to help build a leader's ability (Lombardo, 2014). Here are some example assignments from the book:

1. **Manage Conflict**: Assemble a group of diverse people to address a difficult task and anticipate conflict with an intent to work through the challenges rather than avoid them.
2. **Manage Ambiguity**: Manage a group through a tough crisis with no easy answers. The tension may escalate, giving you a chance to practice keeping your emotions in check.

Leading and promoting an environment of openness and transparency around gender equity among both men and women could be the very answer to developing and practicing both skills. Are you willing to take on that assignment in your place of work? Do you desire to have the ability to manage conflict and ambiguity well? It's uncomfortable to try something new (remember FFTs, Brené Brown's "F***ing First Times," from chapter three?).

It may feel like taking a giant leap without knowing what's on the other side (ambiguity). But if and when conflict arises, you're going to have the opportunity to hone your skills in that kind of environment. This will help develop your leadership abilities.

In previous chapters, we figured out the why. In fact, we covered two "whys" of why men's silence was happening and why we need men to speak out. Next, let's look at an example of a man who turned his knowledge about conversations, conflict, and facing discomfort into a new ability.

Practicing Ability in the Masculine Culture

For more than a year, I traveled to mining locations in the United States and Canada, delivering people-management skills training to supervisors. The content ranged from planning and prioritizing team goals to communication, conflict management, and implicit bias. The company had an 85 percent male workforce, which was even higher in the mines and production areas for which I ran the training. One of the mines I traveled to had, within the past year, added female locker rooms and *covergalls* (coveralls to meet women's body shapes) protective gear.

Talk about breaking the glass ceiling a mile below the earth's surface!

Wyatt was one of nearly one hundred frontline supervisors I trained who made a leap, maybe not in the area of gender equity but toward a mindset shift nonetheless that showed me the power of turning knowledge into ability. He walked into the first training session with a handlebar mustache and skin that had weathered over the years. Like a good pair of leather boots, he was not worn down but worn in. On the first day of training he sat in the back row and, with no pen in hand, appeared to have no intention to take any notes, much less participate in activities.

He was not the only one who looked at me skeptically. Most of the men present looked at each other in a way that implied they were wondering why they had to sit in this room with a woman from the corporate office for a total of six days over the course of three months, talking about communication and people-management skills. I sensed it and pushed through the discomfort.

Wyatt introduced himself as one of the most experienced supervisors, having nearly forty years in the mine. When he was not working at the mine, he and his sons ran a cattle ranch. Outwardly, he embodied rugged male individualism. When I asked him what had changed over the forty years in management, true to form, he said, "We used to be able to manage *jobs*, and now we have to manage *people*."

Internally, I chuckled as many of his colleagues agreed with the sentiment that, in the past, a manager could just say, "Shut up and do what you are told." Now, however, they had to accommodate people's needs—complaints, injuries, basic tools training, and more. I had respect for Wyatt and his years of service, but I thought it unlikely that he would be open to talking about his communication techniques and the increased effectiveness of influence over the command-and-control leadership style.

Over the course of the training, with time to reflect and practice in between each session, I listened, asked questions, reflected on what I heard, and actively engaged with the group. I even changed my own behavior. One of the men called me out because I apologized for the discomfort they experienced at trying something new. He told me that, as the teacher, I had no reason to apologize. He said that was my job.

During the communication-behavior assessment tool debrief, I arranged the groups in a four-square formation based on the results of the assessment they completed prior to the training. Each corner of the room represented a different communication preference style, and the men assembled in the part of the room that corresponded with their own preference. I explained the inclinations for each group, and as they looked across the room at a colleague in the opposite quadrant, some experienced an "aha" moment. They had a framework to help explain the differences in problem-solving practices and communication that at times led to conflict.

When I informed the men that they could apply this newfound knowledge and ability to enhance communication in their personal lives too, I was not surprised when Wyatt, who had a preference for facts and logic over feelings, said he would not share this information with his spouse.

At around session five, something switched for Wyatt.

He shared that he had been practicing the communication-preference-style tips both at home and at work. I resisted every urge to jump up and down in total hysterics of a high-energy celebration, as his style preference would have found that annoying. I calmly encouraged him to tell us more. He told us that he shared his profile, insights, and training materials with his adult kids and spouse, and they had a good conversation. He had such good luck there that he tried it with one of his employees whom he had trouble connecting with on a day-to-day basis. It worked!

The capstone of the training included supervisor-trainees presenting in groups to senior leaders, sharing what they had learned. During Wyatt's portion, he shared these remarks: "Initially, I did not know what to expect from the training and did not really think I needed it. I learned a lot about myself and how my behavior and style impact others. It felt awkward at first, but I shared my profile with my work team and even asked for input. I practiced it here in a safe space, then with my family, and then at work. I saw the difference."

My handlebar-mustache-rough-exterior-weathered-supervisor trainee took a chance and saw a result. He even asked if he could give me a hug as I handed out graduation certificates.

RUN to a New Dance

Ability is all about practice. In her 2017 book, *We Can't Talk about That at Work! How to Talk about Race, Religion, Politics, and Other Polarizing Topics*, Mary-Frances Winters wrote that creating shared meaning and establishing common ground is a key step in her Model for Bold, Inclusive Conversations. While her primary focus is on race, Winters broadened the context to include any polarizing topics. Her premise for "talking about the issue at work" is that people are already discussing, contemplating, and debating the topic more than you think they are, especially with the advancement of social media, which did not exist decades ago.

The Winters Group asked attendees during virtual learning sessions, "What is the impact when your manager and your company are silent about what is going on in the external world?" The most common response was, "We don't think they care."

People interpreted the silence as not caring.

Men-in-the-Middle, who may be silent—not speaking up or out about gender equity in the workplace—said it was about fear and vulnerability, triggered by the uncertainty of how a comment or action may be interpreted or the ambiguity about their role in gender-equity conversations. What if their female colleagues, spouses, and friends interpreted that silence as they just don't care?

The men I spoke with did care. They just did not have the ability to speak out confidently.

Near the end of her book, Winters shares a number of gender-related triggering comments called micro-inequities, or words and phrases that may be considered offensive, and small offhanded comments that build up over time to erode trust. For each statement, she also provided data or a counterpoint that showed a different perspective. Some of the examples Winters included are reflected in the following table:

Triggers or Micro-Inequity Phrase	Data or Counterpoint
Women are too emotional to be good leaders.	Contemporary research suggests successful leaders have a blend of emotional intelligence and competitive spirit.
Are you planning on having a family?	This is an illegal question to ask in the United States, but leaders still ask.
Women are not as committed to their careers.	A 2013 Gallup poll on the state of the workplace, an annual survey input and analysis of global employees, showed that women were more engaged than men.
Work-life balance is a women's issue.	It is a human issue, as men and women both balance work and personal responsibilities.

It's time to leave behind the awkwardness of eggshells and junior high dance floors and take on a new dance called "RUN." The acronym RUN highlights the *ability* that you have gained through knowledge and practice to pave a new path forward for gender equity, one that both engages and benefits men and women. Here is what that looks like:

- **The R is for Reframe**: Pivot the mindset from gender equity as a women's issue to a strategic leadership issue that benefits men, women, and the business.
- **The U is for Understand:** Engage in conversations about gender-related issues with men and women in the office, practicing perspective-taking and finding common ground.
- **The N is for Negotiate:** Agree to common goals, mediate areas of uncertainty, define roles, and embrace collaboration or change. How can we work differently for the benefit of all?

Through conversations and supportive, collaborative relationships, shifting from conflict to curiosity, men and women can identify or build common interests and help each other—inviting men to be allies for women and even women to mentor men. If you feel you are already doing this, I encourage your group to go to the bummock:

1. Women, ask men about the impacts of the Man Box, masculine culture on the work-family balance. What does success look like for the men in your network?
2. Men, ask women about the impacts of working in a masculine culture. What does it look like from a female perspective?

Journalist, speaker, and author Malcolm Gladwell introduced a concept called "the tipping point" in his 2013 book *The Tipping Point: How Little Things Can Make a Big Difference*. It is when a fundamental change takes place, which he also referred to as the moment of critical mass, the threshold, or the boiling point. The author went on to share that sociology suggests that 20 percent of a group tends to influence 80 percent of the outcome—in other words, 20 percent of employees carry out 80 percent of the work (Gladwell, 2013).

Gladwell wrote, "There are exceptional people out there who are capable of starting epidemics. All you have to do is find them." That is the purpose of my book. Men-in-the-Middle, I am looking for you.

Where are the 20 percent of men willing to break the silence about gender equity and have a conversation that can start a movement?

Figure 11: Graphic depiction of a fictitious advertisement to demonstrate the ask for Men-in-the-Middle.

In the next and final chapter, we will focus on *reinforcement* by sharing stories about what the Men-in-the-Middle did well. In their silence, unfortunately, they are also not speaking about or sharing the good behaviors that can be examples for others.

Key Takeaways

- Ability is putting knowledge and skills into practice. The only way to get better at the "awkward gender-equity dance" is to practice in a safe space.
- On average, employees spend 2.1 hours a week in conflict; managing conflict is a core leadership competency, and when you manage it effectively, collaboration improves.
- Work by The Winters Group shows that when managers are silent about an event in the external world, employees think they don't care, thus impacting employee engagement.
- Let's RUN to a new path on gender equity: *reframe* the issue as one of leadership, u*nderstand* perspectives, and *negotiate* roles to find common goals for a novel approach that unites men and women to benefit all.
- Malcolm Gladwell's "tipping point" is defined as when a fundamental change and a spark of an idea or invention hits critical mass; it only takes 20 percent to move the other 80 percent.

Questions to Ask or Ponder

It takes practice to work through the discomfort or stages of uncertainty. How would you respond to the situations that follow? Jot down notes for your answers and then compare with others. This is not a test, and there is no score. These came from the interviews with Men-in-the-Middle.

1. In a staff meeting, you observe that one of your peers talks over another person in a meeting and, in the process, dismisses new ideas. You feel the need to confront the issue. What do you say?

2. Leaders are talking about the skills of a young female professional, considering her for a new assignment. A senior leader provides a rationale for not picking her, saying she just got married and will have babies soon. How do you handle it?

3. At a business dinner, one of your colleagues starts harassing the waitress, at first about the service, but the more he drinks, the more he makes inappropriate sexual advances toward her. What do you say to him?

4. Your boss, an excellent scratch golfer, wants to include eighteen holes of golf as part of a team-building event. You know that half the team does not golf. What do you say to your boss?

5. Your employee approaches you, looking for advice. When her intern talks with her, he does not look her in the eye; he seems to be staring at her chest. What advice do you give her?

CHAPTER ELEVEN

SEND IN THE REINFORCEMENTS

Nicholas did not feel men fit the description of the word 'diverse' as it is used in corporate, but he also believed a conversation about gender equity without men did not meet the criteria for inclusion either.

When I asked Nicholas, a senior leader with a blend of private and public sector experience, what it would take to make more progress in gender equity, he did not hesitate.

"Make men part of the solution," he said.

"Diversity falls short with what I believe is an artificial construct of equality when we focus, for example, on hiring three men and three women," he continued. "Rather than concentrate on numbers, we should highlight and reinforce the value of diversity of thought. In the case of gender equity, this includes the male perspective."

For our Men-in-the-Middle, who see gender equity as a women's issue, hearing a man's take on gender equity is making the effort to be inclusive. That act, just giving men an opportunity to speak up and out, reinforces that male is a gender too, and men are partners in the conversation to change gender equity in the workplace.

Nicholas proposed flipping the narrative from Diversity, Equity, & Inclusion, or DE&I, as it is commonly referred to in corporations, to Inclusion, Equity, & Diversity, IE&D. He wants a culture where people of all types—in this case, men and women—can speak out, ask questions, and be heard. A place where inclusion comes first is also a safe space to learn without fear of repercussions (like judgment or isolation) that can shut down the conversation.

"If we are truly inclusive, we will bring men into the gender equity conversation in a way that acknowledges this is newer territory, and we might get it wrong a time or two. There is a logic to equaling the playing field regarding diverse representation in key positions, equal pay, and more, and I agree we should do these things. It's not the logic that we are up against but emotional uncertainty and the risk of change that makes it a challenge. We are trying to solve one without addressing the other," Nicholas said.

I hear you, Nicholas. Behavior change and taking a risk on something new can be challenging, even when we know there are benefits and there is logic behind the case for change. It is easier to play it safe and revert to what we know, even if that circumstance does not work well for us.

Change is hard, especially when it is worth it!

Men-in-the-Middle, I understand the challenges you face, and I want to meet you where you are now. *Reinforcement* is the final step in the Prosci® ADKAR® change management model. Prosci® experts say we have a physiological tendency to revert to what we know—the status quo—especially when change is difficult or involves risk. Therefore, in light of the proposed changes, we need to put mechanisms in place, like celebrating wins, providing recognition, and issuing regular reminders, to reinforce the new behaviors we want to see so that they stick. Prosci® uses the word "sustained" change to represent a desire for the alternate, new approach to continue after the change process is complete.

Without addressing the strategies of *reinforcement,* people tend to revert to old habits, resist the change, forget what needs to be done, or skip to the next change effort. In short, the organization creeps back to the norm and the new desired behaviors disappear.

In 2022, Prosci®'s Chief Innovation Officer Tim Creasey wrote a blog published on the company website titled "How to Reinforce Change by Celebrating Successes," in which he said to move from change as a check-the-box exercise to a sustainable movement, there are three additional steps after you have gone through *awareness* of the future vision, *desire* to change, *knowledge* of how to change, and the *ability* to put the change in motion. I have paraphrased Creasey's steps of reinforcement to fit more closely within the context of gender equity:

1. Collect and analyze feedback
2. Diagnose gaps between the current and desired state and manage resistance
3. Course correct where needed and celebrate success

Part of celebrating success is the opportunity to "see it to believe it." It is the evidence of others taking the chance to demonstrate new behaviors and publicly acknowledging those actions we want to see more of on a regular basis.

Global management consulting firm McKinsey & Company refers to the "evidence" part of the change process as role modeling, or "I see my leaders, colleagues, and staff behaving differently" (Basford, 2016).

Reinforcement for Sustained Change

Role modeling is not just for high-powered leaders or people in formal positions of authority, according to Tessa Basford and Bill Schaninger, authors of the 2016 article on McKinsey's website, "The Four Building Blocks of Change." The authors say everyone has the power to role model. This "everyone" includes groups, which we have evidence of through social media. We have come full circle. Take, for instance, the impact of the #MeToo movement and the tremendous good it has done to:

- elevate the stories of women and some men who have been victims of assault and harassment
- spotlight lewd behaviors that don't belong in the office or anywhere
- open discourse about behaviors and experiences that had not been previously shared

Now, how do we continue to build momentum to stop harassment and assault in the office and work toward equal pay and leadership opportunities under the broader umbrella of gender equity? What will it take to encourage and engage our gender partners, men, to speak out about gender equity when this has not been their role? Even among the uncertainty, can we make progress and get more men to break the silence, speak out about the impacts of gender stereotypes at work, and even highlight the good things they do that also get lost in the silence?

Reinforcement influences others and is the key to building momentum.

In this sense, role modeling goes beyond the change process to embrace the psychology that involves changing mindset and behavior. Basford and Schaninger wrote that the most *successful transformations,* based on a combination of a global survey, academic research, and practical experience, deploy all four of the actions in their "influence model:"

Building Block	Why It Works
Fostering understanding and conviction: I understand what is being asked of me and it makes sense.	People seek congruence between their beliefs and actions that inspire them to support change.
Reinforcing with formal mechanisms: I see that our structures, processes, and systems support the changes I am being asked to make.	Associations and consequences shape behaviors.
Developing talent and skills: I have the skills and opportunities to behave in new ways.	You can teach an old dog new tricks—our brains remain plastic into adulthood.
Role modeling: I see my leaders, colleagues, and staff behaving differently.	People mimic individuals and groups who surround them, consciously and unconsciously.

Social issues, like gender equity, are large and complex. I enjoy taking business tools, like change management, that are often applied to everyday business problems—from introducing a new business process to updating mandated compliance rules for safety regulations—and applying them to social issues. The tools provide a framework to break down the complex issues to manageable first steps. At times, applying a business tool requires a little latitude in thinking to translate and transfer ideas and best practices.

In this sense, reinforcement encompasses emphasizing where you want to go, bolstering behaviors you want to see, and then finding, sharing, and spreading examples of those, big and small, to spark imitation by others.

The team from the cloud-based platform WalkMe wrote in 2021 on its change management blog, "Reinforcing Change: All Your Questions Answered," that reinforcement starts as soon as the new behaviors are identified and not when the change process is "done." The team also wrote that reinforcement works best when it aligns with the company culture, creates meaningful impact, is personalized to the employees involved, and provides a good balance of constructive feedback and praise.

Before this book ends, I want to reinforce the current and desired state for gender equity so that we are clear on what we are working toward and then highlight behaviors for our Men-in-the-Middle that we want to see more of on a regular basis. Clarity anchors us in a common vision for the future, and reinforcement helps us gain momentum toward engaging men in the conversations. Let's start with some *meaningful* and *personalized* positive consequences of engagement for men.

Rewards Can Outweigh the Risk

Yes, there are risks that come with speaking out, and we've acknowledged those in previous chapters, but let's now discuss the other side of the coin—the rewards.

Throughout this book, I have mentioned a number of sources—*Good Guys* authors Johnson and Smith, WMFDP cofounders Proudman and Welp, Catalyst, McKinsey & Company research, and more—that speak to the business value and impacts of diverse teams and leadership, ranging from enhanced innovation and problem-solving to financial returns.

Let's talk about additional reasons for how speaking up is rewarding for men. Graeme Russell, a professor of organizational psychology and a man who spent nearly fifty years researching, advocating for, and consulting with companies on gender equality and diversity, gave us "10 Reasons Men Should Care about Gender Equity" in his 2012 blog for Catalyst:

For gender equality to be achieved, both women and men need to be active participants in the change process. This is why my initial research in the 1970s focused on men and women sharing in both paid work and in caring for their children. It has been somewhat frustrating, though, over this period of time, being both a participant and an observer of the debate about gender equality. There is both a need and a continuing appetite for responses to questions such as, "Why should men care about gender equality?"

There's the "What's in it for me?" question we touched on in chapter five. Here are a few reasons from his list for why men might be motivated to speak out for change:

- **Lower stress levels** due to a greater investment in life outside of work.

- **More productive and creative work environments** as a result of teaming up with people who have greater diversity of perspectives.

- **Enhanced psychological development and well-being** resulting from being active participants in the process of change to improve outcomes for women, from economic and social resources to health and well-being.

- **Higher-quality personal/intimate relationships**, resulting from having personal lives based on gender equality in relationships. For those who are partnered, this should also result in improved economic security and social well-being.

- **Greater life satisfaction**, resulting from increased involvement in caring for people who are elderly, disabled, or ill.

- **Increased sense of purpose** due to being active participants in a significant process of change.

- **Higher quality of work**, resulting from greater teamwork and collaboration and reduced emphasis on competitiveness.
- **Elevated personal growth and development**, as well as increased skills, resulting from being actively involved as fathers and by making a significant contribution to their children's well-being.

From-To-And: The Context for Reinforcement

With those benefits in mind, let's capture the shift in culture we want to see, moving from the current state to a future state. In chapter ten, I suggested we RUN: *reframe* the issue, *understand* perspectives, and *negotiate* to find common goals that unite men and women in a way that can benefit both. Now, it's time to align on where or toward what we are RUNning. Any good change plan includes a *from-to* page that reflects a shared vision.

It is designed to help people see what the future could look like if change is reinforced and sustained. Figure 12 below, the Gender Equity Mindset Shift, includes concepts that have been covered throughout the book. It visually represents the following mindset shifts to help gain momentum toward attaining gender equity:

- Gender equity is not a women's issue. It is a leadership issue.
- Instead of focusing on gender differences, align on common results to work toward.
- Shift the mindset that women drive gender equity changes to: male is a gender too, and men can benefit.
- Gender equity is not a game of win-lose but win-win.
- When uncertain, shift away from silence and embrace inquiry.
- Leave the toxic frames of the masculine "Man Box" culture and embrace the positive aspects of being a man that embraces masculine and feminine energies.

- Rather than perpetuate the status quo, be a disrupter for good.
- Call out the bad behaviors and reinforce the good as a role model.
- Replace gender-based stereotypes with a focus on effective leadership traits.

Gender Equity Mindset Shift

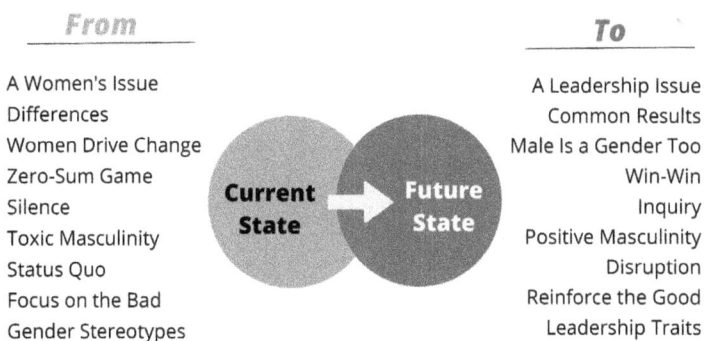

From	*To*
A Women's Issue	A Leadership Issue
Differences	Common Results
Women Drive Change	Male Is a Gender Too
Zero-Sum Game	Win-Win
Silence	Inquiry
Toxic Masculinity	Positive Masculinity
Status Quo	Disruption
Focus on the Bad	Reinforce the Good
Gender Stereotypes	Leadership Traits

Current State → **Future State**

Figure 12: Illustrates a "from-to" mindset shift to promote gender equity.

There is one more shift that will help us change the gender-equity narrative from a women's issue to an "all-of-us" issue, as Nicholas urged at the top of the chapter to include the male perspective. This is a practical tip to reinforce, role model, and reset for a new dialogue that is inclusive of ideas.

Be aware of the buts, especially the "no buts."

I am a fan of shifting from the "but" to the "yes, and" technique when we talk about gender equity. A "but" or "no, but" shuts down and negates idea-sharing, as in "here is my rebuttal to the argument I must win." Here are examples of how "buts" form the interviews and secondary research:

- "I hear the issues being discussed, *but* this is something that doesn't pertain to me," a man might think when he hears someone speak about what he perceives is a women's issue. So he will choose to be silent.
- "This is important, *but* this is unfamiliar to men and I don't know what to say," a man might think. That lack of psychological safety silences another man.
- "I want to speak up and offer my input, *but* I am afraid I'll say the wrong thing," a man might think. Here, that fear of isolation would be the reason he stays mum on the matter.

Shifting to a "yes, and" allows teams to collaborate and build on an idea (Finette, 2017):

- *Yes,* Men-in-the-Middle, it can be tough to speak out when there is so much ambiguity about your role, *and*, at the same time, the benefits and rewards are clear for working through the discomfort, as mentioned in earlier chapters. The payoffs are not just business growth and innovation, but also men individually benefit through reduced stress levels and an increased sense of purpose.
- *Yes,* it might feel risky or unsafe to speak up and work through the discomfort of doing something new, *and* men who are willing to push through that awkwardness can change the culture for sons and daughters, sisters and brothers, and future generations.
- *Yes,* Men-in-the-Middle are silent about gender equity issues due to this uncertainty, *and* they have the influence and power, related to the amount of men in leadership roles, to make a difference.

The "yes, and" also acknowledges the other comment by Nicholas—that we need to address the logic and the emotions, as discussed in chapter nine under "The Turbulence of Emotions."

Reinforcing the Good for Change

Nicholas shared one more piece of sage advice during our interview. He said *reinforcement* falls short when it stays in the safety of a learning lab.

"It is one thing to say in a sterile training room, 'Don't discriminate against women,'" he continued. "In that environment, people will say, 'Of course we respect women.' Now, let's get out of the lab and apply the learning to an actual situation where you are at a sales meeting and have had a few drinks. The say-do gap can grow under those conditions."

You are right, Nicholas. We live in a world that is complex and unpredictable—a VUCA world (introduced in chapter ten). That is why talking about scenarios in advance of a live situation, practicing perspective-taking, and even providing a little bit of grace are so important.

So let's get out of the lab! I love a rallying cry. Please, Men-in-the-Middle, engage with us and speak out about gender equity to be role models, reinforce and socialize a new norm, and ultimately use your influence for good to make positive changes toward advancing gender equity.

After all, the men I interviewed had a lot to say. They shared ideas and stories from a very pragmatic lens. Countless times since my interview with John (chapter two), I have shared his advice to study the effectiveness of other movements, especially the March on Washington, when the leaders made a strategic move to find common ground with the men in power at the time. His words inspired a movement of its own. They became a catalyst for me to write this book in an effort to change the narrative, find common ground with those in a position of influence, and move the gender equity conversation forward toward more action.

While we might understand *why* they remain silent in the discomfort, I want to reinforce what they shared as an example for others. When men don't speak out, we also don't get to hear ideas for change, such as what we want to see more of in the workplace or what they already do to promote equity. We also don't get to know the emotions they might be experiencing that will impact the decision to remain silent, speak out, or do something.

With this book, I want to reinforce what that might look like and create a safe space for men to speak out in real time and share more of their stories in order to spark conversations and lead to positive change.

So, I dedicate the rest of this chapter to sharing the stories, sentiments, and expressions from the heroes of this book, the Men-in-the-Middle who talked about their experiences, feelings, advice, and ideas related to gender equity outside of the training lab. They had a real conversation about their views on gender equity. Judith E. Glaser, author of the book *Conversational Intelligence: How Great Leaders Build Trust and Get Extraordinary Results,* wrote about the importance of conversations that "prime the brain for mutual success." This quote from her book reinforces the importance of communication and storytelling in the change process:

> *Too often we fall into the trap of thinking that if we give employees the facts and explain why change needs to take place from an economic point of view, they'll buy into the change. We overestimate the power of logic and underestimate the power of storytelling, an appeal to belonging and the positive emotions of belonging.*

I have shared the logic for why I want men to engage in this conversation. It is time for the storytelling from the men. These are seeds of change that may go overlooked because they exist in the everyday. These are not the tales that make the headlines of the *Wall Street Journal* or *People* magazine. They are real and raw and, in some cases, may seem amazingly unremarkable. Some of them reinforce the good stuff we want to see more of in the world. Some stories could catalyze a conversation for a sea of change.

The idea here is to suspend judgment and celebrate the men's willingness, even if only in an anonymous format, to talk about gender equity and share their experiences and behaviors. This is about reinforcing more of what we want to see: men participating in gender-related conversations and issues in the workplace to make progress toward equity. At the end of this chapter, I expanded the "Questions to Discuss or Ponder" section so that you can go back and examine your own views in the context of the stories and comments.

These are the stories and words from some of the men I interviewed about taking steps to reinforce change. This is where the conversation starts, on the journey to socialize and normalize the idea that men have a role to play in conversations about gender equity. They shared, and I listened with the goal of starting a broader dialogue and inviting men into the conversation. Men can spark change, disrupt the status quo, and gain momentum on an issue that can benefit them too.

Preparing for the Awkward

Jeff, an experienced sales leader and a dad to two grown sons and no daughters, openly shared with me his concerns about gender equity in the office. As a self-described "unprotected white male," he said he did not feel safe discussing gender issues at work, from #MeToo to pay discrepancies.

That did not stop him, however, from addressing what he called inappropriate behaviors in the office or at work-related events, specifically in the male-dominated field of customer sales, that are typical of the automotive, manufacturing, and technology industries. Here is how Jeff explained the context of his work:

> *I have recruited several female college graduates to go into sales. These professional women are smart and eager to do well in their careers. At the same time, I have seen how some customers and peers behave, especially when there is alcohol at a customer-related event. It can get awkward when a senior-level buyer for a customer or the company owner from a very large, lucrative client is at the event, and they are behaving badly.*
>
> *I trained the new sales associates, especially college graduates, new to the work environment, to understand appropriate behaviors at events and meetings. I taught females in sales what to watch for and how to handle inappropriate situations.*

Jeff described a time when a high-up executive from a key account customer had a few too many drinks and started flirting with one of the new female sales associates. Jeff observed the behavior, determined it was high-risk, and removed her from the situation. He called her out of the room and sent her to another station. Out of earshot of the client, he told her why he moved her and that she did not have to accept that behavior. He also told her she did nothing wrong and they could talk about it more at the office next week.

In the lab, as Nicholas described earlier, the place where we formally talk about sexual harassment, it would be easy to instruct someone to confront the customer and tell him that is not acceptable behavior. However, what happens when you are face-to-face with a multi-million-dollar customer who has had a few drinks that render his behavior unprofessional? If you confront the customer in the moment, what is the chance that the customer gets offended and pulls his account, impacting the sales of your team and division?

It is a real scenario, and Jeff made a decision based on uncertainty, risk, and logic. In the awkwardness, Jeff decided to remove his female associate from that situation for her well-being. He eliminated a risk in the moment. He also committed to educate, train, and talk with his employees, men and women, about appropriate office behaviors.

The Intern Gazes at Employee's Chest

Here is another one that made me think twice. At the end of his call, Peter told me a story that happened years ago, but he still thinks about it because he was shocked at the way his boss handled it. He shared:

> *My really talented employee came to me for advice as she had often noticed that her male summer intern would stare at her chest during one-on-one meetings. I gave her advice on how to discuss it with him, which she did. The intern denied that he was doing it, but did acknowledge that she was uncomfortable. However, the intern continued to stare at her chest, despite their conversation. She then sought additional advice from my boss, so we set up a meeting to discuss it with him. He listened to her. He looked at me, hesitated, and then gave this advice and direction:*

> *'Look, guys are going to stare at your chest. It happens a lot, but of course, it does not make it right. Now, having said that, fire him. You told him not to do it, and he continued to do it. We don't want someone who won't take coaching and clearly doesn't get it.'*

> *I couldn't believe he said the thing about her chest, but in the end, he did the right thing by advising her to let him go.*

In the lab, we probably would have corrected Peter's boss, saying, "Don't talk about a woman's anatomy." In general, I agree it is best to avoid talking about boobs, genitals, and butts in the office. In the awkwardness, Peter's boss made a decision to be transparent and take action. I thanked Peter for sharing a vulnerable story. His employee sought additional advice, and he said the conversation had been uncomfortable. But he felt his boss offered the right solution—there was just some rough turbulence on the delivery.

Thank You and Pay It Forward

The Prosci® ADKAR® model suggests tactics to foster reinforcement, including a desire to establish systemic visible ways to acknowledge behaviors positively, say thank you, and provide recognition. Looking back on the process used to gather insights and stories for this book, there are parallel reinforcements:

- I provided a $100 gift card for the men interviewed as a visible acknowledgment of time spent, willingness to talk about a potentially uncomfortable topic, and a cooperative nature to impart experiences and wisdom under anonymous identities.
- I thanked the men after the interviews in this book. Although it took longer to write than I initially anticipated, I sent them a summary and offered to send an early copy of the manuscript if they wanted to see it.
- In recognition of the men I spoke with and the pages of interview notes I took of their words to study and analyze, I highlighted some of the wisdom and suggestions they shared.

This is about reinforcing more of what we want to see: men talking about gender equity and sharing their perspectives. The extreme, lewd, and inappropriate behaviors have gotten media attention, and that will continue. To promote dialogue in the workplace, I am interested in elevating the behaviors and comments from men that will open a dialogue for a new conversation.

No Slate If It Is an All-Male Slate

Bruce shared another one of those stories that I processed well after our interview call. He worked at a large, global-branded company where posters on the wall said, "We value an inclusive culture where all employees can bring their whole selves to work each day." One of his female bosses had posted a prestigious vice president position in the company.

When the human resource team handed her the final slate of candidates and she saw that all-male applicants had made it through the screening process, she threw out the entire panel, saying she refused to hire for the position from an all-male candidate pool.

"I asked, what about our inclusive culture? Men are part of that culture too," said Bruce. "I want women, including my daughter, to have opportunities. At the same time, I don't want them doing that to my son."

In Diversity & Inclusion training, "the training lab" as Nicholas described it, would this scenario be included as a case study to discuss? Does it seem far-fetched or even uncomfortable when, as discussed earlier, some men, especially white men, don't see themselves as qualifying under the diversity umbrella? We are human, after all. Even good intentions taken to an extreme can create inequity.

From Creep to Pay Champion

I would be remiss at this point if I did not share this story about a boss in my life who told me I had been compensated well under the pay range for my education and experience. He put a plan in place to correct it over the course of eighteen months.

Here is the twist.

This man is the same one I mentioned in my introduction who massaged my shoulders in the office and made me feel uncomfortable. He did not touch my shoulders again, and his advocacy for equal pay did not justify the other. I am simply saying the more we talk about these situations and get them out in the open, the better prepared we are to deal with both the logical and emotional issues. We can also acknowledge that people are complex, and we mess up at times on both a conscious and subconscious level.

Stories, Advice, and Ideas from Our Men-in-the-Middle

Below is the highlight reel of behaviors and comments shared by our Men-in-the-Middle during the anonymous interviews that became a catalyst for this book. These are not stories like the ones above but quips in the form of a short response. These may seem like simple examples, and that is by design. New behaviors take hold in the everyday moments, often inspired by others who prepare the way, even if the identity of the others is incognito.

Sustainable change is incremental.

Every little thing counts. It is better than silence and inaction. I am acknowledging that small actions lead to big changes. My goal in doing so is to reinforce and even normalize men sharing perspectives on gender-related issues in the workplace.

Call Out Bad Behaviors from Your Male Peers

In our interview guide, we asked the men if they have observed any harassment or discrimination behaviors by male peers and what they did about it. Some men spoke up:

- "I was out to dinner with a supplier and our management team—eight men and one woman—and a man on our team was telling an inappropriate story with bad language. It was offensive to me whether a woman was there or not. I called it out. I told all the people there it was not appropriate."
- "My peers and I were discussing talent succession plans. One leader discounted a good-performing female employee for a role because she had just had a child. He said she probably would not move for the promotion. I responded that if we think she can do the job, we ought to ask her and not decide for her based on our assumptions about her family life. I reminded him that the previous candidate we had discussed, a male, had also welcomed a child that year, and we did not second guess his desire to move for the role."
- "Working around politics in the Eighties, I often had to pull men aside and say, 'You can't say that.' I told them they might think it is funny, but others might find it offensive."
- "I am a man of color, so when [my boss] said something offensive about women, my relationship as a guy allowed me to approach him with feedback. I could also use my own experiences of people using discriminatory language about me that would help him see the situation from a different perspective. I would never embarrass him, but I am okay with healthy tension, enough for him to question his bias and be open to seeing the situation through a new lens."
- "I call people out on behaviors that I think suck, but that is just the right thing to do."

Reframe Gender Equity as a Business Issue

There is overwhelming evidence that leadership teams with more women, as one form of diversity, will have positive impacts on the top and on the bottom line of the profit and loss statement. Here is how some men suggested a shift in thinking:

- "Why aren't more men involved? Again, it goes back to the fact that gender equity is not seen as a business driver; it's not talked about that way. So there is no motivation for men to talk about #MeToo and gender equity. Men have not thought through these things. We need to address topics that address both personal and work lives for men."

- "Recruiting and retaining engineers is an ongoing challenge for this company. Some of the men on our leadership team had a bias against hiring young female candidates, concerned they might leave at some point to start a family. When we had some excellent female candidates, I finally said, 'Look, we lose ten to twenty engineers anyway over time [with a 16 percent turnover], so why should we worry if women leave or might leave due to pregnancy?'"

- "One challenge we face getting women into leadership roles is that they mainly progress in support positions like Human Resources, not in the money-making functions, including running a line of business. We need to get more women into positions where they manage a profit and loss statement for a part of the business. That is the path to the executive suite."

Acknowledge People's Emotions, Not the Stereotypes

We have already established that emotions and logic work hand-in-hand. Emotions and feelings—including anger, fear, and stress—can manifest in different ways for men and women. For example, anger might make a man yell but a woman may be brought to tears. Here is a viewpoint from one of the men we interviewed:

- "It's important not to let stereotypes determine the value of a response. Today, we have to be more open-minded about people's reactions and help them through that. People work a lot of hours and often under strenuous conditions that are physically and mentally demanding. Emotions could be shutting down or disengaging. In the past, if a woman were to cry at work, they would dismiss her, as, you know, she can't handle it. I no longer think that is the case."

Engage Men in Discussions about Work-Life Balance

The majority of the home-family management falls to women. In some cases, women are working at a full-time day job and then running the family home. According to a 2020 study at Comparably, a technology platform to collect and compare company data, 44 percent of men and 46 percent of women reported they felt burned out and could use a vacation.

- "We fall short of workplace culture and practices. More needs to be done to accommodate a work-life balance, supporting men and women in home responsibilities."
- "Early in my career, we had determined a fifty-fifty split of household duties before we had kids. Before we started a family, we negotiated roles of who would manage what in the household. Yes, my wife does more in the home now, but we negotiated that when we had kids. We decided for our family that we would go to one income, and she would stay home. I continue to do a lot at home."
- "We acknowledge that golf is not the only pastime people enjoy. When we have a quarterly team meeting, we intentionally alternate activities to be more inclusive. Last month, we did a team cooking challenge at a restaurant that supported a charitable cause."

Ask For Help, How to Have Inclusive Conversations

On the surface, conversations are something we engage in every day. Yet, men acknowledge gender equity-related conversations feel unfamiliar, made complex by the emotions of uncertainty and the fear of what might happen if they speak up and out to share concerns.

- "We need to reduce the cost of candor on the issue of diversity and create a more welcoming environment for all."

- "I wouldn't describe it as fear for the reason why men don't talk about gender equity, but it is uncertainty around addressing topics like the #MeToo movement. If men were provided information on leading those discussions, it might help."

- "What is the concern for men? How do we talk openly about gender equity? How can we change the business or structure that has been going on for years? How do we operationalize this in an environment that has not done this, and, at the same time, how do we avoid doing counterproductive things?"

So, What's Next?

The Men-in-the-Middle had a lot to say, and there are a lot of different ways to catalyze a conversation. Any one of the above quotes from the Men-in-the-Middle gives us a place to start the dialogue. If you found yourself making judgments about the actions or statements as you read them, go back to reexamine those. When you read the quote again, make an observation, note the men's actions and comments, and do some perspective-taking. You can always go back to the discussion questions to review it from your lens, as in what *you* would have done in this real-life scenario.

Whether we agree with the comments, statements, questions, or decisions is not as relevant as the potential to open the conversation that leads to better understanding and positive results. It may require a shift from placing judgment to embracing curiosity. In the words of Shadé Zahrai, an award-winning leadership strategist consultant and coach who has amassed millions of followers across social media platforms, change the narrative in your head:

> *The next time you catch yourself thinking, "I can't do this," redirect to "how could I make this happen?" Shift, "I should do this or I have to do that" to "I get to do this or I choose to do that." Instead of combating disempowering thoughts, redirect your mind to empowering language that reflects personal control. Finally, move from why to what; instead of "why don't I feel motivated?" ask yourself, "What can I do to get excited about getting this done?"*

Zahrai said this in her March 16, 2023 talk titled "Three Habits that Kill your Confidence" at TEDxMonash University. The first of these "mind pits," as she called them, that kills confidence to take action is the "failure to launch." To exemplify this concept, she shared the story of a successful software engineer who felt stuck in an unfulfilling career and had aspirations to launch startups that solve compelling global problems. He believed in his skill set and did his homework, yet he constantly second-guessed himself.

The "failure to launch" pit keeps people stuck in a perpetual cycle of research, learning, and preparation. Endlessly consuming books, podcasts, Googling, taking courses, acquiring extra qualifications—constantly doubting if they're ready enough. Zahrai also referred to a 1999 *Harvard Business Review* article, "The Smart Talk Trap," by Jeffrey Pfeffer and Robert Sutton where they called it the "knowing-doing gap"—knowing too much and doing too little.

Do we have a "knowing-doing gap" for gender equity? The knowledge is there. The research on the business case as well as personal benefits to pursue gender equity have been listed in this book and are well documented in academic journals and other high-integrity organizations, like Catalyst. This book has also provided data, key takeaways, and questions to spark a conversation.

Can we shift our mindsets about our approach, as Zahrai put it, to avoid getting stuck in the failure-to-launch phase? Think: "I get to *choose* to be part of building momentum for gender equity. I am excited about doing this for the next generation of sons and daughters! How can I make gender equity conversations between men and women happen?"

It's Time to Launch

In the beginning of this book, I wrote that if we listen to understand and engage men in the gender-related conversations in the office, we may be able to break through that next barrier and make even more progress in the gender equity movement. Let's RUN—*reframe* the issue, *understand* perspectives, and *negotiate* to find common goals—together in healthy, open dialogue that values leading with curiosity, asking questions, and listening actively.

Men-in-the-Middle, we see you.

We know gender equity and gender-related topics are unpracticed conversations for you, especially with women. These discussions have not been "the water"—i.e., fish in water—you swim in each day. Amid the sex-role stereotypes and the toxic masculinity, we acknowledge this can be an uncomfortable space.

You are concerned that you might say something that leads to a woman accusing you of harassment or a man removing your "bro card." Your choice to remain silent or to only meet with other men for one-on-one work-related dinners or drinks may not be intended to exclude others; in that space, you can be vulnerable and don't have to worry as much about every word you say and how you act.

Even in your silence, we hear you.

We don't know, however, if the silence means you don't care or you are caught in a conundrum about your role that leads to uncertainty, and, in the complexity of it all, you decide staying quiet is the safer bet.

We acknowledge this is an uncomfortable space—us asking you to do something that is unfamiliar. We hear that the competitive zero-sum game is your jam, and we are asking you to reframe and see that together we can be more competitive in the marketplace. Throughout this book, we tried to practice perspective-taking— seeing the world from your lens. We listened to you in one-on-one conversations without judgment, and we reflected on what we heard. If we did not get it all correct, we can listen again and reflect until we get it right.

We see you, we hear you, and we *need* you to speak out.

In corporate America, you hold the most leadership seats—by far. Not only do you influence the most people, but you are also in a position to advocate for policy change that will benefit men and women. It has been almost one hundred years since the Equal Rights Amendment was proposed and recently ratified, but the nation is still determining the next steps.

Other changes have happened at a local and national level to equal the playing field. Still, the sweeping statement of the ERA remains unseen, and there is no apparent sense of urgency, even if men stand to benefit too.

We are not asking you to march for the ERA, although you are welcome if that is your interest. Instead, we are asking you to break the silence, speak out, and be a disruptor for growth. We invite you to engage in the conversation on gender equity to move the dial sooner, making progress together faster than we can alone. We are asking you to join the conversation.

You are invited.

This book is written with that intent in mind. Invite others to join you to have a dialogue via the takeaways and questions at the end of each chapter. Conversations are an opportunity to lead toward a new and better way. I hope your voice and experiences find representation here and that gives you the courage to create a conversation. If not, I welcome the opportunity to open a new conversation.

Key Takeaways

- Reinforcement is the final step in the ADKAR® change management model. Reinforcement helps solidify the change process and make it more sustainable.
- Role modeling, leading by example so that others can imitate you, is a form of reinforcement and is a step to influence others to behave in alignment with the transformation process.
- In any change effort, there is a *from-to* state—where you are today and where you want to be. Shifting from a "no, but" to a "yes, and" response can open new conversations.
- Several thought-provoking remarks from the Men-in-the-Middle in this chapter reinforce the idea of sharing and opening up the conversation.
- Men-in-the-Middle, we see the discomfort you face when talking about gender equity, we hear you when you go against the status quo, and we understand that you have ideas, your own concerns to discuss, and stories to share about when you took action and promoted equity in your own way. We invite you into the gender equity conversation, and we need you to speak up and out.

Questions to Discuss or Ponder

1. Nicholas referred to the lab as diversity and inclusion training that takes place in a company. What do you think of his statement: "It is different to apply what you learn in a real-life setting"? When have you seen this challenge?

2. What is your view on the rewards for men speaking out about gender equity (listed earlier in this chapter)?

3. What type of reinforcement works for you, especially when you have to change behavior patterns that you are used to? What would reinforce your desire or ability to speak out?

4. When you see a man or woman treated disrespectfully in a meeting, do you speak out to help shift the culture and reframe behaviors? Why or why not?

5. When Jeff removed his female colleague from a flirty, inebriated guest, he removed her from a potentially unsafe situation. What would you have done? Sharing this example, invite others to discuss and discern how they might handle an event like this in the future.

6. If your female employee was uncomfortable with a male intern's inappropriate behavior, what would you say if she came to you for advice?

7. Can you share a time when you saw someone do the right thing, specific to gender in the workplace, and you thought, "Wow, that was cool, we should talk about that"? Or maybe you have done something in the spirit of gender equity that you don't discuss today?

8. If we could remove the fear or uncertainty about any reaction to your comments, what are three things that you want your female colleagues to know or questions you want to ask them about gender equity?

9. What would it take for you to actively engage in gender equity conversations in the workplace? What ideas do you have to engage more men and start the conversation?

10. What will change for you now, having read this book?

ACKNOWLEDGMENTS

A special thank you goes out to the men who said "yes" to letting us interview you. Your insights have been invaluable, and they inspired a lot of thinking, additional inquiry, and conversations!

Thank you to Donna Malone of Fusion Marketing Power. You heard my idea and agreed to work with me anyway! Your wisdom created a process and interview guide that allowed for consistency, thought-provoking questions, and a path toward qualitative insights. Even after the interviews, you encouraged me to continue. You are truly amazing.

A special thanks also goes to my friend, Sue Arment. We met in my corporate role and have continued to continue to admire each other's skills long after our first meeting. You graciously volunteered to help with interviews, which also led to a richness in the data-gathering process. You rock!

Thank you to family and friends, including PSDK, and people in my network. For some, I directly asked you to test my logic; for others, unbeknownst to you, you helped me test ideas in the live lab of life. You expanded my sandbox.

I cannot forget my editor, Elina Oliferovskiy. Clarity, accuracy, and attention to detail matter to me. You pushed me, poked at me, and helped me produce a much better product. A talented editor is a treasured partner, especially one who is willing to press and tell you that you can do better. Thanks for having my back!

Thank you, Leila Summers, and the team at Pure Ink Press! Your attention to detail is a gift. I appreciate the way you set quality standards and work with authors from a place of mutual respect.

ABOUT THE AUTHOR

With an undergrad in journalism, a master's in communication, and extensive corporate experience, Kori Reed has spent years inspiring conversations that fuel connection and ignite change. She delights in pursuing the unspoken undercurrents of a topic to get to the root cause and address the crux of the matter. For more than two decades, she worked for large, complex Fortune 500 companies, including Goodyear Tire & Rubber Company, Quaker Oats, PepsiCo, and Conagra Brands. These experiences instilled the value of authentic dialog and finding clarity amid conflict and chaos. As a mom of four—two women and two men—she is fervent about gender equity and creating a world where a rising tide lifts all boats for the world's daughters and sons.

BIBLIOGRAPHY

Disclaimer & Author's Notes

Newman, Tim. "Types of Gender Identity: Types and Definitions." *Medical News Today,* May 11, 2021. Accessed on June 20, 2022. https://www.medicalnewstoday.com/articles/types-of-gender-identity#gender-as-a-spectrum.

Study.com. "America's Core Values: Liberty, Equality & Self-Government." *Social Sciences Courses.* June 29, 2014. Accessed June 8, 2022. https://study.com/academy/lesson/americas-core-values-liberty-equality-self-government.html.

Introduction

Bruggeman, Jacob A. "For Male Survivors of Sexual Assault — Like Me — #MeToo Can Help Change Culture of Silence." *USA Today,* July 26, 2019. https://www.usatoday.com/story/opinion/2019/07/26/sexual-assault-among-men-needs-discussed-metoo-column/1807577001/.

Carmichael, William. "Book Look–Good Guys: How Men Can Be Better Allies for Women in the Workplace." *HR Professionals Magazine,* October 2020. *https://hrprofessionalsmagazine.com/2020/09/28/book-look-good-guys-how-men-can-be-better-allies-for-women-in-the-workplace/.*

CJR Editors. "The Reach of #MeToo." *Columbia Journalism Review.* 2019. https://www.cjr.org/special_report/reach-of-metoo.php.

Faruqi, Osman. "Why Is It So Hard for Men to Link Their Personal Behaviour to Gender Inequality?" *ABC Everyday,* updated December 15, 2020. https://www.abc.net.au/everyday/why-men-struggle-to-link-behaviour-to-gender-equality/11314468.

Filipovic, Jill. "'Bombshell' Exposes Some Very Ugly Truths." *CNN,* December 18, 2019. https://www.cnn.com/2019/12/17/opinions/bombshell-sends-this-message-filipovic/index.html.

Fuhrmans, Vanessa. "What #MeToo Has to Do with the Workplace Gender Gap." *The Wall Street Journal,* October 23, 2018. https://www.wsj.com/articles/what-metoo-has-to-do-with-the-workplace-gender-gap-1540267680.

Gerber, David, producer. "Police Woman." Created by Robert L. Collins. Aired on September 13, 1974, on the NBC network. https://tubitv.com/series/300007077/police-woman.

Horowitz, Juliana Menasce and Ruth Igielnik. "A Century after Women Gained the Right to Vote, Majority of Americans See Work to Do on Gender Equality." *Pew Research Center,* 2020. https://www.pewresearch.org/social-trends/2020/07/07/a-century-after-women-gained-the-right-to-vote-majority-of-americans-see-work-to-do-on-gender-equality/.

Kerr, Geoffrey and Alix Pollack. "Engaging Men: Barriers and Gender Norms (Report)." *Catalyst.* April 7, 2022. https://www.catalyst.org/research/engaging-men-barriers-norms/.

Koeze, Ella and Anna Maria Barry-Jester. "What Do Men Think It Means to Be a Man?" *FiveThirtyEight | ABC News,* 2018. https://fivethirtyeight.com/features/what-do-men-think-it-means-to-be-a-man/.

Merriam-Webster OnLine, s.v. "zero-sum game," accessed May 20, 2022. https://www.merriam-webster.com/dictionary/zero-sum%20game.

Prosci. "The Prosci® ADKAR Model." *Prosci*. Accessed May 28, 2022. https://www.prosci.com/methodology/adkar.

Reed, Kori. "#MeToo Silenced the Men Who Can Make a Difference. What Now?" Lakeshore. TED video. TEDx Talk video. 10:24. https://www.ted.com/talks/kori_reed_metoo_silenced_the_men_who_can_make_a_difference_what_now.

Roach, Jay, dir. *Bombshell*. IMDb. United States: Lionsgate, 2020.

Thomas, Rachel, Marianne Cooper-Ph.D., Kate McShane Urban, Gina Cardazone-Ph.D., Mary Noble-Tolla-Ph.D., Sonia Mahajan, Briana Edwards, Lareina Yee, Alexis Krivkovich, Ishanaa Rambachan, Wei Wei Liu, Monne Williams, Nicole Robinson-Ph.D. and Hilary Nguyen. "Women in the Workplace 2022." *McKinsey & Company & LeanIn.Org*. Accessed March 5, 2023. https://www.mckinsey.com/~/media/mckinsey/featured%20insights/diversity%20and%20inclusion/women%20in%20the%20workplace%202022/women-in-the-workplace-2022.pdf.

United States Census Bureau. "United States Census Bureau QuickFacts: United States." *Census.gov*. July 1, 2022. https://www.census.gov/quickfacts/fact/table/US/PST045222.

Chapter One

American Psychological Association Dictionary of *Psychology.org*. s.v. "perspective-taking." Accessed May 20, 2022. https://dictionary.apa.org/perspective-taking.

Anderson, Monica and Skye Toor. "How Social Media Users Have Discussed Sexual Harassment since #MeToo Went Viral." *Pew Research Center,* October 11, 2018. https://www.pewresearch.org/

fact-tank/2018/10/11/how-social-media-users-have-discussed-sexual-harassment-since-metoo-went-viral/.

Buchholz, Katharina and Felix Richter. "Infographic: Only 15 Percent of CEOs at Fortune 500 Companies Are Female." *Statista.* March 8, 2022. https://www.statista.com/chart/13995/female-ceos-in-fortune-500-companies/.

Cormier, Danielle. "How to Use Hashtags in Your Social Media Marketing." *Constant Contact,* August 19, 2022. https://www.constantcontact.com/blog/how-to-use-hashtags/#:~:text=A%20hashtag%20consists%20of%20words,or%20trend%20of%20your%20choosing.

Garofalo, Amanda Van Hoose. "You Think #MeToo Is Over? Think Again." *Employment Law Spotlight* (blog), February 15, 2022. https://www.employmentlawspotlight.com/2022/02/you-think-metoo-is-over-think-again/.

Griffin, Riley, Hannah Recht, and Jeff Green. "#MeToo: One Year Later." *Bloomberg,* October 5, 2018. https://www.bloomberg.com/graphics/2018-me-too-anniversary/.

Jones, Paula. "Benedict Cumberbatch: I'll Turn Down a Role If My Female Co-star Isn't Paid the Same." *RadioTimes,* May 13, 2018. https://www.radiotimes.com/tv/drama/benedict-cumberbatch-equal-pay-women-female-co-star-patrick-melrose/.

Keegan, Rebecca. "How Benedict Cumberbatch's Sunnymarch Grew into a Major Production Player." *Hollywood Reporter,* September 8th, 2021. https://www.hollywoodreporter.com/movies/movie-news/benedict-cumberbatch-sunnymarch-production-company-1235008552/.

Koeze, Ella and Anna Maria Barry-Jester. "What Do Men Think It Means to Be a Man?" *FiveThirtyEight: ABC News,* June 20, 2018. https://fivethirtyeight.com/features/what-do-men-think-it-means-to-be-a-man/.

Krivkovich, Alexis, Wei Wei Liu, Hilary Nguyen, Ishanaa Rambachan, Nicole Robinson, Monee Williams, and Lareina Yee. "Women in the Workplace 2022 Article." *McKinsey & Company.* October 18, 2022. https://www.mckinsey.com/featured-insights/diversity-and-inclusion/women-in-the-workplace.

Langone, Alix. "#MeToo and Time's Up Founders Explain the Difference Between the 2 Movements—And How They're Alike." *Time*, March 8, 2018. https://time.com/5189945/whats-the-difference-between-the-metoo-and-times-up-movements/.

McConnell, Liv. "This Man's Post Perfectly Sums up What's Wrong with #MeToo." *Fairygodboss.* Accessed May 20, 2022. https://fairygodboss.com/articles/this-man-s-post-perfectly-sums-up-what-s-wrong-with-metoo.

Medin, Douglas and Megan Bang. "Perspective Taking, Diversity and Partnerships." *American Psychological Association.* February 2008. Accessed May 20, 2022. https://www.apa.org/science/about/psa/2008/02/medin.

Merriam-Webster OnLine, s.v. "hashtag," accessed February 25, 2023, https://www.merriam-webster.com/dictionary/hashtag.

Milano, Alyssa (@Alyssa_Milano). "If you've been sexually harassed or assaulted write 'me too' as a reply to this tweet." *Twitter,* Oct 15, 2017. 1:21 p.m. https://twitter.com/alyssa_milano/status/919659438700670976?lang=en.

Milano, Alyssa (@Alyssa_Milano). "I was just made aware of an earlier #MeToo movement, and the origin story is equal parts heartbreaking and inspiring." *Twitter,* October 16, 2017, 4:24 p.m. https://twitter.com/alyssa_milano/status/920067975016624128?lang=en.

Nai, Indigo. "Women are owning the internet today. Every woman I know is speaking up and reaching out." Facebook, October 16, 2017. https://www.facebook.com/indigo.nai/posts/10155856522186383.

Reiner, Rob, dir. *When Harry Met Sally*. Beverly Hills: MGM Home Entertainment, 1989. DVD video.

Richards, Katie. "The #TimesUp Movement Dominated Social Media during the Golden Globes." *Adweek*, January 8, 2018. Accessed May 20, 2022. https://www.adweek.com/brand-marketing/the-timesup-movement-dominated-social-media-during-the-golden-globes/.

Rueckert, Phineas. "Benedict Cumberbatch Won't Take a Role If Female Co-star Isn't Paid Equally." *Global Citizen*, May 14, 2018. Accessed May 20, 2022. https://www.globalcitizen.org/en/content/benedict-cumberbatch-gender-wage-gap/.

Sayej, Nadja. "Alyssa Milano on the #MeToo movement: 'We're Not Going to Stand for It Any More.'" *The Guardian*, December 1, 2017. Accessed May 20, 2022. https://www.theguardian.com/culture/2017/dec/01/alyssa-milano-mee-too-sexual-harassment-abuse.

TimesUp Now. "Leveling the Playing Field: Establishing Equity at Work." *TimesUpNow.org*. October 28, 2019. https://timesupnow.org/work/equity/leveling-the-playing-field-establishing-equity-at-work/.

TimesUp Now. "Time's Up Now. Join Us." November 21, 2022. *https://timesupnow.org/*.

UN Women | United Nations Entity for Gender Equality and the Empowerment of Women. "Prohibition of Discrimination, Harassment, Including Sexual Harassment, and Abuse of Authority." *United Nations*. 2013 Accessed April 27, 2022. https://www.un.org/womenwatch/uncoordination/antiharassment.html.

United States Census Bureau. "United States Census Bureau QuickFacts: United States." *Census.gov*. July 1, 2022. https://www.census.gov/quickfacts/fact/table/US/PST045222.

Wiessner, Daniel. "US Agency Saw Sharp Rise in Sexual Harassment Complaints after #MeToo." *Reuters,* October 4, 2018. https://www.reuters.com/article/us-usa-harassment/u-s-agency-saw-sharp-rise-in-sexual-harassment-complaints-after-metoo-idUSKCN1ME2LG.

Zacharek, Stephanie, Eliana Dockterman, and Haley Sweetland Edwards. "The Silence Breakers." *Time,* 2017. Accessed May 20, 2022. https://time.com/time-person-of-the-year-2017-silence-breakers/.

Chapter Two

Academy of Achievement. "Ruth Bader Ginsburg on Integrity." *American Academy of Achievement.* Aug. 28, 2020. Accessed May 20, 2022. https://achievement.org/video/ruth-bader-ginsburg-20/.

Carmon, Irin and Shana Knizhnik. *Notorious RBG: The Life and Times of Ruth Bader Ginsburg.* New York: Dey Street Books, 2015.

Cohen, Alex and Wilfred U. Codrington III. "The Equal Rights Amendment Explained." *Brennan Center: For Justice.* 2020. Accessed on May 15, 2022. https://www.brennancenter.org/our-work/research-reports/equal-rights-amendment-explained.

EqualityNow.org. "ERA Explainer." *Resource Center.* Accessed May 22, 2022. https://www.equalitynow.org/era_explainer/?gclid=-Cj0KCQjw-daUBhCIARIsALbkjSYJO_hvpBik3_BTCa-BsKI0QOQQolppR8Bxef5w-fY3Jk77HNYVVwMAaAiZPEALw_wcB.

ERA. "EqualRightsAmendment." Accessed February 10, 2022. https://www.equalrightsamendment.org/.

Gray, Robert J. "'An Amendment That Requires Both Sexes to Be Treated Equally': A Men's Rights Activist Voices Support for the ERA." Submitted in 1984 to a House committee considering a new bill to enact the ERA.

History Matters—The U.S. Survey Course on the Web. Accessed February 10, 2022. http://historymatters.gmu.edu/d/7028/.

Harvey, Paul. "Martin Luther King Jr. Had a Much More Radical Message than a Dream of Racial Brotherhood." *The Conversation*, March 30, 2018. Accessed June 1, 2022. https://theconversation.com/martin-luther-king-jr-had-a-much-more-radical-message-than-a-dream-of-racial-brotherhood-92795.

History.com Editors. "March on Washington." *History.* Updated January 11, 2022. Accessed June 20, 2022. https://www.history.com/topics/black-history/march-on-washington.

Hruby, Emma. "NCAA Volleyball Championship Draws Record 1.2 Million Viewers." *Just Women's Sports.* December 22, 2021. https://justwomenssports.com/ncaa-volleyball-championship-viewers-wisconsin-nebraska/.

Justia. "Charles E. Moritz, Petitioner-Appellant, v. Commissioner of Internal Revenue, Respondent-Appellee, 469 F.2D 466 (10TH Cir. 1972)." *US Court of Appeals for the Tenth Circuit.* November 22, 1972. Accessed May 20, 2022. https://law.justia.com/cases/federal/appellate-courts/F2/469/466/79852/.

Law, Tara. "Virginia Just Became the 38th State to Pass the Equal Rights Amendment. Here's What to Know About the History of the ERA." *Time,* updated January 15, 2020. https://time.com/5657997/equal-rights-amendment-history/.

Leder, Mimi, dir. "On the Basis of Sex." Aired on September 25, 2020, on Netflix. Accessed June 1, 2021. https://www.netflix.com/be-en/title/8099898.

MAKERS. "Ruth Bader Ginsburg: Free to Be... You and Me... and a Feminist." July 2, 2012. Video, 0:55. https://youtu.be/IwkhV-q0V20.

Merriam-Webster OnLine,. s.v. "feminism," accessed May 20, 2022. https://www.merriam-webster.com/dictionary/feminism.

Scholar, Megan A. "The History of Family Leave Policies in the United States." *Organization of American Historians.* 2016. Accessed May 28, 2022. https://www.oah.org/tah/issues/2016/november/the-history-of-family-leave-policies-in-the-united-states/.

Study.com. "The March on Washington in 1963: Definition, Facts & Date." *History Courses.* June 28, 2015. Accessed on April 15, 2022. https://study.com/academy/lesson/the-march-on-washington-in-1963-definition-facts-date.html.

Tenreyro, Tatiana. "Ruth Bader Ginsburg Reveals Thoughts on Felicity Jones-Starring Biopic 'On the Basis of Sex.'" *The Hollywood Reporter,* December 18, 2018. https://www.hollywoodreporter.com/news/general-news/what-rbg-thinks-biopic-basis-sex-starring-felicity-jones-1170140/.

The King Center. "About Dr. Martin Luther King Jr." *Who We Are.* Accessed June 8, 2022. https://thekingcenter.org/about-tkc/martin-luther-king-jr/.

The US National Archives and Records Administration. "Civil Rights Act (1964)." *National Archives and Records Administration.* Accessed February 8, 2022. https://www.archives.gov/milestone-documents/civil-rights-act.

Thompson, Krissah. "In March on Washington, White Activists Were Largely Overlooked but Strategically Essential." *The Washington Post,* August 25, 2013. https://www.washingtonpost.com/lifestyle/style/in-march-on-washington-white-activists-were-largely-overlooked-but-strategically-essential/2013/08/25/f2738c2a-eb27-11e2-8023-b7f07811d98e_story.html.

Thulin, Lila. "The True Story of the Case Ruth Bader Ginsburg Argues in 'On the Basis of Sex.'" *Smithsonian Institution Magazine,* December 24,

2018. https://www.smithsonianmag.com/history/true-story-case-center-basis-sex-180971110/.

United States Department of Health & Human Services. Office for Civil Rights (OCR). *Title IX of the Education Amendments of 1972.* Washington, D.C.: HHS, October 27, 2021. https://www.hhs.gov/civil-rights/for-individuals/sex-discrimination/title-ix-education-amendments/index.html.

United States Equal Employment Opportunity Commission. *The Equal Pay Act of 1963.* Washington, D.C.: EEOC, 1963. Accessed February 15, 2022. https://www.eeoc.gov/statutes/equal-pay-act-1963.

United States Equal Employment Opportunity Commission. *The Pregnancy Discrimination Act of 1978.* Washington, D.C.: EEOC, 1978. Accessed February 15, 2022. https://www.eeoc.gov/statutes/pregnancy-discrimination-act-1978.

Weinberger, Jillian. "Transcript: Interview with Supreme Court Justice Ruth Bader Ginsburg." In *The Takeaway.* Produced by Jillian Weinberger. 2013 Podcast, MP3 audio, 27:01. https://www.wnycstudios.org/podcasts/takeaway/segments/transcript-interview-justice-ruth-bader-ginsburg.

West, Betsy and Julie Cohen, dir. "RBG." Originally aired at Sundance March 4, 2018. Aired on Netflix October 21, 2021. https://www.netflix.com/title/80240086.

Chapter Three

Associated Press. "Some Male Sexual Assault Victims Feel Left behind by #MeToo." *NBC News,* updated April 19, 2018. Accessed May 20, 2022. https://www.nbcnews.com/news/us-news/some-male-sexual-assault-victims-feel-left-behind-metoo-n867386.

Audette, Andre P. and Sean Lam. "Gender Equality Supports Happiness and Well-Being." *The Gender Policy Report*. Accessed May 20, 2022. https://genderpolicyreport.umn.edu/gender-equality-supports-happiness/.

Audette, Andre P., Sean Lam, Haley O'Connor, and Benjamin Radcliff. *(E)Quality of Life: A Cross-National Analysis of the Effect of Gender Equality on Life Satisfaction*. J Happiness Stud 20, 2173–2188 (2019). https://doi.org/10.1007/s10902-018-0042-8.

Basile, Kathleen C., Sharon G. Smith, Marci-jo Kresnow, Srijana Khatiwada, and Ruth W. Leemis. "The National Intimate Partner and Sexual Violence Survey: 2016/2017 Report on Sexual Violence." *National Center for Injury Prevention and Control, Centers for Disease Control and Prevention. June 2022. Accessed March 2, 2023* https://www.cdc.gov/violenceprevention/pdf/nisvs/nisvsReportonSexualViolence.pdf.

Bertotti, Candace and David Maxfield. "Most People Are Supportive of #MeToo. But Will Workplaces Actually Change?" *Harvard Business Review*, July 10, 2018. Accessed June 8, 2022. https://hbr.org/2018/07/most-people-are-supportive-of-metoo-but-will-workplaces-actually-change.

Biller, Henry B. "The Father and Personality Development: Paternal Deprivation and Sex-Role Development," in Michael E. Lamb, ed., *The Role of the Father in Child Development* New York: Wiley & Sons, 1981, p. 104.

Bing, Elizabeth. "Effect of Childrearing Practices on Development of Differential Cognitive Abilities." *Child Development* 34, no. 3, 1963, pp. 631–48. https://doi.org/10.2307/1126757.

Black, Michele C., Kathleen C. Basile, Matthew J. Breiding, Sharon G. Smith, Mike L. Walters, Melissa T. Merrick, Jieru Chen, and Mark R. Stevens. *The National Intimate Partner and Sexual Violence Survey (NISVS): 2010 Summary Report*. November 2011. Atlanta, GA: National Center for Injury Prevention and Control, Centers for Disease Control and Prevention. https://www.cdc.gov/violenceprevention/pdf/nisvs_report2010-a.pdf.

Bradley, Laura. "'I Was Terrified, and I Was Humiliated': #MeToo's Male Accusers, One Year Later." *Vanity Fair*, October 4, 2018. Accessed June 8, 2022. https://www.vanityfair.com/hollywood/2018/10/metoo-male-accusers-terry-crews-alex-winter-michael-gaston-interview.

Breitman, Kendall. "Lauer Defends GM Mom Question." *Politico*. Politico LLC, June 26, 2014. Accessed December 17, 2022. https://www.politico.com/story/2014/06/matt-lauer-mary-barra-108346.

Brown, Brené. "Brené on FFTs." In *Unlocking Us*. March 20, 2020. Podcast, MP3 audio, 37:52. https://brenebrown.com/podcast/brene-on-ffts/.

CapeTalk. "Male Survivor of Sexual Abuse Speaks Out." Video, 37:37. November 21, 2019. https://youtu.be/BEMA3_zHOV8.

Catalyst. "Why Diversity and Inclusion Matter: Financial Performance (Appendix)." Catalyst, Inc. June 24, 2021. https://www.catalyst.org/research/why-diversity-and-inclusion-matter-financial-performance/.

Chen, Jie, Woon Sau Leung, and Kevin P. Evans. "Female Board Representation, Corporate Innovation and Firm Performance." *Journal of Empirical Finance* 48 (September 2018): 236–54. https://doi.org/10.1016/j.jempfin.2018.07.003.

Croft, Alyssa, Toni Schmader, Katharina Block, and Andrew Scott Baron. "The Second Shift Reflected in the Second Generation." *Psychological Science* 25, no. 7, 2014, pp. 1418–28. https://doi.org/10.1177/0956797614533968.

Davie, Gavin. "Spiral of Silence." Mass Communication Theory: Mass Communication Theory: From Theory to Practical Application." May 21, 2014. Accessed May 5, 2022. https://masscommtheory.com/theory-overviews/spiral-of-silence/.

Elsesser, Kim. *Sex and the Office.* Barricade Books 2004. Quoted in Smith, David G., and W. Brad Johnson. *Good Guys: How Men Can Be Better Allies for Women in the Workplace.* Harvard Business Review Press, 2020: 25.

Fisher Phillips. "'Sexual Horseplay' or 'Sex Discrimination'? The Half-Million Dollar Question." Fisher Phillips LLP. September 27, 2018. Accessed December 17, 2022. https://www.fisherphillips.com/news-insights/sexual-horseplay-or-sex-discrimination-the-half-million-dollar-question.html.

Gold Star Law. "Hold Your Horses!" BlueFireMediaGroup, October 6, 2021.Accessed December 17, 2022. https://www.goldstarlaw.com/hold-your-horses/.

Harmon, Barbara. *Framing, Spiral of Silence, and Coverage of the #MeToo Movement.* Middle Tennessee State University: Barbara Harmon, 2021. https://jewlscholar.mtsu.edu/server/api/core/bitstreams/2e111f01-20cb-4006-a734-99a40cafb5bd/content.

Hegde, Sushmitha, trans. "What Is the Spiral of Silence?" *Science ABC*, updated, June 3, 2022. Accessed, April 11, 2023. https://www.scienceabc.com/social-science/what-is-the-spiral-of-silence.html.

Heracleous, Loizos and David Robson. "Why the 'Paradox Mindset' Is the Key to Success." *Worklife: BBC* (blog), November 11th, 2020. Accessed May 28, 2022. https://www.bbc.com/worklife/article/20201109-why-the-paradox-mindset-is-the-key-to-success.

Johnson, Matthew D., Nancy L. Galambos, and Jared R. Anderson. "Skip the Dishes? Not So Fast! Sex and Housework Revisited." *Journal of Family Psychology* 30, no. 2 (2016): 203–13. https://doi.org/10.1037/fam0000161.

Johnson, W. Brad and David G. Smith. *Athena Rising: How and Why Men Should Mentor Women.* Boston: Harvard Business Review Press, 2019.

Kersley, Richard, Eugene Klerk, Anais Boussie, Bahar Sezer Longworth, Joelle Anamootoo Natzkoff, and Darshana Ramji. "The CS Gender 3000 Report 2019. Diversity and Company Performance." Credit-Suisse Research Institute: October 10, 2019. Pages 22-23. https://www.credit-suisse.com/about-us-news/en/articles/news-and-expertise/cs-gender-3000-report-2019-201910.html.

Kim, Daehyun and Laura T. Starks. "Gender Diversity on Corporate Boards: Do Women Contribute Unique Skills?" *American Economic Review*, 106 (5): 267-71. May 2016. https://www.aeaweb.org/articles?id=10.1257%2Faer.p20161032.

Koestner, Richard, Carol Franz, and Joel Weinberger. "The Family Origins of Empathic Concern: A 26-Year Longitudinal Study." *Journal of Personality and Social Psychology*, 58, no. 4 (1990): 709–717. https://doi.org/10.1037/0022-3514.58.4.709.

Lapiano, Arielle. "Dear Sir–Don't Let #MeToo Make You Afraid of Me." *Forbes*, January 9, 2019. https://www.forbes.com/sites/ellevate/2019/01/09/dear-sir-dont-let-metoo-make-you-afraid-of-me/?sh=198bd09c3b59.

Liu, Chelsea. "Are Women Greener? Corporate Gender Diversity and Environmental Violations." *Journal of Corporate Finance* 52 (October 2018): 118–42. https://doi.org/10.1016/j.jcorpfin.2018.08.004.

National Head Start Training and Technical Assistance Resource Center. "Building Blocks for Father Involvement, Building Block 1: Appreciating How Fathers Give Children a Head Start." Head Start Bureau, Administration on Children, Youth and Families, United States Department of Health and Human Services. Contract No. 233-02-0002 Arlington, VA: June 2004. https://files.eric.ed.gov/fulltext/ED543023.pdf.

Neubaum, German and Nicole C. Krämer. "What Do We Fear? Expected Sanctions for Expressing Minority Opinions in Offline and Online

Communication." *Communication Research* 45, no. 2 (2016): 139–64. https://doi.org/10.1177/0093650215623837.

Noelle-Neumann, Elisabeth. *The Spiral of Silence: Public Opinion–Our Social Skin.* 2nd ed. London: The University of Chicago Press, Ltd, 1993.

Osborne, Cynthia, Rachel Boggs, and Bethany McKee. University of Texas at Austin Policy brief. *The Importance of Father Involvement.* Austin, TX: LBJ School of Public Affairs, 2021. https://www.fatherhoodresourcehub.org/wp-content/uploads/2021/08/CFRPBrief_B0450821_ImportanceofFatherInvolvement.pdf.

Parke, Ross. *Fatherhood.* Cambridge, MA: Harvard University Press, 1996.

Parker, Ashley. "Karen Pence Is the Vice President's 'Prayer Warrior,' Gut Check and Shield." *The Washington Post,* March 28, 2017. Accessed May 20, 2022. https://www.washingtonpost.com/politics/karen-pence-is-the-vice-presidents-prayer-warrior-gut-check-and-shield/2017/03/28/3d7a26ce-0a01-11e7-8884-96e6a6713f4b_story.html.

Perryman, Alexa A., Guy D. Fernando, and Arindam Tripathy. "Do Gender Differences Persist? an Examination of Gender Diversity on Firm Performance, Risk, and Executive Compensation." *Journal of Business Research* 69, no. 2 (February 2016): 579–86. https://doi.org/10.1016/j.jbusres.2015.05.013.

Petersen, Thomas. "The 'Spiral of Silence' Theory." *Elisabeth Noelle-Neumann: Her Life and Scientific Work.* Accessed May 20, 2022. https://noelle-neumann.de/scientific-work/spiral-of-silence/.

Post, Corinne, Boris Lokshin, and Christophe Boone. "Research: Adding Women to the C-Suite Changes How Companies Think." HBR.org. Harvard Business Publishing, September 17, 2021. https://hbr.org/2021/04/research-adding-women-to-the-c-suite-changes-how-companies-think.

PricewaterhouseCoopers. "2021 PricewaterhouseCoopers's Annual Corporate Director Survey." *PwC.* 2021. https://www.pwc.com/us/en/ services/governance-insights-center/assets/pwc-2021-annual-corporate-directors-survey.pdf.

Pruett, Kyle D. *Fatherneed: Why Father Care Is as Essential as Mother Care for Your Child.* New York, NY: Broadway Books, 2001, page 45-52.

Radin, Norma and Rena Goldsmith. "Predictors of Father Involvement in Childcare." University of Michigan, School of Social Work Research Paper. Presented at the Society for Research in Child Development: April 21, 1983. (Also cited in Pruett, 2000, p. 45.) https://files.eric.ed.gov/ fulltext/ED248031.pdf.

Reeves, Arin, Nextion. Quoted in Lapiano, Arielle. "Dear Sir–Don't Let #MeToo Make You Afraid of Me." *Forbes,* January 9, 2019. https://www. forbes.com/sites/ellevate/2019/01/09/dear-sir-dont-let-metoo-make-you-afraid-of-me/?sh=198bd09c3b59.

Reguera-Alvarado, Nuria, Pilar de Fuentes, and Joaquina Laffarga. "Does Board Gender Diversity Influence Financial Performance? Evidence from Spain." *Journal of Business Ethics* 141, no. 2 (July 1, 2015): 337–50. https:// doi.org/10.1007/s10551-015-2735-9.

Rosenberg, Jeffrey and William Bradford Wilcox. "The Importance of Fathers in the Healthy Development of Children." Washington, D.C: United States Department of Health and Human Services, Office on Child Abuse and Neglect, 2006. https://www.childwelfare.gov/pubPDFs/ fatherhood.pdf.

Sandberg, Sheryl and Marc Pritchard. "The Number of Men Who Are Uncomfortable Mentoring Women Is Growing." *Fortune.* Fortune Media LP, May 17, 2019. Accessed May 20, 2022. https://fortune.com/2019/05/17/ sheryl-sandberg-lean-in-me-too/.

Sears, Robert R., Eleanor E. Maccoby, and Harry Levin. *Patterns of Childrearing.* Evanston, IL: Row Peterson, 1957.

Smith, David G. and W. Brad Johnson. *Good Guys: How Men Can Be Better Allies for Women in the Workplace.* Boston: Harvard Business Review Press, 2020.

Soken-Huberty, Emmaline. "7 Reasons Why Gender Equality Is Good for Everyone." *Human Rights Careers,* April 16, 2020. Accessed June 8, 2020. https://www.humanrightscareers.com/issues/why-gender-equality-is-good-for-everyone/.

Talbot, Margaret. "Men Behaving Badly." *The New York Times Magazine,* October 13, 2002. Access December 16, 2022. https://www.nytimes.com/2002/10/13/magazine/men-behaving-badly.html.

United States Department of Health and Human Services Administration for Children and Families Administration on Children, Youth, and Families Head Start Bureau. *Building Blocks for Father Involvement, Building Block 1: Appreciating How Fathers Give Children a Head Start.* Arlington, VA: No. 233-02-0002, June 2004. Arlington, VA. https://eclkc.ohs.acf.hhs.gov/sites/default/files/pdf/building-blocks-01-appreciating-how-fathers-give-children.pdf.

Wooll, Maggie. "How to Build Trust in the Workplace: 10 Effective Solutions." How to Build Trust in the Workplace: 10 Effective Solutions. *BetterUp,* October 21, 2022. https://www.betterup.com/blog/how-to-build-trust.

Chapter Four

American Rhetoric Movie Speeches. *American Rhetoric: Star Trek.* Accessed May 20, 2022. https://www.americanrhetoric.com/MovieSpeeches/startrekintro.html.

Brown, Brené. "FFTs with Brené Brown." In *Unlocking Us.* Podcast, MP3 audio, 37:52. March 20, 2020. https://brenebrown.com/podcast/brene-on-ffts/.

Chamorro-Premuzic, Tomas. "The Business Case for Women in Leadership." *Forbes,* May 2, 2022. https://www.forbes.com/sites/tomaspremuzic/2022/03/02/the-business-case-for-women-in-leadership/?sh=2e27dea79cbb.

Christensen, Clayton M., Michael E. Raynor, and Rory McDonald. "What Is Disruptive Innovation?" *Harvard Business Review*, April 19, 2022. https://hbr.org/2015/12/what-is-disruptive-innovation.

Chugh, Abhinav. "What Is the 'Great Resignation?' an Expert Explains." *World Economic Forum,* November 29, 2021. https://www.weforum.org/agenda/2021/11/what-is-the-great-resignation-and-what-can-we-learn-from-it/.

Daniels, Mark, dir. "Star Trek." Created by Gene Roddenberry. Aired September 4, 1966, on NBC.

Deloitte. "Fortune 500 Boards Still Decades Away from Representation Parallel to the Presence of Women and Minorities in the US Population." *Alliance for Board Diversity (ABD).* June 8, 2021. Accessed May 20, 2022. https://www2.deloitte.com/us/en/pages/about-deloitte/articles/press-releases/number-of-fortune-500-boards-with-over-40-percent-diversity-nearly-quadrupled-since-2010.html.

Deloitte & Alliance for Board Diversity. "Missing Pieces Report: The Board Diversity Census of Women and Minorities on Fortune 500 Boards, 6th edition." Deloitte Development, LLC June 8, 2021. https://www2.deloitte.com/content/dam/Deloitte/us/Documents/center-for-board-effectiveness/missing-pieces-fortune-500-board-diversity-study-sixth-edition.pdf.

Dixon-Fyle, Sundiatu, Vivian Hunt, Kevin Dolan, and Sara Prince. "Diversity Wins: How Inclusion Matters." *McKinsey & Company.* May 19,2020. Accessed May 20, 2022. https://www.mckinsey.com/featured-insights/diversity-and-inclusion/diversity-wins-how-inclusion-matters.

Gebhardt, Jillesa. "On Equal Pay Day 2019, Lack of Awareness Persists." *Curiosity at Work* (blog), March 23, 2019. https://www.surveymonkey.com/curiosity/equal-pay-day-2019/.

Gonzales, Matt. "Nearly 2 Million Fewer Women in Labor Force." *SHRM.* February 17, 2022. https://www.shrm.org/resourcesandtools/hr-topics/behavioral-competencies/global-and-cultural-effectiveness/pages/over-1-million-fewer-women-in-labor-force.aspx.

Madgavkar, Anu, Kweilin Ellingrud, and Mekala Krishnan. "The Economic Benefits of Gender Parity." *McKinsey & Company.* January 8, 2016. https://www.mckinsey.com/mgi/overview/in-the-news/the-economic-benefits-of-gender-parity.

McKinsey Quarterly. "Five Fifty: The Pandemic's Gender Effect." *McKinsey & Company.* December 2020. Accessed May 20, 2022. https://www.mckinsey.com/featured-insights/diversity-and-inclusion/five-fifty-the-pandemics-gender-effect.

PayScale, Inc. "2023 State of the Gender Pay Gap Report." *Research & Insights.* 2022. Accessed March 26, 2023. https://www.payscale.com/research-and-insights/gender-pay-gap/.

Rodsky, Eve. *Fair Play: A Game-Changing Solution for When You Have Too Much to Do (and More Life to Live).* New York: G.P. Putnam's Sons, 2019.

Turley, Jim. "Why Business Needs Women." Workplaces That Work for Women (blog). *Catalyst.* September 13, 2013. https://www.catalyst.org/2013/09/13/why-business-needs-women/.

United States Bureau of Labor Statistics, United States Department of Labor. *Number of Quits at All-Time High in November 2021.* Washington, D.C.: The Economics Daily, 2022. Accessed March 10, 2022. https://www.bls.gov/opub/ted/2022/number-of-quits-at-all-time-high-in-november-2021.htm.

United States Census Bureau. "United States Census Bureau QuickFacts: United States." *Census.gov.* July 1, 2021. https://www.census.gov/quickfacts/fact/table/US/PST045221.

World Economic Forum. "Global Gender Gap Report 2020." *Insight Reports.* Published December 16, 2019. Accessed May 20, 2022. https://www.weforum.org/reports/gender-gap-2020-report-100-years-pay-equality.

Chapter Five

Amaechi, John. "What Is White Privilege?" *Bitesize: BBC,* March 30, 2022. Accessed May 20, 2022. https://www.bbc.co.uk/bitesize/articles/zrvkbqt.

American Psychological Association Dictionary of Psychology s.v. "perspective-taking." Accessed June 20, 2022. https://dictionary.apa.org/perspective-taking.

Bommelje, Rick. "Listening Legend Interview, Dr. Ralph Nichols." International Listening Association. Listening Post, Summer 2003, Vol 84, 2003. https://listen.org/Legend-Interview.

Brown, Brené. "Brené on FFTs." In *Unlocking Us.* Podcast, MP3 audio, 37:52. March 20, 2020. https://brenebrown.com/podcast/brene-on-ffts/.

CMOE Team. "Workplace Conflict: Statistics That Reveal Its Cost." *Center for Management & Organization Effectiveness* (blog), 2022. Accessed on May 25, 2022. https://cmoe.com/blog/workplace-conflict-costs/#How.

Covey, Stephen. "'The 7 Habits of Highly Effective People' Update: A Win-Win Is Always the Best Negotiating Strategy." Entrepreneur. Entrepreneur Media, Inc., May 26, 2020. https://www.entrepreneur.com/growing-a-business/the-7-habits-of-highly-effective-people-update-a-win-win/349409.

Cridland, Caryn. "Why Perspective Take—Part 1." *Mediate.* September 13, 2013. https://www.mediate.com/why-perspective-take-part-1/.

D'Aprix, Roger. "Communicating Culture Down the Line—Roger D'Aprix." *ROI.* December 1, 2014. Accessed May 28, 2022. https://roico.com/2014/12/01/communicating-culture-down-the-line/.

Geher, Glenn. "10 Human Universals That Should Be Fully Embraced." *Psychology Today* (blog), January 24, 2014. Accessed May 28, 2022. https://www.psychologytoday.com/us/blog/darwins-subterranean-world/201401/10-human-universals-should-be-fully-embraced.

Goodwin, Rachael Dailey. *Rachael Dailey Goodwin.* 2022. Accessed on May 29, 2022. https://www.rachaeldaileygoodwin.com/.

Hammond, Sue Annis. *The Thin Book of Appreciative Inquiry, 3rd Edition.* Bend: Thin Book Publishing Company, 2013. https://www.readpbn.com/pdf/The-Thin-Book-of-Appreciative-Inquiry-Sample-Pages.pdf.

Leading Effectively Staff. "The Importance of Empathy in the Workplace." *Center for Creative Leadership.* November 28, 2020. Accessed May 28, 2022. https://www.ccl.org/articles/leading-effectively-articles/empathy-in-the-workplace-a-tool-for-effective-leadership/.

Linver, Sandy. *Speak and Get Results: Complete Guide to Speeches & Presentations Work Bus.* Revised ed. May 31, 1994. New York: Fireside, 1994.

Mcleod, Saul. "Maslow's Hierarchy of Needs." *Simply Psychology,* December 29, 2020. Accessed, March 15, 2021. https://www.simplypsychology.org/maslow.html.

Merriam-Webster OnLine, s.v. "empathy," accessed May 20, 2022. https://www.merriam-webster.com/dictionary/empathy.

Mills, Charles Wright and Alan Wolfe. *The Power Elite*. New Edition. New York, NY: Oxford University Press, 2000.

Morris, Jim and Noah Prince. "US White Male Culture (a.k.a. Western Business Culture): A Deeper Look." *WMFDP*. August 26, 2019. Accessed May 20, 2022. https://wmfdp.com/u-s-white-male-culture-aka-western-business-culture-a-deeper-look/.

Newkirk, Pamela. "Diversity Has Become a Booming Business. So Where Are the Results?" *Time*, 2019. Accessed Jan. 14, 2023. https://time.com/5696943/diversity-business/.

Nichols, Ralph G., and Leonard A. Stevens. *Are You Listening? The Science of Improving Your Listening Ability for a Better Understanding of People*. New York: McGraw Hill, 1957.

Proudman, Bill. "The Roots of White Male Culture: From the British Isles through the American Prairie to the Boardroom." *WMFDP*. July 30, 2019. Accessed May 20, 2022. https://wmfdp.com/whitepapers/the-roots-of-white-male-culture-from-the-british-isles-through-the-american-prairie-to-the-boardroom/.

Silver, Nicole Serena. "Feminine and Masculine Workforce Dynamics (Series 2 of 5)." *Forbes*. Forbes Magazine, January 30, 2023. https://www.forbes.com/sites/nicolesilver/2023/01/24/feminine-and-masculine-workforce-dynamics/?sh=5fab738454a2.

Team Tony. "6 Human Needs: Why Are They So Important?" *Tony Robbins,* June 29, 2021. Accessed May 28, 2022. https://www.tonyrobbins.com/mind-meaning/do-you-need-to-feel-significant/.

Tsai, Yafang. "Relationship between Organizational Culture, Leadership Behavior and Job Satisfaction." BMC Health Services Research. BioMed Central, May 14, 2011. https://doi.org/10.1186/1472-6963-11-98.

VanBommel, Tara. "The Power of Empathy in Times of Crisis and Beyond (Report)." *Catalyst,* October 21, 2021. Accessed May 28, 2022. https://www.catalyst.org/reports/empathy-work-strategy-crisis/.

White Men as Full Diversity Partners. "Our Approach." *WMFDP.* Accessed May 20, 2022. https://wmfdp.com/.

Wilkie, Dana. "How DE&I Evolved in the C-Suite." *SHRM Executive Network.* February 16, 2022. https://www.shrm.org/executive/resources/articles/pages/evolving-executive-dei-diversity-c-suite.aspx.

Wirtschafter, Valerie. "How George Floyd Changed the Online Conversation around BLM." *Brookings,* June 17, 2021. Accessed May 28, 2022. https://www.brookings.edu/techstream/how-george-floyd-changed-the-online-conversation-around-black-lives-matter/.

Zweigenhaft, Richard L. and G. William Domhoff. *Diversity in the Power Elite: Ironies and Unfulfilled Promises.* 3rd ed. Lanham, MD: Rowman & Littlefield, 2018.

Chapter Six

Cherry, Kendra. "What is Cognitive Dissonance?" *Verywell Mind,* updated on February 8, 2022. https://www.verywellmind.com/what-is-cognitive-dissonance-2795012.

Harper, Pam S. *Preventing Strategic Gridlock: Leading over, under & around Organizational Jams to Achieve High Performance Results.* Hilton Head Island, SC, NC: Cameo Publications, 2003.

Harper, Pam S. and D. Scott Harper. "How Financial Executives Can Achieve Long-Term Performance in a Short-Term World." *Daily Financial Executives* (blog), December 12, 2021. https://daily.financialexecutives.org/FEI-Daily/December-2021/How-Financial-Executives-Can-Achieve-Long-Term-Per.aspx.

Hunt, Vivian, Sara Prince, Sundiatu Dixon-Fyle, and Lareina Yee. "Delivering through Diversity—McKinsey & Company." *McKinsey & Company.* January 2018. https://www.mckinsey.com/~/media/mckinsey/business%20functions/people%20and%20organizational%20performance/our%20insights/delivering%20through%20diversity/delivering-through-diversity_full-report.pdf.

Johnson, David W. "The Importance of Taking the Perspective of Others." Psychology Today. Sussex Publishers, June 5, 2019. https://www.psychologytoday.com/us/blog/constructive-controversy/201906/the-importance-taking-the-perspective-others#:~:text=Perspective-%2Dtaking%20also%20communicates%20that,people%20feel%20understood%20and%20respected.

Kennedy, Julia Taylor and Pooja Jain-Link. "What Majority Men Really Think About Diversity & Inclusion (And How to Engage Them in It)." *Coqual.* August 2, 2020. Accessed on May 20, 2022. https://coqual.org/reports/what-majority-men-really-think-about-di-and-how-to-engage-them-in-it/.

Kohll, Alan. "5 Reasons Social Connections Can Enhance Your Employee Wellness Program." *Forbes Magazine.* January 31, 2018. Accessed December 10, 2021. https://www.forbes.com/sites/alankohll/2018/01/31/5-ways-social-connections-can-enhance-your-employee-wellness-program/?sh=188bee41527c.

Leading Effectively Staff. "What Is Psychological Safety at Work?" *Center for Creative Leadership.* January 15, 2022, Accessed December 10, 2022. https://www.ccl.org/articles/leading-effectively-articles/what-is-psychological-safety-at-work/.

Levs, Josh. "To Make the Case for Paternity Leave, Dads Will Have to Work Together." *Harvard Business Review.* Harvard Business Publishing, March 19, 2019. Accessed September 28, 2022. https://hbr.org/2019/03/to-make-the-case-for-paternity-leave-dads-will-have-to-work-together.

Lorenzo, Rocio, Nicole Voigt, Miki Tsusaka, Matt Krentz, and Katie Abouzahr. "How Diverse Leadership Teams Boost Innovation." *Boston Consulting Group*, January 23, 2018. https://www.bcg.com/en-us/publications/2018/how-diverse-leadership-teams-boost-innovation.

Marder, Andrew. "How After-Hours Events Can Make Your Business Stronger." *Capterra* (blog), October 30, 2017. https://blog.capterra.com/how-after-hours-events-can-make-your-business-stronger/.

Morris, Chris. "Disconnecting to Spend Time with Your Kids Could Sabotage Your Career." *CNBC*, May 11, 2019. https://www.cnbc.com/2019/05/10/disconnecting-to-spend-time-with-your-kids-could-sabotage-your-career.html.

Prime, Jeanine, Heather Faust-Cummings, Elizabeth Salib, and Corinne A. Moss-Racusin. "Calling All White Men: Can Training Help Create Inclusive Workplaces? (Report)." Catalyst. Catalyst, Inc., July 8, 2012. https://www.catalyst.org/research/calling-all-white-men-can-training-help-create-inclusive-workplaces/.

Riordan, Christie M. and Rodger W. Griffeth. "The Opportunity for Friendship in the Workplace: An Underexplored Construct." *Journal of Business and Psychology,* volume 10 (December 1995): 141–54. https://link.springer.com/article/10.1007/BF02249575#citeas.

Sattari, Negin, Sarah DiMuccio, and Ludo Gabriele. "When Managers Are Open, Men Feel Heard and Interrupt Sexism." *Catalyst.* Accessed May 15, 2022. https://www.catalyst.org/reports/managers-openness-sexism/.

Smith, David and W. Brad Johnson. *Good Guys How Men Can Be Better Allies for Women in the Workplace.* Boston, MA: Harvard Business Review Press, 2020.

TEDx Talks. "White Men: Time to Discover Your Cultural Blind Spots | Michael Welp | TEDxBend." July 16, 2017. Video, 16:47. https://youtu.be/rR5zDIjUrfk.

Turban, Stephen, Dan Wu, and Letian (LT) Zhang. "Research: When Gender Diversity Makes Firms More Productive." *Harvard Business Review,* February 11, 2019. Accessed September 17, 2021. https://hbr.org/2019/02/research-when-gender-diversity-makes-firms-more-productive.

Weber Shandwick. "Gender Equality in the Executive Ranks: A Paradox—The Journey to 2030." *Weber Shandwick,* October 20, 2015. Accessed May 28, 2022. https://www.webershandwick.com/uploads/news/files/gender-equality-in-the-executive-ranks-report.pdf.

Welp, Michael. *Four Days to Change: Twelve Radical Habits to Overcome Bias and Thrive in a Diverse World.* Portland: Equal Voice, 2016.

Chapter Seven

Abbas, Tahir. "Iceberg Model of Change Management." *Change Management Insight.* January 2, 2021. https://changemanagementinsight.com/iceberg-model-of-change-management/.

American Psychological Association (APA). "Boys and Men Guidelines Group." APA Guidelines for Psychological Practice with Boys and Men. pdf, August 2018. Accessed May 15, 2022. http://www.apa.org/about/policy/psychological-practice-boys-men-guidelines.pdf.

Billan, Rumeet. "The Tallest Poppy: How the Workforce Is Cutting Ambitious Women Down." https://www.womenofinfluence.ca/tps/. Women of Influence, March 1, 2023. https://www.womenofinfluence.ca/wp-content/uploads/2023/02/tp-whitepaper.pdf.

Blum, Robert MD, John Hopkins Bloomberg School of Public Health. Quoted in Bonnie Chiu, "Gender Inequality Harms Not Only Women and Girls, But Also Men and Boys." *Forbes,* May 28, 2019. https://www.forbes.com/sites/bonniechiu/2019/05/28/gender-inequality-harms-not-only-women-and-girls-but-also-men-and-boys/?sh=21f74e154d9f.

Bobinski, Daniel. "The Role of Fear in Conflict Resolution." OR Today. MD Publishing, December 31, 2019. https://ortoday.com/the-role-of-fear-in-conflict-resolution/.

Burns, Alexander, Maggie Haberman, and Jonathan Martin. "Donald Trump Apology Caps Day of Outrage Over Lewd Tape." *The New York Times*, October 7, 2016. Accessed on June 1, 2020. https://www.nytimes.com/2016/10/08/us/politics/donald-trump-women.html.

Chu, Judy Y, Ph.D. Quoted in Fortin, Jacey. "Traditional Masculinity Can Hurt Boys, Say New A.P.A. Guidelines." *New York Times*, January 10, 2019. https://www.nytimes.com/2019/01/10/science/apa-traditional-masculinity-harmful.html.

CollinsEnglishDictionary Online. s.v. "bummock." Accessed May 20, 2022. https://www.collinsdictionary.com/us/dictionary/english/bummock.

Devine, Patricia G., Patrick S. Forscher, Anthony J. Austin, and William T.L. Cox. "Long-Term Reduction in Implicit Race Bias: A Prejudice Habit-Breaking Intervention." *Journal of Experimental Social Psychology* 48, no. 6 (November 2012): 1267–78. https://doi.org/10.1016/j.jesp.2012.06.003.

Edmondson, Amy. "Creating Psychological Safety in the Workplace." January 22, 2019. In *HBR IdeaCast* from Harvard Business Review. Hosted by Curt Nickisch. Podcast, MP3 audio29:46. https://hbr.org/podcast/2019/01/creating-psychological-safety-in-the-workplace.

Fortin, Jacey. "Traditional Masculinity Can Hurt Boys, Say New A.P.A. Guidelines." *New York Times*, January 10, 2019. https://www.nytimes.com/2019/01/10/science/apa-traditional-masculinity-harmful.html.

Galinsky, Adam D. and Gordon B. Moskowitz. "Perspective-Taking: Decreasing Stereotype Expression, Stereotype Accessibility, and in-Group Favoritism." *Journal of Personality and Social Psychology* 78, no. 4 (April 1, 2000): 708–24. https://doi.org/10.1037/0022-3514.78.4.708.

Grant Thornton LLP. "Psychological Safety in a Speak-up Culture." *Grant Thornton*, March 4, 2020. https://www.grantthornton.com/library/articles/advisory/2020/psychological-safety-speak-up-culture.aspx.

Greene, Mark. "Why Calling It 'Toxic Masculinity' Isn't Helping." *Medium.com*, August 11, 2018. Accessed March 2, 2023. https://remakingmanhood.medium.com/why-we-must-stop-saying-toxic-masculinity-cfe83b9034dc.

Goodwin, Rachael Dailey. *Rachael Dailey Goodwin*. 2022. https://www.rachaeldaileygoodwin.com/.

Horowitz, Juliana Menasce and Ruth Igielnik. "A Century after Women Gained the Right to Vote, Majority of Americans See Work to Do on Gender Equality." *Pew Research Center,* July 7, 2020. https://www.pewresearch.org/social-trends/2020/07/07/a-century-after-women-gained-the-right-to-vote-majority-of-americans-see-work-to-do-on-gender-equality/.

Kerr, Geoffrey and Alix Pollack. "Engaging Men: Barriers and Gender Norms (Report)." *Catalyst*. April 7, 2022. Accessed May 15, 2022. https://www.catalyst.org/research/engaging-men-barriers-norms/.

Kouchaki, Maryam, Keith Leavitt, Luke Zhu, and Anthony C. Klotz. "Research: What Fragile Masculinity Looks like at Work." *Harvard Business Review*. Harvard Business School Publishing, January 26, 2023. https://hbr.org/2023/01/research-what-fragile-masculinity-looks-like-at-work.

Kuchynka, Sophie L., Jennifer K. Bosson, Joseph A. Vandello, and Curtis Puryear. "Zero-Sum Thinking and the Masculinity Contest: Perceived Intergroup Competition and Workplace Gender Bias." *Journal of Social Issues* 74, no. 3 (2018): 529–50. https://doi.org/10.1111/josi.12281.

Landsbaum, Claire. "Obama's Female Staffers Made Sure Their Voices Were Heard With a Genius Strategy." *The Cut*, September 13, 2016.

Accessed on May 25, 2022. https://www.thecut.com/2016/09/heres-how-obamas-female-staffers-made-their-voices-heard.html.

Mental Health America. "Infographic: 5 Minutes to Men's Mental Health." Accessed June 4, 2022. https://www.mhanational.org/infographic-mental-health-men.

Merriam-Webster Online, s.v. "cancel culture" accessed March 30, 2023. https://www.merriam-webster.com/dictionary/cancel%20culture#:~:text=For%20those%20of%20you%20who,Twitter%2C%20Instagram%2C%20or%20Facebook.

Merriam-Webster OnLine, s.v. "mansplaining," accessed May 20, 2022. https://www.merriam-webster.com/words-at-play/mansplaining-definition-history.

Meyer, Chris. "Tall Poppy Syndrome: How to (Not) Cope with Success." *The Mind Collection,* November 21, 2022. https://themindcollection.com/tall-poppy-syndrome/.

Morin, Amy. "What Is Toxic Masculinity?" *Verywell Mind,* November 26, 2020. https://www.verywellmind.com/what-is-toxic-masculinity-5075107.

Pappas, Stephanie. "APA Issues First-Ever Guidelines for Practice with Men and Boys." *American Psychological Association.* Accessed May 22, 2022. https://www.apa.org/monitor/2019/01/ce-corner.

Perception Institute. "Implicit Bias Explained." *Perception Institute.* May 17, 2017. Accessed May 20, 2022. https://perception.org/research/implicit-bias/.

Shaffer, Emily, Negin Sattari, and Alixandra Pollack. "Interrupting Sexism at Work: How Men Respond in a Climate of Silence." *Catalyst.* June 9, 2020. Accessed May 22, 2022. https://www.catalyst.org/research/interrupting-sexism-silence/.

Thompson, Edward H. and Joseph H. Pleck. "The Structure of Male Role Norms." *American Behavioral Scientist* 29, no. 5 (May 1, 1986): 531–43. https://doi.org/10.1177/000276486029005003.

Yousaf, Omar, Aneka Popat, and Myra S. Hunter. "An Investigation of Masculinity Attitudes, Gender, and Attitudes toward Psychological Help-Seeking." *Psychology of Men & Masculinity* 16, no. 2 (2015): 234–37. https://doi.org/10.1037/a0036241.

Chapter Eight

Bates-Duford, Tarra. "Female vs. Male Friendships." *Psych Central* (blog), January 26, 2018. https://psychcentral.com/blog/relationship-corner/2018/01/female-vs-male-friendships-10-key-differences#1.

Berdahl, Jennifer L. and Sue H. Moon. "Workplace Mistreatment of Middle Class Workers Based on Sex, Parenthood, and Caregiving." *PsycEXTRA Dataset* 69, no. 2 (2013): 341–66. https://doi.org/10.1037/e521512014-116.

Bright Horizons Family Solutions LLC. *Seventh Annual Modern Family Index—New Data Shows the Pandemic Is Making the Mental Load a Family Affair.* Bright Horizons, May 9, 2022. Accessed May 22, 2022. https://www.brighthorizons.com/-/media/Corporate/MFI-2021/2021-MFI-Report-FINAL.

Bright Horizons Family Solutions LLC. *Sixth Annual Modern Family Index.* Bright Horizons, February 6, 2020. Accessed May 28, 2022. https://www.brighthorizons.com/-/media/2019_MFI.ashx.

Coltrane, Scott, Elizabeth C. Miller, Tracy DeHaan, and Lauren Stewart. "Fathers and the Flexibility Stigma." *Journal of Social Issues* 69, no. 2 (2013): 279–302. https://doi.org/10.1111/josi.12015.

Dorment, Rich. "Men Can't Have It All Either, Struggle with Work-Life Balance." *New York Post,* March 10, 2020. https://nypost.com/2020/03/10/men-cant-have-it-all-either-struggle-with-work-life-balance/.

Harrington, Brad, Fred Van Deusen, Jennifer Sabatini Fraone, and Iyar Mazar. Rep. "The New Dad: Portrait of Today's Father." Boston College Center for Work and Family." Boston College Center for Work & Family, 2015. file:///Users/korireed/Downloads/The%20New%20Dad%20 2015_A%20Portrait%20of%20Todays%20Fathers%20(2).pdf.

Hastwell, Claire. "What Are Employee Resource Groups (ERGs)?" *Great Place to Work Institute* (blog), January 7, 2020. https://www.greatplacetowork.com/resources/blog/what-are-employee-resource-groups-ergs.

Hewlett, Sylvia Ann. "Executive Women and the Myth of Having It All." *Harvard Business Review Magazine,* 2002. Published online August 21, 2014. https://hbr.org/2002/04/executive-women-and-the-myth-of-having-it-all.

Johnson, W. Brad and David G. Smith. "How Men Can Become Better Allies to Women." *Harvard Business Review,* October 12, 2018. https://hbr.org/2018/10/how-men-can-become-better-allies-to-women.

LeBlanc, Cameron. "Judge Rules Dads Can Get Fired for Taking Paternity Leave." *Fatherly,* October 27, 2021. https://www.fatherly.com/news/paternity-leave-fired-disney-lawsuit-federal-ruling.

Levs, Josh. *All In: How Our Work-First Culture Fails Dads, Families, and Businesses—and How We Can Fix It Together.* New York, NY: HarperOne, 2015.

Lewin, Tamar. "Men in Dual-Career Families May Face 'Daddy Penalty.'" *Tampa Bay Times,* October 7, 2005. https://www.tampabay.com/archive/1994/10/16/men-in-dual-career-families-may-face-daddy-penalty/.

Livingston, Gretchen and Deja Thomas. "Among 41 Countries, Only US Lacks Paid Parental Leave." *Pew Research Center,* August 7, 2020. https://www.pewresearch.org/fact-tank/2019/12/16/u-s-lacks-mandated-paid-parental-leave/.

Miller, Claire Cain. "Men Say They Want Paid Leave but Then Don't Use All of It. Shat Stops Them?" *The New York Times,* December 4, 2019. https://www.nytimes.com/2019/12/04/upshot/fathers-parental-leave-unequal.html.

Miller, Claire Cain. "The Motherhood Penalty vs. The Fatherhood Bonus." *The New York Times,* September 6, 2014. https://www.nytimes.com/2014/09/07/upshot/a-child-helps-your-career-if-youre-a-man.html.

Petts, Richard J., Kevin M. Shafer, and Lee Essig. "Does Adherence to Masculine Norms Shape Fathering Behavior?" *Journal of Marriage and Family* 80, no. 3 (2018): pp. 704–20. https://doi.org/10.1111/jomf.12476.

Reed, Kori and Mike Becker. *ZagZig Parenting: (Mis)Adventures of a Career-Driven Mom and a Stay-at-Home Dad.* Omaha, NE: Reed Imagine LLC., 2017.

Rudman, Laurie A., and Kris Mescher. "Penalizing Men Who Request a Family Leave: Is Flexibility Stigma a Femininity Stigma?" *Journal of Social Issues* 69, no. 2 (2013): pp. 322–40. https://doi.org/10.1111/josi.12017.

Shockley, Kristen M., Winny Shen, Michael M. DeNunzio, Maryana L. Arvan, and Eric A. Knudsen. "Disentangling the Relationship between Gender and Work-Family Conflict: An Integration of Theoretical Perspectives Using Meta-Analytic Methods." *Journal of Applied Psychology* 102, no. 12, (July 27, 2017): pp. 1601–35. https://doi.org/10.1037/apl0000246.

TET Staff. "Men Struggle as Much as Women to Maintain Work-Life Balance." *The Economic Times | Panache,* July 29, 2017. https://

economictimes.indiatimes.com/magazines/panache/men-struggle-as-much-as-women-to-maintain-work-life-balance/articleshow/59823097.cms.

Tucker, Reed. "Men Can't Have It All Either, Struggle with Work-Life Balance." *NY Post*, March 10, 2020. https://nypost.com/2020/03/10/men-cant-have-it-all-either-struggle-with-work-life-balance/.

Williams, Joan C. "The Pandemic Has Exposed the Fallacy of the 'Ideal Worker.'" *Harvard Business Review*, May 11, 2020. https://hbr.org/2020/05/the-pandemic-has-exposed-the-fallacy-of-the-ideal-worker.

Williams, Joan C., Mary Blair-Loy, and Jennifer L. Berdahl. "Cultural Schemas, Social Class, and the Flexibility Stigma." *Journal of Social Issues* 69, no. 2 (June 12, 2013): pp. 209–34. https://doi.org/10.1111/josi.12012.

Chapter Nine

Barone, Emily. "Many American Men Have a Skewed View of Gender Inequality, Time Poll Finds." *Time*, September 26, 2019. https://time.com/5667397/gender-equality-opinions/.

Boris, Vanessa. "How Leaders at All Levels Are Taking on Change Management." *Harvard Business* (blog), April 8, 2020. https://www.harvardbusiness.org/how-leaders-at-all-levels-are-taking-on-change-management/.

Braley, Nicole. "Council Post: Why Change Management Is the Most Critical Leadership Skill." *Forbes*, December 10, 2021. https://www.forbes.com/sites/forbescommunicationscouncil/2021/11/19/why-change-management-is-the-most-critical-leadership-skill/?sh=4c50dfa73f22.

Dakin Kirby, Erika L. Creighton University Faculty Directory, 2023. Accessed April 12, 2023. https://www.creighton.edu/faculty-directory-profile/205/erika-dakin-kirby.

Eckstrom, Bill and Sarah Wirth. *The Coaching Effect: What Great Leaders Do to Increase Sales, Enhance Performance, and Sustain Growth*. Austin: Greenleaf Book Group Press, 2019.

Fry, Richard. "US Women Near Milestone in the College-Educated Labor Force." Pew Research Center. Pew Research Center, June 20, 2019. https://www.pewresearch.org/fact-tank/2019/06/20/u-s-women-near-milestone-in-the-college-educated-labor-force/.

Groenewegen, Astrid. "Kahneman Fast and Slow Thinking: System 1 and 2 Explained by Sue." SUE. Behavioural Design, April 5, 2022. https://suebehaviouraldesign.com/kahneman-fast-slow-thinking/.

Lerner, Jennifer S., Ye Li, Piercarlo Valdesolo, and Karim S. Kassam. "Emotion and Decision Making." *Annual Review of Psychology* 66, no. 1 (2015): 799–823. https://doi.org/10.1146/annurev-psych-010213-115043.

Lipman, Joanne. *That's What She Said: What Men (and Women) Need to Know about Working Together*. London: John Murray Publishers, 2019.

Logie, Jamie. "Why Change Can Be Difficult for Men." *The Good Men Project*, September 18, 2015. https://goodmenproject.com/featured-content/why-change-can-be-difficult-for-men-kcon/.

Mather, Mara and Nichole R. Lighthall. "Risk and Reward Are Processed Differently in Decisions Made Under Stress." *Current Directions in Psychological Science* 21, no. 1 (2012): 36–41. https://doi.org/10.1177/0963721411429452.

Metivier, Anthony. "Logical vs Rational Thinking: What's the Difference?" Web log. *https://www.magneticmemorymethod.com/* (blog). Anthony Metivier · Advanced Education Methodologies Pty Ltd, June 13, 2022. https://www.magneticmemorymethod.com/logical-vs-rational/.

Mind Tools Content Team. "Managing in a VUCA World: Thriving in Turbulent Times." MindTools. Accessed May 29, 2022. https://www.mindtools.com/pages/article/managing-vuca-world.htm.

Morse, Gardiner. "Decisions and Desire." *Harvard Business Review Magazine*, 2006. Harvard Business Publishing online, August 1, 2014. https://hbr.org/2006/01/decisions-and-desire.

Pendell, Ryan. "Customer Brand Preference and Decisions: Gallup's 70/30 Principle." *Gallup*, October 6, 2022. https://www.gallup.com/workplace/398954/customer-brand-preference-decisions-gallup-principle.aspx#:~:text=Gallup's%20own%20research%20has%20found,are%20based%20on%20rational%20factors.

Peterson, Tanya J. "Why Is Even Good Change Sometimes So Hard?" HealthyPlace. September 28, 2015.Accessed on April 6, 2023. https://www.healthyplace.com/other-info/mental-health-newsletter/why-is-even-good-change-sometimes-so-hard.

Pixar. "Purl | Pixar SparkShorts." Video, 8:43. February 9, 2019. https://youtu.be/B6uuIHpFkuo.

Prosci. "Change Management Process." *Prosci.* 2022. Accessed May 28, 2022. https://www.prosci.com/resources/articles/change-management-process.

Prosci. "The Prosci ADKAR Model." *Prosci.* Accessed May 28, 2022. https://www.prosci.com/methodology/adkar.

Segami, Amy. "Everything New Emerges from Turbulence." Filmed January 31, 2017 at TEDxWilmette Women. Video, 14:08. https://www.ted.com/talks/amy_segami_everything_new_emerges_from_turbulence_may_2020.

Smith, David G. and W. Brad Johnson. *Good Guys: How Men Can Be Better Allies for Women in the Workplace.* Boston: Harvard Business Review Press, 2020.

Smith, Deborah. "Psychologist Wins Nobel Prize." Monitor on Psychology. *American Psychological Association,* December 2002. https://www.apa.org/monitor/dec02/nobel.html.

Statista. "US Population by Gender 2010-2024." *Statista.* September 30, 2022. Accessed March 20, 2023. https://www.statista.com/ statistics/737923/us-population-by-gender/.

TEDx Talks. "Bill Eckstrom: Why Comfort Will Ruin Your Life." January 31, 2017. Video, 12:34. https://youtu.be/LBvHIlawWaI.

TEDx Talks. "White Men: Time to Discover Your Cultural Blind Spots | Michael Welp | TEDxBend." July 6, 2017. Video, 16:47. https://youtu. be/rR5zDIjUrfk.

Thurman, Chris. *Stop Shoulding All Over Yourself: Making the Journey from Condemnation to Compassion.* Chicago. Kharis Publishing, 2021.

VUCA-World. "Leaders with Vision, Understanding, Clarity, Agility!" VUCA. Waltruad Glaeser, Accessed April 10, 2023. https://www.vuca-world.org/.

Wiens, Kandi and Darin Rowell. "How to Embrace Change Using Emotional Intelligence." *Harvard Business Review,* March 17, 2019. https:// hbr.org/2018/12/how-to-embrace-change-using-emotional-intelligence.

"Women in Leadership: Public Says Women Are Equally Qualified, but Barriers Persist." *Pew Research Center,* Washington, D.C. January 14, 2015. https://www.pewresearch.org/social-trends/2015/01/14/women-and-leadership/.

Woolley, Kaitlin and Ayelet Fishbach. "Motivating Personal Growth by Seeking Discomfort." Psychological Science 33, no. 4 (2022): 510–23. https://doi.org/10.1177/09567976211044685.

Chapter Ten

Boyle, Kari. "5 Benefits of Workplace Conflict: Queen's University IRC." Queen's University IRC | Building - Better - Leaders. Queen's University

IRC, December 5, 2017. Accessed March 8, 2021. https://irc.queensu.ca/5-benefits-of-workplace-conflict/.

Brown, Brené. "Brené on FFTs." In *Unlocking Us.* Podcast, MP3 audio, 37:52 March 20, 2020. https://brenebrown.com/podcast/brene-on-ffts/.

CPP Global Human Capital Report. *Workplace Conflict and How Businesses Can Harness It to Thrive.* Mountain View, CA: CPP, Inc, 2008. https://img.en25.com/Web/CPP/Conflict_report.pdf.

De Vries, Deanne. *Africa: Open for Business.* St. Augustine, FL: Best Seller Publishing, 2022.

De Vries, Deanne. "Dr. Deanne De Vries Speaker and Author." Dr. Deanne De Vries, 2022. https://www.drdeannedevries.com/.

Dictionary Online. s.v. "conflict." Accessed Feb 8, 2023. https://www.dictionary.com/browse/conflict.

Gladwell, Malcolm. *The Tipping Point.* New York: Back Bay Books, 2002.

Grenny, Joseph. "Avoiding Conflict Is Killing Your Bottom Line." *Crucial Learning* (blog) Accessed June 7, 2022. https://cruciallearning.com/blog/avoiding-conflict-is-killing-your-bottom-line/.

Grenny, Joseph, Kerry Patterson, Ron McMillan, Al Switzler, and Emily Gregory. *Crucial Conversations: Tools for Talking When Stakes Are High.* 3rd ed. New York: McGraw Hill, 2021.

Korn Ferry. *Korn Ferry Leadership Architect Legacy Competency Mapping.* Los Angeles, CA: Korn Ferry, 2020. https://www.kornferry.com/content/dam/kornferry/docs/article-migration/KFLA_LegacyCompetencyModelsMapping.pdf.

Latham, Ann. "Don't Deal with Conflict, Eliminate It with a Culture of Clarity." *Forbes,* September 29, 2015. https://www.forbes.com/sites/

annlatham/2015/09/29/dont-deal-with-conflict-eliminate-it-with-a-culture-of-clarity/?sh=2b9b6dab799e.

Leading Effectively Staff. "The 7 Costs of 'Conflict Incompetence.'" *Center for Creative Leadership.* March 11, 2021. https://www.ccl.org/articles/leading-effectively-articles/the-cost-of-conflict-incompetence/.

Lombardo, Michael M. *FYI: For Your Improvement - Competencies Development Guide.* Edited by Heather Barnfield. 6th ed. New York: Korn Ferry, 2014.

Prosci Inc. "Ability—The Prosci ADKAR Model." *Prosci.* Accessed May 28, 2022. https://www.prosci.com/resources/articles/adkar-model-ability.

Prosci Inc. "The Prosci ADKAR Model." *Prosci.* Accessed May 28, 2022. https://www.prosci.com/methodology/adkar.

ThoughtForm Staff. "Four Business Benefits of Clear Communication." ThoughtForm, Inc., February 23, 2023. https://thoughtform.com/conversations/blog/four-ways-clear-communications-can-help-advance-strategic-initiative/.

VitalSmarts Research. "The Cost of Conflict Avoidance." Provo, UT: VitalSmarts, April 2010. Accessed on May 28, 2022. http://www.norskstyrebase.no/uploads/9/4/6/7/9467257/005_cost-of-conflict-avoidance.pdf. In 2021, VitalSmarts became Crucial Learning, and the links in the press release are no longer accessible. This one-page PDF summary is on the web. Also see Grenny, Joseph entry, as he refers to the report in his blog on Crucial Learning.

Vocabulary.com. s.v. "conflict." Accessed Feb 8, 2023. https://www.vocabulary.com/dictionary/conflict.

Winter, Mary-Frances. *We Can't Talk about That at Work! How to Talk about Race, Religion, Politics, and Other Polarizing Topics.* Oakland: Berrett-Koehler, 2017.

Chapter Eleven

Basford, Tessa and Bill Schaninger. "The Four Building Blocks of Change." McKinsey.com. McKinsey & Company, April 11, 2016. https://www. mckinsey.com/capabilities/people-and-organizational-performance/our-insights/the-four-building-blocks--of-change.

Comparably. "Study: Work-Life Balance in the Modern Workplace | Comparably." *Comparably*, January 10, 2020. https://www.comparably.com/news/study-work-life-balance-in-the-modern-workplace/.

Creasey, Tim. "How to Reinforce Change by Celebrating Successes." *Prosci*. Prosci Inc, August 10, 2022. https://www.prosci.com/blog/how-to-reinforce-change-by-celebrating-successes.

Finette, Pascal. "Yes, And… vs. No, But…" *The Heretic*, July 28, 2017. https://theheretic.org/2017/yes-and-vs-no-but/.

Glaser, Judith E. *Conversational Intelligence: How Great Leaders Build Trust and Get Extraordinary Results*. New York, NY: Bibliomotion Inc, 2014.

Pfeffer, Jeffrey, and Robert I Sutton. "The Smart-Talk Trap." *Harvard Business Review*, May-June, 1999 Harvard Business Publishing, Online August 1, 2014. https://hbr.org/1999/05/the-smart-talk-trap.

Prosci Inc. "Change Management Process." *Prosci*. Accessed May 28, 2022. https://www.prosci.com/resources/articles/change-management-process.

Prosci Inc. "Reinforcement—The Prosci ADKAR Model." *Prosci*. Accessed May 28, 2022. https://www.prosci.com/resources/articles/adkar-model-reinforcement.

Prosci Inc. "The Prosci ADKAR® Model." *Prosci*. Accessed May 28, 2022. https://www.prosci.com/methodology/adkar.

Russell, Graeme. "10 Reasons Men Should Care about Gender Equality (blog)." *Catalyst*, March 23, 2012. https://www.catalyst.org/2012/03/23/reasons-men-care-gender-equality/.

TEDx Talks. "Three Habits that Kill Your Confidence" | Shadé Zahrai | TEDxMonashUniversity. March 16, 2023. Video, 11:25. https://youtu.be/YUdiyhiyVVc.

WalkMe Team. "Reinforcing Change: All Your Questions Answered." The Change Management Blog. WalkMe, November 1, 2021. https://change.walkme.com/reinforcing-change/.

Zahrai, Shadé. *ShadéZahrai.* 2023 Shadé Zahrai and Influenceo Global LLC. https://www.shadezahrai.com/about.